The Substance of Capital

The Substance of Capital is the first book in a series of pamphlets and books under the heading of *The Life and Death of Capitalism* that Chronos Publications will be publishing over the next few years. The essays that are to be presented are not academic exercises, but provocations designed to goad an intellectually and politically complacent milieu to question the basis of capitalist society and the complicity of the old Left, postmarxism, postmodernism and theory-lite activists in maintaining that society.

The works of the late Robert Kurz and his comrades in the EXIT! Collective will feature prominently in the series. Further titles will be announced shortly, followed by meetings and discussions to disseminate their contents.

The Life and Death of Capitalism

Pamphlets:
1. *No Revolution Anywhere*   October 2012

Books:
1. *The Substance of Capital*   October 2016
   Robert Kurz

Robert Kurz

THE SUBSTANCE OF CAPITAL

Translated from German by Robin Halpin

The Life and Death of Capitalism

CHRONOS PUBLICATIONS

The Substance of Capital was originally published in two parts in the first two issues of the German theoretical journal *Exit!* as:

Die Substanz des Kapitals, Erster Teil: *Die negative historisch-gesellschaftliche Qualität der Abstraktion* in **Exit!** *Krise und Kritik der Warengesellschaft,* Issue 1, August 2004
and
Die Substanz des Kapitals, Zweiter Teil: *Das Quantitätsproblem der Realabstraktion – die Entsubstantialisierung des Kapitals und die marxistische Krisentheorie* in **Exit!** *Krise und Kritik der Warengesellschaft,* Issue 2, February 2005

The Life and Death of Capitalism
Chronos Publications
October 2016

Chronos Publications
B.M. Chronos
London
WC1N 3XX

Designed and typeset by Lithobolia

ISBN 978-0-9956095-0-1

Contents

Part I
The negative sociohistorical quality of the abstraction 'labour'

{1} Abstract labour as the real metaphysics of society and the absolute intrinsic limits to valorisation 8

{2} The philosophical concept of substance and the real metaphysics of capitalism 14

{3} The negative substance concept of abstract labour in Marx's critique of political economy. 23

{4} The positive concept of abstract labour in Marxist labour ontology 33

{5} Critique of Moishe Postone's concept of labour. 60

{6} Abstract labour and value as social *a priori* 70

{7} What is really abstract about abstract labour? 84

{8} The concrete-historical time of capitalism 112

Part II
The failure of labour-ontological Marxist theory of crisis and the ideological barriers against the further development of the radical critique of capitalism

{9} 'Breakdown theory' as loaded term and counterfeit concept in the history of Marxist theory. 120

{10} Reductive breakdown theories as Marxist minority position in the era of the world wars, part one: Rosa Luxemburg 126

{11} Reductive breakdown theories as Marxist minority position in the era of the world wars, part two: Henryk Grossman 137

{13} From Grossman's demonisation to the passing away of the Marxist debate on crisis and breakdown theory 147

{14} Subject and object in crisis theory. The apparent solution to the problem in mere relations of will and force 158

{15} Crisis and critique, political illusion and the relation of gender-dissociation 173

{16} The quantitative concept of abstract labour and the accusation of 'naturalism' 190

Bibliography 215

Index 221

Part I

The negative sociohistorical quality of the abstraction 'labour'

Abstract labour as the real metaphysics of society and the absolute intrinsic limits to valorisation

The absolute and relative in history. Towards a critique of the phenomenological simplification of social theory.

Looking closely we can almost always establish the existence of something like correspondences and correlations between quite different historical changes in scientific fields or arenas of life that are apparently far removed from one another. In the commodity producing system of Modernity, even in its original formation, such fields as philosophy, medicine, economics, natural science, language, etc. developed in a common direction, even though not at the same pace, but always objectively referring to each other. Naturally, the reason for this sometimes surprising correspondence or correlation is to be sought in the development of each society which forms the common inner bond of the different areas of life, fields of knowledge and perceptions. This implies that there can be no absolute knowledge in the realm of temporal existence: all knowledge, even in the seemingly purely objective, transhistorical and 'hard' sciences is sociohistorically conditioned and thereby in a certain (although not arbitrary) way relative.

This awareness of relativity seems to constitute progress in the sciences of the 19th and 20th Centuries, ranging from the study of history (since historicism), political economy (subjective or relational value theory), natural science (quantum physics), linguistics (Saussure) and philosophy (postmetaphysical thinking, linguistic turn) and flows into the general postmodern anti-essentialism and relativism.

But it only seems to be so. For precisely because science and knowledge are always sociohistorically determinate, they are subject to conditioning by social forms that imply relations of fetishism, power and force (alternatives remain to date unknown), and also always in the wake of apologetic thinking. It could not be otherwise where knowledge is innately knowledge for the benefit of power. In the commodity-producing system of Modernity these apologetics take on the form of ideology. For this reason it is not enough just to see science and knowledge simply in relative terms, but rather to go further and subject this relativity itself to a critique of ideology which must then be related to the relevant real sociohistorical process. This is in any case necessary if the reflection is to be placed within the context of an emancipatory requirement critical of power relations.

But should this ideology critical level of reflection be embraced, then the awareness of relativity itself must be tested for its ideological and apologetic potential. Postmodern thinking attempts to make itself impregnable in this respect by casting suspicion of 'metaphysics' and 'essentialism' on the critique of ideology as such. It is as if the standpoint or measure of the critique of ideology were always a totalitarian, ontological or metaphysical one. In this way, however, the perception is displaced in a direction that is itself metaphysical by paradoxically raising the relativity of everything to an absolute. What falls by the wayside is the concept of critique in the strict sense, since the referential level of relativity is not elucidated.

In fact this relativity can only refer to the tie that science and knowledge have to a particular historical place, not in the sense of an immediate contemporaneity, but rather in the sense of a comprehensive, determinate social formation. This may either be affirmative in a positive (positivistic) way, or critical in a negative way. So the critique cannot detach itself from its historical location since it has made the social formation belonging to this location and its corresponding power relations into the object that it negates. This also points, by the way, to the possibility of transcendence emerging from immanence as movement. However, this does mean that critique can only be a determinate critique, namely in relation to this historical location understood as an *historical social formation*, and in so far as an aspect of critique negates absolutely, even if only in respect of this specific aspect, that is to say its radical rejection of the governing social structural form, it still does not cease to be thoroughly relative in respect of the wider context and to reflect this context.

Negation must be absolute in respect of its content which itself is nothing other than a negative social form and so must itself be negated. This negative form is the destructive, fetishistic reproduction form and subject form from which nothing is to be allowed to remain apart from the associated traumatic experience remaining in the collective memory of humanity. Regarding this fetish form which constitutes the object of critique, the negation has to be absolute, because if it were not, it would not be any critique at all.

The problem with postmodern thought, and with those intellectual movements since the 19th Century out of which it has been composed and constructed, consists precisely in the failure to develop any criterion for keeping apart the reference levels of relativity within human history as a history of 'cultures' or social formations on the one hand, and determinateness or the absolute in a limited historical space of determinate formation that is itself relative, on the other. In other words, no essential differentiation has been made between historically distinct social structural-forms and accordingly no fashioning of a specific concept of the modern commodity-producing system and the fundamental categories of its form. In this strict sense postmodern theories, like their predecessors, reflect precisely their own sociohistorical relativity, but therefore not fundamentally relativity itself. (Abstract) labour, value, commodity, money, market, competition, state, nation, politics, etc. may count as 'cultural constructs' just like all and every other social appearance, but they appear no less ontological than in the usual bourgeois ideology, which was also inherited by labour movement Marxism.

Consequently unreflective relativism also relativises, in this respect, the difference between the relativity of a determinate historical location on the one hand and determinateness, or absoluteness, within this location on the other hand. It does not interest itself in the total historical space of humanity, within which the various sociohistorical constitutions and their forms of knowledge and cognition stand in a relative relationship to one another, and the interior space of a particular formation, in which an internal absoluteness or at least an appropriate real claim exists, namely that of the respective formal constitution of the fetish which needs to be broken.

This blurring has consequences for the concept of critique, that also becomes blurred and indeterminate itself. The basic categories of the constitution of society disappear behind their internal movement. Critique becomes phenomenologically simplified, relating only to a particular activity or omission in the occluded categories. For the most part these are not positively affirmed in an unmediated way, but only because they are not even made into an object of reflection. *Where everything is equally a 'construct', there is no longer any different degree of hardness and dimension of depth; the difference between ideological apparent explanations and the real appearances of the fetish form are levelled down.* The categorial essence or *substantiality* of the historical social formation remains unreflected and therefore also uncriticised.

A paradoxical reversal of the relationship between the real social process and ideology emerges as the result; or more precisely, this relationship is denied in a certain way and because of this relativism itself is made into bad ideology. The negative real substance of the fetish relationship evades radical critique, because 'substantiality' itself appears fundamentally as emerging from nothing more than a totalitarian claim of thought or picture-thinking. This stands the matter on its head. Radical critique is made to take the blame for that for which the real social relation should be held guilty. It is the critique of ideology that appears as 'totalitarian' instead of the underlying real relationships.

This is therefore the way in which the awareness of relativity transforms itself into apologetic ideology. In relation to the modern commodity producing system this means that its concept, that of capital, dissolves itself into a conceptless system of interconnected 'power relations', which, despite all the postmodern critique of the subject amounts to a falling back into bourgeois illusions of the will, which has, however, been reduced to the displacement within these relations of social 'constructs', *which have all been mapped on the same surface level.* This relativity which is already ideological is then further 'differentiated' and run through one after the other the most varied areas of life and social reproduction. In this way the critique remains stuck at the level of particularity of the phenomena (from the power relations in medicine to the deportation policies of the border agencies, from the 'constructs' of racism to the political rhetoric of practical constraints), without ever being able to move as a whole to the level of the formal connections in society, which then no longer have any substantial concept.

This dissolving of the sociohistorical 'essence' into the phenomenological connectedness of the power relations and their construction, or deconstruction, protects, willingly or unwillingly, the negative substantiality of the real categories of capitalism, which cannot even be named. In so doing, however, the critical potential of relativity is lost. For socially this relativity could only manifest itself in an emancipatory movement of transformation through the breaking of the real claim to absoluteness of the ruling fetishistic form, precisely in its substantial content.

It might be that different fields of being and activity each have their own logic, their own claims, their own sense, etc. and that they are not to be grasped by the claim to absoluteness of one single totalitarian principle, but rather only form a whole in the relativity of their interconnectedness that cannot be reduced to a standard form and its likewise standard substance, is an awareness that must actually first be asserted against the powerful real substantialism of the modern commodity producing system.

There is no critique to be had without the concept of a *negative substantiality* of the value relation and the capital relation. On the other hand the absoluteness claim of this negative substantiality also fractures on the physically constituted nature of the world itself and makes its appearance as a life-destroying process; above all, however, this absoluteness claim fractures just as much on the self-contradictory nature of capitalist substantiality as such and makes its appearance at the same time as an endemic crisis of this sociohistorical formation. For this reason there can also be no adequate theory of crisis without the concept of negative substantiality. Denial or ignorance in respect of the negative social real substantiality is to a large extent identical to denial or ignorance in respect of the crisis in its purport as absolute inner limit of the modern commodity producing society.

The ideological and apologetic character of a relativistic thought that does not even pose this problematic connection essentially consists in imputing sociohistorical relativity and 'openness' where in truth false absoluteness and systematic closedness exists, and for this reason postulates an (only ever partially understood) emancipation utterly independent from a critique of the negative real substance and its formal categories; perhaps by means of the just simply stupid concept of 'democratisation'. The negative substantiality of the capital relation is occluded, denied, made invisible and dissolved in an ideological pseudo-relativity. Exactly for this reason the phenomenological reduction and simplification of the critique corresponds to just that reduction and simplification of crisis theory. This relativism, which is ideological rather than emancipatory is nothing but another camouflage of the bourgeois subjectivity of all classes that does not want to see the truth of its historical obsolescence.

It is no coincidence that traditional Marxism to a large extent shares with postmodernist relativism the rejection of radical crisis theory. For a particular kind of ideological relativist reduction and simplification is also inherent to labour movement Marxist theory in all its variants, as Moishe Postone has shown. What postmodern theory has as an explicit programme appears in Marxism as an implicit simplification; it cannot distinguish between an overarching concept of the value-relation or of the capital-relation based on the historical logic of their formation, and the inner historical states of the aggregation and development of that relation, so that the level of abstraction of the essential concepts (that are only relative on a metahistorical scale to the essential concepts of other formations) is fundamentally false:

> The complete inadequacy of theories of modern capitalism, that take one specific historical configuration of capitalism for the essence of this social formation (the free market or the bureaucratic command state) has become historically... manifest... All these critiques are... incomplete. As we can now see, none of these configurations exhaust capitalism... An adequate critical theory of the present has to be grounded on a non-reified concept of the relations that constitute the essence of capitalism, and the difference between this essence and the changing historical configurations of capitalism.[1]

In this respect the decisive level of the concept of the formation-logical substantiality of capital is what matters, and this level cannot be reached either by traditional Marxism, or by postmodern theory, because of their false, ideological relativism.

1. Foreword to the German edition: Moishe Postone, *Zeit, Arbeit und gesellschaftliche Herrschaft. Eine neue Interpretation der kritischen Theorie von Marx* (Freiburg 2003) 12 ff.
   Hereafter all references to original English edition: Moishe Postone, *Time, Labor, and Social Domination: A reinterpretation of Marx's critical theory* (Cambridge 1993).

2

The philosophical concept of substance and the real metaphysics of capitalism

In order to be able to define the ideological character of the supposedly postmetaphysical bourgeois thought, and particularly its pseudo-relativistic upshot, it is necessary to relate the philosophical concept of substance to the capitalist constitution of Modernity. As a matter of fact there is no generally recognised meaning of the concept of substance given in the history of philosophy. Substance in the philosophy of Antiquity and the Middle Ages means the essential core as distinct from the mere properties (accidents), or the persisting, self-maintaining and therefore the identity as contrasted with the mere 'states' or developments. Aristotle's concept of substance has the meaning both of the material, in the sense of a substrate of 'things', as well as the form of what is essential about these material things.

What the different meanings or levels of meaning of most of the pre-modern philosophical concepts of substance have in common, however, is that they do not necessarily postulate a substantial abstract generality or absoluteness, or in any case not in the physical and social world known to us. There is an assumption, explicit or implicit, that there exist qualitatively different substances capable of stepping into relation with one another. Substance would therefore be something relative in a certain way. For the older philosophies and theologies stars, stones, trees, dogs, human beings, etc. represent different substances, both according to their form and content. And what is identical about a particular substance, for example a human individual, can be regarded as the totality of her or his natural, social, cultural, personal and other relationships in their unique make-up. Only God appears as the absolute, general, 'highest' substance; but this substance is transcendent with respect to the world.

However, one moment of the absolute or abstract-general in respect of the substance of the earthly world is already hinted at in the atomistic theories, and that is through the mode of reduction. For Democritus, say, there 'exists' nothing but void and bodies composed of qualitatively largely homogeneous atoms, differing only in form and size, as the smallest components. In this way the thought of an absolute substantial unity of the world as immanent principle was anticipated. It is no coincidence that this physical reductionism was again systematically taken up by modern natural science where it celebrates its real triumph. Newton's mechanical 'clockwork universe' consists, as he himself writes in the *Opticks*, of "solid, massy, hard, impenetrable, movable particles"[1] that act externally upon each other through "forces". In this homogeneous universe God is merely a sort of watchmaker, but as soon as it has been wound up this mechanical world system runs all by itself. So the Enlightenment does entirely without any transcendent 'highest and first' creative substance.

The reductionist physical standardisation of the world into dead, homogenous building blocks or units located in an absolute, uniform space-time continuum that was only hinted at in Antiquity, has become to some extent radicalised and generalised to a dogma in Modernity. In this way the atomistic concept of substance extends itself beyond physical nature onto every area of determinate being, for instance in Leibniz's concept of 'windowless monads'. This corresponds to a concept of human society that no longer emanates from a commonality, however that is defined, but on the contrary, from the separation of its members, who arrange things among themselves only retrospectively and in an external and mechanical way. It is already clear here that the apparently pure knowledge of nature that Modernity has, that is the 'construct' of the Newtonian clockwork universe, reflects in reality a definite *social relation*, one containing a paradigm of atomistic or abstract individuals, whereby this paradigm in its apparently sheer abstraction of 'individuality as such' includes a thoroughly historical relative particularity, namely that of the *white Western male* subject. However, with this we are already no longer dealing with a mere idea of presuppositionless actors of knowledge about 'the' world, but rather with a definite sociohistorical constitution, namely that of the dawning capitalist one of the modern commodity producing system.

What concerns us here is not, for instance, the overcoming of metaphysics, which is presumed to happen with the progress of the social formation. Both modern natural science as well as the apologetic philosophy and social theory connected with it have quite obvious metaphysical

1. Quoted in Shimon Malin, *Dr. Bertlmanns Socken. Wie die Quantenphysik unser Weltbild verändert* (Leipzig 2003) p40

foundations. These foundations could only be gradually denied and finally cast overboard, because they did not represent metaphysics in the sense of mere philosophical or theological reflections, but rather a *real social relation*, that is to say a *real metaphysics* that is in a certain sense incarnated or folded into the social reproduction process. To the same extent that this real metaphysics has prevailed and been internalised it has also been possible to shade out its philosophical reflections, because the apparently self-evident, axiomatic, and everyday no longer needed extra thought and no longer appeared as a distinct entity.

One might in a certain sense say that all social fetish-constitutions, even those in premodern times, represent a kind of real metaphysics inasmuch as the respective metaphysics never exhausts itself in mere ideas or images, but moreover and at the same time insofar as real social reproduction, social relations and the "metabolism with nature" (Marx) are being regulated. However, the premodern social real metaphysics of social relations, reproduction relations and power structures is in a certain sense 'determined by the beyond', that is mediated through the projection of a sheer transcendent absolute substance, an absolute divine being outside the world who is represented in a personalised-mythological or religious way. As representations of this projected transcendent being the real structures of social reproduction and domination present themselves in a personalised way; namely as a system of personal relations of dependence and obligation.

However, the concept of 'personal dependence' is usually funda-mentally misunderstood (even by Marx, who did not deal precisely with premodern relations) as 'persons' in the sense of pre-modern social fetish-constitutions are taken to mean 'natural persons' or even interest groups according to modern linguistic usage. It then appears as if the structure of 'personal dependence' were a matter of direct, unmediated domination in contrast to modern, indirect and mediated domination. The truth is that premodern relations are just as mediated, only in another way in that the persons themselves become projection screens and therefore representatives of the fetishistic transcendence. Such transcendental persons and personal dependency relations in this sense are kept strictly apart from natural persons and their personal relations; incidentally, even up to bizarre contradictions between the transcendental and natural personality that are in no way inferior to the absurdities of modern value socialisation, for instance in the concept of the "two bodies of the King"[2].

The persons are here in the context of their fetishistic constitution not for themselves as people having will and responsibility, but as worldly representatives of the projected transcendental substantial entity. Since the absolute substance always remains transcendent and takes on no immediate earthly form (except in symbolic representation), it cannot also have a totalitarian grasp of the real world. There exists no social abstract universality, but a manifold gradation of personal representatives and relational contexts at all levels.

On the other hand the capitalist real metaphysics of Modernity is completely different. Here transcendence has been superseded in a certain way; the projected fetishistic substance or the entity as absolute became in the form of the 'self-expansion of value' immediately earthly and social (and only in this sense of a world-immanence 'direct' and no longer 'determined by the beyond', i.e. no longer derived from an otherworldly principle). It is true that the moment of transcendence insofar as it is maintained as the fetishistic essential form 'value' is not a matter of any directly physical or social entity, but rather of an intangible *social abstraction* that to a certain extent has incarnated itself in a paradoxical way in the 'metabolism with nature' and in social relations. In this respect the social relation so constituted represents a real abstraction, not merely an ideological or (in the premodern sense) religious, mythological or other projected image and no mere nominal abstraction.

The projection has become in a certain sense immediately real and thereby also palpably earthly, even if it continues to be mediated to the extent that it only *appears* in real social relations and things (commodities and money), while the essence 'value' being an abstraction cannot be immediate and therefore also not tangible. The paradox of real abstraction consists in the fact that the abstraction, in itself not physical, material or bodily, a thing made of thought, and therefore a *socially objectified* mental creation as fetishistic projection, but nonetheless appearing as a real social relation and real physical materiality, and indeed in objects that essentially are not abstract, but which have been made into objects of real abstraction by the social *projection mechanism*.

2. Ernst H. Kantorowicz, *The King's Two Bodies: A Study in Medieval Political Theology* (Princeton 1997, 1957)

'A thing made of thought' and 'mental creation' are here not to be misunderstood as something 'contrived', say in the sense of an (original) 'social contract' in the ideology of the Enlightenment, a problem of willpower or as ideology; a fetishistic projection mechanism is much more like an objectified form of consciousness and action that must first be decoded and is always already a presupposition of the 'contrived.'

In a certain sense we may almost speak of a regression, since the modern projection mechanism is a throwback into a kind of secondary animism, in that it is no longer the transcendental representative persons, but rather the dead things that appear to have souls, as Marx in his chapter on the fetish showed ironically with his example of the table that falls into metaphysical caprices. To be sure it is no longer a case of things having souls on an individual basis, but of something identically reproduced in the selfsame form of value and price in which the negative sociality of the commodity soul appears, and social relations as reified forms. This secondary animism does not so much impute a soul to things (nature) as it, so to say, makes a thing of, or reifies, the soul (the human complex of relationships); it is to this extent the false immediacy of the real metaphysical projection that no longer makes a detour.

Since projection's transcendence has been superseded to the extent that this projection now appears immediately in earthly things and relationships themselves, it can no longer also be personalised, but has to appear in reified, 'objectified' form and moreover to regulate the social reproduction process, social mediation in every respect. Putting it more precisely: projection 'is' this mediation which for this reason requires no more otherworldly transcendent authority and no personal mediator as representative of this absolute authority, for it is itself already established as absolute. Value, the fetish projection, that appears really material in money, constitutes itself as the worldly social absolute through the feedback movement of money as capital into itself, as the valorisation process or "automatic subject" (Marx), to which the whole of social reproduction and all worldviews are subjected. Every variegation of natural, cultural and social complexes of relationships ceases and is replaced by the claim to absoluteness of the one abstract essential principle 'value' and its negative substantiality.

Ideologically or 'philosophically', as form of reflection *ex post* or in the sense of an accompanying, flanking apologetic, thinking about this real abstract projection mechanism falls back on some definite purport of premodern religious and philosophical concepts of substance, which however appear in completely new configurations that correspond to the capitalist real metaphysics. In the place of the transcendent absolute divinity steps the immanent absolute essential principle 'value' or the valorisation process. Since it is a matter of the projection of a socially objectified process of abstraction, this absolute essential principle can, however, have no immediate material or social determinate being for itself, even though it appears immediately in things and relationships and therefore is immanent. As such it remains intangible, impossible to grasp, 'non-empirical' despite its undoubtable immanence. In this respect the positive, apologetic reflection of capitalist real metaphysics can fall back on the 'idealist' strand of earlier religious and philosophical metaphysics, in particular that of Platonic provenance. The transcendent ideality of the essential Form for Plato and his successors now appears as the immanent ideality of the essential principle in Modernity, especially in German Idealism.

On the other hand there is, however, an important difference in the concept of this ideality. With Plato and his successors it is a case of the transcendent ideality of the essential Forms in the plural, of the ideal Forms of the various things that only appear as 'shadows' in earthly material. In this respect the Platonic idealism of Forms remains just as pluralistic and therefore relativistic as the traditional concept of substance, whose component it is. 'Above' the ideality of the world of plural Forms there rises, however, the sphere of the 'Good' the highest stage and origin of all being, an all-one that is, however, so far removed in its transcendence that it no longer appears as such in its immanence.

The immanent form ideality of Modernity, on the other hand, knows no pluralism of forms and therefore no corresponding relativity any more. The value-form or the 'automatic subject' can tolerate no other God beside itself. The transcendent absolute of the ideal all-one has come down to Earth as the immanent absolute of the essential principle 'value'. Just as with Plato empirical, earthly things possess no independent existence, but are rather merely an 'expression' of the form ideality, but it is in the first place no longer a transcendent ideality of form, but an immanent one appearing in the value based organisation of society, and secondly it is no longer a plural ideality of forms, but a monistic, absolute and totalitarian one. Whether as the Kantian 'form in general' or the Hegelian 'world spirit', as 'absolute will' etc., it is always a matter of a total formal principle of immanence in the last instance and every thing and every relation are only to be its 'mode of appearance'. The world does not build itself from the relationality or different entities, but monistically from the earthly all-one of the self-expansion of value.

It only takes a glance to recognise that Newton's clockwork universe with its uniform atomic building blocks and its uniform absolute continuum of space and time corresponds more or less exactly to this absolute, totalitarian formal idealism. The apparent opposition between the 'idealism' of the form and the 'materialism' of the physical world disappears as soon as both constructs are decoded on the strength of their sociohistorical ground. This is in all probability also true of the ancient early forms of the opposition between Platonic formal idealism and atomic substance materialism in so far as the Western philosophy of Antiquity already represented a still incomplete reflection within the context of the immature connection between the form of the commodity and the form of thought.

In Modernity the complementarity of both these constructs has been accomplished, corresponding in sociohistorical respect to the emergence of the social formation "based on value" (Marx) that is capitalism. The formal idealism of modern philosophy (that only manifests its vulgar degeneration in positivist theories) may be decoded as the essential principle of value, of the paradoxically secularised social fetish form, whereas the substance materialism of mechanistic physics may be decoded as the natural world that has been mauled and in a certain sense put to death by this dictate of form. It is a world of uniform elements and mechanical 'forces' that even in their physical and biological quality have been degraded to mere 'modes of appearance' of the social real abstraction. Today's cultural environment and life-world of the increasingly standardised global capitalist society approximates in a ghostly way to the Newtonian construct of a monotonous mechanical universe. However, what this means for the planetary biosphere as well as for human culture in the broadest sense is step by step destruction.

The classical philosophical concept of substance first differentiates itself clearly into form (immanent-transcendent or 'transcendental' ideal form, value-form) and content (mechanistically shaped, physically reduced world) in the capitalist real metaphysics of Modernity. *What however is still missing in this relation of form and content in the metaphysical real substance is the social agency of the whole real metaphysical arrangement, the mediating moment of movement.* The connection between value-form and the mechanistically reduced substance of nature cannot be static, but only a dynamic process in which nature that has essentially not yet been reduced first becomes reduced in reality to the value abstraction by means of the social mediation, through a social force in the specifically capitalist 'metabolism with nature'.

This force is itself a material substance, not a natural one, though, but rather a social one. The natural substance of modern real abstraction as the formal abstraction of the essential principle 'value' is the physically and mechanistically reduced abstract matter, the social substance of this real metaphysical formal principle is – "abstract labour" (Marx). 'Labour' as a form of activity and at the same time as substance of capital forms the socio-material force and the process whereby the real metaphysical formal principle with its negative, destructive claim to absoluteness can first assert itself in the earthly world. The mediating movement of abstract labour is the self-mediation of substance and consequently the end in itself and self-aggregation in the value-form (appearing in the money-form) and as permanent 'objectification' in the natural material and in the social relations from their shaping to their destruction, in order to make them into the likeness of the self-moving real abstraction.

It has already become clear at this point that traditional Marxism has remained utterly fixed in the real metaphysics of Modernity. Its 'materialism' with its eternal celebration of the corresponding line in the history of Western philosophy represents nothing more than the affirmative reflection of one side of the value-relation or capital-relation, namely the substantial materialism of the physical reduction in which the natural world already appears as fashioned by the capitalist real abstraction. It is the destructive materialism of a fetishistic form of reproduction in which the earth's biosphere is hacked to pieces and ground down. *Logically, the positive substantial materialism of 'labour' corresponds in Marxist thought to the positive physical substantial materialism of a destructively treated nature, with this labour constituting the agent of this treatment.* This 'materialism' of the Marxist ontology of labour and the mechanistic belief in natural science that belongs to it far from overcoming the formal idealism of the apparently opposed philosophical tradition, in fact, exactly as in bourgeois thought and as its modified continuation, merely behaves as its' complement.

In this respect, the Hegel who stands on his head is not turned the right way up and stood on his feet, but rather his feet are always running under the command of his head, the formal-ideal capitalist essential principle. If they are decoded socially, fetishistic relationships as 'real metaphysics' are always at the same time *'real idealisms'* that have been carried to extremes for the first time by the immanent capitalist real idealism of the 'automatic subject' in the shape of the self-expansion of value, the cybernetic feedback mechanism of the real abstraction value back into itself. *In this way the real materialism of labour and capitalist natural science is ironically nothing other than the practical form of appearance of the real idealism of the value-form, and not the other way round.* The real abstraction of value represents an aggregation or a form of determinate being of the *real-abstract praxis* of labour and also the converse; just for this reason does abstract labour constitute the mode in which the non-material social essential principle seizes the material world in its ghostlike way.

Hegel's 'objective idealism' is closer to the point in a certain respect than the 'objective materialism' of Marxist thought; but Hegel thinks the capitalist real idealism apologetically as a positive movement of self-mediation of the real-abstract essence thus fundamentally missing its negative, destructive, murderous quality. On the other hand Marxist materialism buys into the transition to the (largely simplified, stuck in immanence) critique so that for its part it misses the character of social real abstraction. As an abstraction value and abstract labour remain in a certain sense a thing made of thought and consequently a (negative) ideality. What it is not, however, is a *subjective*, merely *reflexive* ideality, not an ideality of mere (linguistic-mental) nominal abstractions, but an ideality objectified by historical processes, an ideality 'materialised' by forced praxis.

In order to attain a complete critique of the negative substantiality of the capitalist fetish relationship it is not Hegel's objective idealism that must be stood on its feet instead of its head, it is rather that the head of real abstraction must be guillotined. Only that would be the liberatory, transcending praxis that no longer forcibly shapes the social and natural world, but itself destroys the essential principle of this destructive praxis.

3

*The negative substance concept of abstract labour in
Marx's critique of political economy*

It is an old, long-established matter that labour movement Marxism largely suppressed or relativised, simplified and watered down the concept of critique in Marx's critique of political economy in order to arrive at a completely positive 'political economy' upon the uncritically presupposed ground of the modern form of the fetish. For this reason the textbooks of the lost world of 'real existing socialism' always spoke in deadly seriousness of a 'political economy of capitalism' and a 'political economy of socialism', instead of conceptualising and developing socialism as the practical critique of political economy as such. It was therefore inevitable that in the understanding of Marxism even Marx's substance concept of abstract labour had to appear in the end totally positive, as the mere definition of an objective, 'given by a law of nature' ontological fact that was not to be transcended.

This point of view, however, does not accord at all with the way in which Marx introduces the concept of abstract labour already on the fourth page of the first volume of *Capital* one can read:

> If we then disregard the use-value of commodities, they have only one property left, that of being products of labour. However, the product of labour has already undergone a change in our hands. If we abstract from the use-value of the product of labour, then we abstract at the same time from the bodily constituents and forms that make it a use-value. It is no longer a table, a house, yarn, or any other useful thing. All its sensual properties are extinguished. It is therefore no longer the product of carpentry, masonry, spinning, or any other specific kind of productive labour. Along with the useful characteristics of the products of labour, the useful characteristics of the various kinds of labour represented in them disappear. Therefore, also the different concrete forms of these labours disappear. They

> no longer differ from each other, but are altogether reduced
> to equal human labour, human labour in the abstract.
> Let us consider now what remains of the products of labour.
> Nothing has remained of them except the same ghostlike
> material, a mere congelation of undifferentiated human
> labour, i.e. of the expenditure of labour-power without
> regard to the form of its expenditure. These things represent
> nothing but that in their production human labour-power
> has been expended, human labour has been accumulated.
> As crystals of this social substance which they have all in
> common they are values - commodity values.[1]

What cannot be overlooked here is that the concept of abstract labour
is not at all a matter of a dry, positivistic definition, but of how to approach
the conceptual critique of a really negative fact. The "abstraction from
use-value", in which "all its sensual properties are extinguished", so as to
arrive at a "ghostlike material", "a mere congelation of undifferentiated
human labor", already characterises a really destructive tendency against
the sensual and social world. What is at issue here is precisely the
practical, active side of a real social abstraction and not a mere linguistic
one expressing things made of thought, without thereby immediately
stretching actively out into the natural and social world. The abstraction
'labour' more closely represents an immediate practical dimension, in fact
as the *a priori of social reproduction*, with unpredictable consequences.

Here Marx approaches a critique that he himself does not follow
through to its conclusion. He does develop (unlike most Marxists) a radical
critique of the real abstraction contained in the modern concept of labour,
but at the same time he remains stuck in the Protestant-Enlightenment
ontology of labour, as was the labour movement that arose within the
same historical context as his theory and which also inscribed it upon
its banners. Marx had therefore to attempt to separate the supposedly
ontological principle of 'labour' from the specific capitalist real abstraction
of which it is an expression. An enterprise that was largely lost on his
followers who wholly absorbed the concept of labour in transhistorical

1.   Karl Marx, *Capital I*, trans. Ben Fowkes (London 1976) p128
     Emended translation by Hans G. Ehrbar, *Annotations to Marx's Capital* (2002)
     (see: http://content.csbs.utah.edu/~ehrbar/akmc.htm) p80-98

ontologisation – with a few exceptions who stand out as particularly reflective, although they did not go further than the reproduction of Marx's aporia in the concept of labour as being at the same time capitalist real abstraction and also an ontological principle.

Marx formulates his aporia quite openly in the *Grundrisse* when he defines his terms in the *Introduction*:

> Labour seems to be a very simple category. The notion of labour in this universal form, as labour in general, is also extremely old. Nevertheless 'labour' in this simplicity is economically considered just as modern a category as the relations which give rise to this simple abstraction. [...]
>
> It was an immense advance when Adam Smith rejected all restrictions with regard to the activity that produces wealth for him it was labour as such, neither manufacturing, nor commercial, nor agricultural labour, but all types of labour. The abstract universality which creates wealth implies also the universality of the objects defined as wealth: they are products as such, or once more labour as such, but in this case past, materialized labour. [...]
>
> The fact that the specific kind of labour is irrelevant presupposes a highly developed complex of actually existing kinds of labour, none of which is any more the all-important one. The most general abstractions arise on the whole only when concrete development is most profuse, so that a specific quality is seen to be common to many phenomena, or common to all. Then it is no longer perceived solely in a particular form. This abstraction of labour is, on the other hand, by no means simply the conceptual resultant of a variety of concrete types of labour. The fact that the particular kind of labour employed is immaterial is appropriate to a form of society in which individuals easily pass from one type of labour to another, the particular type of labour being accidental to them and therefore irrelevant. Labour, not only as a category but in reality, has become a means to create wealth in general, and has ceased to be tied as an attribute to a particular individual. This state of affairs is most pronounced in the United States, the most

modern form of bourgeois society. The abstract category 'labour', 'labour as such', labour *sans phrase*, the point of departure of modern economics, thus becomes a practical fact only there. The simplest abstraction, which plays a decisive role in modem political economy, an abstraction which expresses an ancient relation existing in all social formations, nevertheless appears to be actually true in this abstract form only as a category of the most modern society. [...]

The example of labour strikingly demonstrates how even the most abstract categories, despite their validity in all epochs - precisely because they are abstractions - are equally a product of historical conditions even in the specific form of abstractions, and they retain their full validity only for and within the framework of these conditions.[2]

This reflection on the concept of labour is aporetic in many respects. In the way it is presented, the abstraction as well as its social content, is on the one hand positive, 'progress', general 'wealth-creating activity', the development of a diversity; and on the other hand as negative, as 'irrelevant' in relation to its content. Likewise, 'labour' presents itself on the one hand as a 'rational' abstraction, as the merely general term for a profuse "concrete development" of activities; on the other hand Marx corrects himself immediately and points out that this abstraction is a matter of "by no means simply the conceptual resultant of a variety of concrete types of labour"; but rather of the correspondence of a 'social formation' in which this abstraction becomes real and thereby determines actual practice. However, Marx holds firmly above all to the notion that the abstraction 'labour' is "ancient" and "valid for all epochs"; on the other hand though, he clarifies at the same time that it is "just as modern a category" as "the relations which give rise to this simple abstraction", so that this category is in the end indeed the "product of historical conditions", and namely

2.   Karl Marx, *Grundrisse*, trans. Martin Nicolaus (London 1973) p103
Emended translation by Hans G. Ehrbar, *Annotations to Karl Marx's Intoduction to Grundrisse* (2010) (See: http://content.csbs.utah.edu/~ehrbar/akmc.htm) p83-90

modern ones, and it possesses its "full validity only for and within the framework of these conditions."

This aporetic reasoning can only be resolved by solely identifying the category 'labour' as a real abstraction and so as historical, modern and capitalist, and therefore giving up the ontology of labour altogether. If Marx claims sloppily that this abstraction (surely in the sense of a mere nominal abstraction) is an "ancient" one, then this identification is obviously not based on a historical investigation. In fact there have been many societies in history, among which are included the so-called high cultures, such as ancient Egypt, in which there is absolutely no abstract-universal category of activity. Even in societies in which such a nominal general concept (precisely not a real abstraction) seems to be found it is a matter of very limited areas of activity and never of a *social universality* of "activity in general". If the modern reading of 'labour' is inserted here, then it leads astray and is an anachronism; actually, it is a translation error (by the way, this is also true for other specifically modern categories belonging to the fetish relation of the self-expansion of value, such as for example, politics and the state, etc.) Insofar as the abstraction 'labour' as a concept of modern society was adopted from the Indogermanic language, it had to be completely redefined, because in these languages the term 'labour' consistently refers to the specific activity of slaves, dependants, minors, etc. That is to say it is not a mentally constructed general term for various areas of activity, but is a social abstraction (and insofar also a real abstraction in this specific pre-modern sense), but is exactly for this reason not a social universality, not a category of social synthesis as it is in Modernity.

Marx's aporia continues in the analysis of 'capital' as he introduces the determinations of 'abstract labour' and 'concrete labour'. Strictly speaking the term 'abstract labour' is a logical pleonasm (like 'black darkness') since the attribute is already contained in the concept; 'labour' being already an abstraction. Conversely, the term 'concrete labour' is a contradiction in terms (like 'bright darkness') since the adjective stands in contradiction to the concept; as an abstraction (which even conceptually has only arisen on the ground of a real social abstraction) 'labour' cannot *per se* be 'concrete' in the sense of a definite kind of activity.

It could be said that these Marxist determinations reflect the real para-dox of the capital relation and its socialisation by value, since that really is the way that what is in itself concrete, the diversity of the world, is reduced to an abstraction, standing the relation of universal and particular on its head. The universal is no longer a manifestation of the particular, but on the contrary the particular is just a manifestation of the totalitarian universal. Consequently the concrete no longer represents the structured diversity of the particular, but rather it 'is' nothing more than the 'expression' of the real abstraction of the universal, the universal substance.

Marx, however, is not totally aware of what he is actually reflecting here, because he wants to hold fast to an ontological and transhistorical moment of the abstraction "labour". He attempts to fix this moment to a concept of use-value:

> So far as labour forms use-values, i.e., as useful labour, it is therefore a necessary condition, independent of all forms of society, for the existence of the human race; it is an eternal nature-imposed necessity, in order to mediate the metabolism between man and nature, and thus human life.[3]

The concept of 'usefulness for specific purposes' is, however, not a category of social synthesis and therefore also not to be equated without further ado with the concept of 'use-value' as Marx does throughout. The category of use-value is merely abstract usefulness (a further real-paradoxical determination) and insofar itself a component part of modern real abstraction; it is not a concept related to need, but rather a conceptual representation of the value-form mediation (the use-value of the one commodity expresses as equivalent form only the exchange-value of the other commodity).

The term use-value only makes any sense at all in mediation with exchange-value, as the polarity of the value relation, and is therefore far from being "a necessary condition, independent of all forms of society, for the existence of the human race".[4] Insofar as "labour" posits 'use-value' this is no transhistorical, ontological determination outside of the value abstraction, but *nothing other than the specific way in which the real abstraction takes possession of objects that in themselves are not abstract*. What Marx paradoxically calls 'concrete labour', for this reason does not

3. Marx, *Capital I* p133 as emended by Ehrbar p217
4. Ibid. p133 and p217 respectively

represent an 'eternal nature-imposed necessity', but is *nothing other than the specific material way that 'abstract labour' accesses the natural or social 'stuff'*. Once this has been clarified it might be possible to make further use of Marx's established concepts with, however, a changed meaning.

At this point it is necessary to anticipate a line of argument that will be developed later at greater length. This concerns the material character of the substance of abstract labour that Marx, as is well known, conceived of as "expenditure of human brain, nerves, muscles" independently of the concrete manner of this expenditure, whether as the labour of the joiner or the weaver, etc. Representatives of a certain line (often today with a postmodern spin) in the postmarxist debate pride themselves in speaking pejoratively of a false 'substantialism' or physiological 'naturalism' in Marx and the traditional Marxists, and it is through this 'naturalising' that abstract labour is transformed into a transhistorical ontological fact, since after all human beings always have to expend 'nerve, muscle, brain'. Incidentally, Moishe Postone unfortunately also subscribes to this point of view.[5]

It is indeed true that traditional Marxism ontologises abstract labour, as will be shown in detail in the next section. Nonetheless, the critique of 'substantialism' outlined above is quite wrongly applied. At issue, however, is not so much the clarification of the concept of substance and labour as the defence of a substantial theory of crisis which argues for the historical decline of labour-substance as value-substance of capital (desubstantialisation). In this sense abstract labour is understood as a relation of quantity, as a concept of substance in the quantitative sense. For in order for something to be increased or decreased, it has to really be there in the sense of material content; a mere form as substance cannot represent a relation of quantity. For this reason the critique of the materially substantial character of abstract labour serves as a defence against the substantial theory of crisis and thus the denial of any absolute inner limit to the self-expansion of capital. Crisis is then reduced to the superficiality of the market as an 'operational error' of the market mechanism that may be corrected through political regulation, or it disappears entirely from the basic theoretical discussion.

Since this line of argument against 'substantialism' belongs more to the abstract labour theory of quantity and crisis, it will be dealt with at

5. See Postone, *Time, Labor, and Social Domination* p144

length only in the second section of this study. In anticipation the issue can be briefly addressed here in the sense of the negative quality concept of abstract labour which plays a role in it. The apparently reflective postmarxist anti-substantialists even fall behind the level of traditional Marxism, because they overlook something quite essential. Marx speaks explicitly of the physiological expenditure of nerve, muscle, brain etc. but by no means at all in an unmediated naturalistic or transhistorical sense. Since the physiological expenditure of human energy is in a purely 'natural' way not separable from the concrete form of this expenditure. However, this is exactly what happens socially in the labour abstraction. And this abstraction from the concrete form of expenditure is neither rational nor transhistorical. If one were to say, for example, to an ancient Egyptian catching fish that he was here not simply catching fish, but essentially expending 'nerve, muscle, brain' in the abstract sense, he would quite rightly shake his head. An abstraction like this only makes 'sense' in the context of the modern real abstraction.

However, the abstract substance of labour is not without material or 'physical' content, even if it is not a case of an unmediated natural substance (since an expenditure of nerve, muscle, brain lacking in content is simply not possible), but of a social substance as abstraction. It is a case of one side of the *materialisation of the fetishistic form-ideality* (the other would be the reductionistically treated natural stuff itself), in that under the dictates of this negative form-ideality only the expenditure as such is posited as essential, independently of its concrete determination and also in practice ignoring the concrete manner of its expenditure (that naturally takes place nonetheless) in a definite social context.

In the abstraction as real abstraction there then remains a thoroughly material content as a residue, namely the expenditure of 'human energy in general'. For the 'automatic subject' of the process of self-expanding value it is completely inessential whether trousers or hand-grenades are manufactured; all that is essential is that *bodily human combustion processes* (expenditure of energy) take place that can present themselves as a quantum of value, in itself an utterly absurd procedure. But these combustion processes do indeed take place in reality; what is absurd is only treating and 'representing' them independently of their concrete form and thereby of the purpose of their material content, which happens because the social purpose is exactly this fetishistic 'representation'. The reduction to the bodily combustion process is a social abstraction, but for this reason is no mere thing made of thought (like, for instance a nominal generic term), but it refers to a thoroughly real moment for which reason it is also a real abstraction.

'Representation' here is an essential process of what Marx characterised as the fetishism of the value-form. For the quantum of expended human energy is not only not to be separated from the concrete form of this expenditure, but it is also, as soon as the product has been produced, something past and no longer ready to hand, for which reason it is also, of course, not 'contained' in the products in any natural or physical sense. The 'representation' as an objective process takes place therefore only in the heads of the social subjects constituted in this way, namely as the fetishised practical perception and 'treatment' of their own society. However, this 'representation' refers to something that necessarily does not take place only in the heads of the subjects as form of perception and action, but is physically real, and that is namely the past combustion processes in human bodies, the expenditure of units of energy.

Since the quantum of energy consumed in the process of its expenditure cannot really be separated from the concrete form or determination of this expenditure, and since as definitively past expenditure it cannot be literally contained in the objects, the social representation is indeed in this respect unreal in a double sense. However, this quantum of energy must really have been burnt up in the past, so it does represent (even if paradoxically 'represented') an actual physical substance. The *form of this representation*, however, has nothing physical about it, but is a real abstraction, a socially constituted manner of perception and action in which natural materials and produced goods are in fact treated as if they were the physical objects of the pure representation of past combustion processes taken place in human bodies.

Abstract labour is therefore a definite aggregated state of the fetishistic modern form-ideality which refers completely, however, to an energetic quantum of actually expended labour-power, that is to say to a material, quantifiable content (not in respect of the individual commodity, but of the social average of commodities). This content is, however, as an abstraction, 'ghostlike', not only in the result of the value quasi-material, but already in the process of expenditure itself, therefore in practical respect as a determination of an expended mass of nerve, muscle, brain that is separated from its material form. Undertaking definite transformations of natural materials under the *a priori* essential determination that quanta of abstract human energy are here expended regardless of the concrete form of their expenditure, this determination is substantial in a material sense, though not in a natural one, but rather in a social one, and not in a transhistorical one, but in a historically specific one in the modern constitution of the fetish.

4

The positive concept of abstract labour in Marxist labour ontology

Marx came close to a critique of the concept of labour as the substance of capital, but he was unable to accomplish this critique since he still had one leg on the ground of modern labour ontology. While Marxism (as traditional or labour movement Marxism) completely set its heart on the ontological moment in Marx's presentation and wanted to critique capitalism from the transhistorical standpoint of 'labour', the concept of abstract labour necessarily had to remain underexposed and thereby the substance of capital also remained unconceptualised. Addressing this theme as a central issue beyond a merely positivist definition is found in a very few theoreticians. In the 1920s for example I.I. Rubin, in his 1924 work *Essays on Marx's Theory of Value*, promptly came to the opinion that:

> When we see the decisive importance which Marx gave to the theory of abstract labour, we must wonder why this theory has received so little attention in Marxist literature.[1]

However, Rubin himself in no way goes beyond Marx's aporia in respect of the concept of labour. He gives a positivist rendering of abstract labour in a twofold manner, once as historical progress in the establishment of social universality:

> Only on the basis of commodity production, characterized by a wide development of exchange, a mass transfer of individuals from one activity to another, and indifference of individuals towards the concrete form of labour, is it possible to develop the homogeneous character of all

---

1. Isaak Illich Rubin, *Essays on Marx's Theory of Value,* trans. Miloš Samardźija and Fredy Perlman (Detroit 1972) p138

> working operations as forms of human labour in general...
> We would not be exaggerating if we said that perhaps the
> concept of man in general and of human labour in general
> emerged on the basis of the commodity economy. This is
> precisely what Marx wanted to point out when he indicated
> that the general human character of labour is expressed in
> abstract labour.[2]

Here Rubin stresses the role of real abstraction (which does not yet
appear to him as such) in a positively connoted 'development', although
he incidentally (like Marx) also speaks of the "indifference of individuals
towards the concrete form of labour." Without, however, having Marx's
radical critical orientation.

Nevertheless, he displays on the other hand a differentiation in order
to bridge Marx's aporia somehow: the abstract labour of commodity
production, that appears in Rubin without further ado as capitalist, is to
disappear along with capitalism. However, a moment of it has to remain,
but with another character:

> Although abstract labor is a specific property of a
> commodity economy, socially equalized labor can be found,
> for example, in a socialist commune... Every abstract labor
> is social and socially equalized labor, but not every socially
> equalized labor can be considered abstract labor.[3]

Rubin therefore postulates a transhistorical continuity of 'labour'
along the horizon of Enlightenment progress, whereby capitalist abstract
labour is to be only a special case of labour abstraction in the sense of the
abstract and general as 'socially equalised' labour. In truth, however, it is
only a matter of paraphrasing abstract labour in a commodity producing
system, as is very clearly shown with the definition of 'socialist labour':

> Let us imagine some socialist community where labor
> is divided among the members of the community. A
> determined social organ equalizes the labors of various

2. Ibid. p138
3. Ibid. p139

individuals with each other, since without this equalization a more or less extensive social plan cannot be realized. But in such a community, the process of equalization of labor is secondary and supplements the process of socialization and allocation of labor. Labor is first of all socialized and allocated labor. We can also include here the quality of socially equalized labor as a derived and additional characteristic. The basic characteristic of labor is its characteristic of being social and allocated labor, and a supplementary characteristic is its property of being socially equalized labor.[4]

The only thing that makes a difference between socialist 'equalised' labour and abstract labour in the capitalist sense is the supposedly merely 'secondary' and 'supplementary' character of the abstracting, which, however, is then denied in the same breath as according to Rubin no 'social plan' would be possible without this equalisation. However, a plan is defined by being made in advance, otherwise it would not be one and consequently the 'process of equalisation' according to Rubin's own logic cannot be merely secondary and supplementary, but constitutes the presupposition of the whole thing. Furthermore, that which precedes the supposedly merely supplementary equalisation process is once again 'labour', therefore that (real) abstraction. What is obviously so difficult to think here is the problem of overcoming the destructive real abstraction itself, that is the awareness that this 'equalisation' always means subjugating the various fields of reproduction and life with their own different intrinsic logics, time scales and requirement profiles to a uniform logic of subsumption, but exactly that constitutes the uniform, totalitarian substance logic of abstract labour.

That planning in the sense of assigning resources to different areas could not be based on this equalisation, which is solely conditioned by the value abstraction and not by some real technical requirement, is not even called into question. That is shown particularly crassly when Rubin speaks without further ado about a "total mass of homogeneous social labour" under socialism.[5] It matters little that it is the same individual

4. Ibid. p96
5. Ibid. p141

who, for instance, lays electrical wiring, plants an apple tree, writes a letter or looks after children. It still does not mean in the slightest that she or he deals with all these qualitatively quite different 'objectifications' as a 'homogeneous mass' of substantial expenditure of energy on one and the same timescale of an abstract flow of time. Nor, does it mean in the least, that a whole society need behave in this way once it has left the commodity form behind it.

A society that has organised itself consciously as a total being of freely associated individuals means precisely that it is no longer subjugated to a fetishistic principle of 'equalisation' and also need never suffer because of a 'lack of time', which represents a specific feature of self-expanding value as an end in itself. Just because there is not an infinite amount of time available by no means implies that it would be 'lacking' in itself and necessitate an equalisation process of 'homogenous' units of expended human energy with the aim of facilitating 'optimal efficiency'. In general, this completely crazy notion could only arise under the dictate of abstract labour in the process of socialisation by value.

That something else is at issue, other than the material or social necessity of resource allocation, is made clear by Rubin when he attempts to describe the modalities of this ominous equalisation:

> We suppose that the organs of the socialist community equalize labor of different types and of different individuals. For example, one day of simple labor is taken as 1 unit, and a day of qualified labor as 3 units; a day of the labor of experienced worker A is taken as equal to two days of the labor of inexperienced worker B, and so on. On the basis of these general principles, the organs of social accounting know that worker A expended in the social process of production 20 units of labor, and worker B, 10 units of labor.[6]

In reality the problem consists not in a planned resource distribution among qualitatively different areas of reproduction and life, but rather in the *cost-allocation* by the distribution of goods and services. It is the problem of attributing an abstract 'output' that this 'homogenisation' is

6. Ibid. p152

to enforce, in spite of the supposed overcoming of specifically capitalist abstract labour. In this way, a moment of abstract labour under the capitalist logic of valorisation is dragged forward. Incidentally, it also manifests itself with Proudhon and generally in all the 'time-chitting' utopias.

An element of this illogicality is even found in Marx himself when he speaks of the infamous 'two stages' of socialism/communism. At first the abstract work ethic, and so too a moment of valorisation logic, still holds: "From each according to his ability, to each according to his work". Only in the far-distant communism – when, incidentally, 'labour' has also characteristically become 'life's prime want' – is it permitted that: "From each according to his ability, to each according to his need." There is, however, no necessity for this. If Marx did not consider the development of productivity under the capitalist form-determination in the 19th Century sufficient to throw the bourgeois work ethic overboard, then this is the fault of his adhering to elements of the Protestant work ethic. Quite apart from the fact that this abstract work ethic is a specifically modern one, that paradoxically has only arisen with the blind development of capitalist productive forces as destructive forces, and therefore not tied to the premodern situation of a relatively minimal development of productive forces.

Thereby in Marxism the aporia in Marx's concept of labour was dissolved one-sidedly into the positive ontology of labour; and for this very reason the critical concept of abstract labour had to remain underexposed and reduced to a positivistic definition. Rubin marked out a line of argument for the reflective theoretician that has sufficed until today by his doubling up of this concept into, on the one hand, the definition of a purely capitalist category (for him it was still identical with social commodity production in general) and, on the other hand, into the definition of an abstract universal 'social equalisation' that holds for all forms of society. In this manner the aporia was far from being dissolved, it was only raised to a higher level. However, even that was far too much reflection for Stalinism and Rubin was sent to the camps in 1931, as were so many disagreeable intellectuals, since when he has counted among the disappeared.

Rubin's fate indicates that the 'socialism' that emerged in Russia, following the October Revolution, needed to suppress every theoretical reflection that approached Marx's aporia, because this 'socialism' had no use for even the least differentiation. Theoretical determinations, such as Rubin's, that still tried to grapple with the problem of demarcating the abstract labour (that Marx unequivocally ascribed to the capital relation) from an 'equalisation of labours' no longer conceived of as making commodities in a postcapitalist society, were bound to appear in the same measure dangerous and subversive to this 'socialism'. Since, it was quite openly shown in practice how the character of the social synthesis rested on abstract labour, value, commodity and the money-form.

Thus was the character of the whole epoch identified, which in retrospect may be decoded as a history of 'recuperative modernisation'. The historical movements on the capitalist periphery could not burst the integument of the modern fetish form, but aimed at exactly the opposite by implementing socially the real categories of a modern commodity producing system. In the industrialised countries of Europe, where this system was already established, the same was also true in another way of the Western labour movement that went to court to attain 'recognition' of citizens and subjects with rights in precisely the form that logically presupposed abstract labour. This historical context is the reason why the critical content of Marx's concept of abstract labour was lost, and both the Western labour movement and Eastern state socialism, as well as the later national liberation movements in the South, were caught within the bourgeois ontology of labour.

If in Marx himself the concept of abstract labour still had clearly negative connotations, even if the facts of the matter were presented aporetically, in traditional Marxist theory, and not only there, it was completely obscured. Either: by not understanding the concept of abstract labour as a negative real abstraction, but only as a conceptual and definitional abstraction; or, if understood as real abstraction (and at any rate only in the reflexive line of Western Marxism) *then not as such a priori, but only as a real abstraction a posteriori, that is to say purely referring to the products of labour as commodities on the market.* Consequently, abstract labour was understood as the way in which real, supposedly always concrete and 'useful', labour is only retrospectively perceived in an abstract form in the finished commodities as objects on the market, to some extent as a socially constructed product quality. In the Eastern state socialist ideology this happened positively, in Western Marxism negatively; in both cases nonetheless the determination of abstract labour limited itself in the same degree to a process of abstraction that would only be undertaken on the market in the act of exchange. And so it has remained in Marxist literature.

In other words: Marxism prides itself on its 'foundation in production' only in the positivistic sense of an ontological 'dignity of labour', while its critique of capitalism has in truth merely a 'foundation in circulation' and precisely for this reason remains superficial. Since understanding the process of real abstraction as undertaken only in retrospect on the product of labour as commodity on the market, means nothing other than limiting the critique of real abstraction and thereby of the commodity producing system, as far as it is done at all, to the sphere of circulation. The problem of capitalist negativity is thus wholly narrowed down to the sphere of circulation and the mode of distribution linked to it and only perceived from this superficial perspective, as Moishe Postone was the first to establish:

> The focus of Marx's historical critique, according to this interpretation, is the mode of *distribution*.
>
> This statement may seem paradoxical, because Marxism is generally considered to be a theory of *production*. Let us, therefore, briefly consider the role of production in the traditional interpretation. If the forces of production (which, according to Marx, come into contradiction with capitalist relations of production) are identified with the industrial mode of producing, then that mode is implicitly understood as a purely technical process, intrinsically independent of capitalism. Capitalism is treated as a set of extrinsic factors impinging on the process of production: private ownership and exogenous conditions of the valorization of capital within a market economy. Relatedly, social domination in capitalism is understood essentially as class domination, which remains external to the process of production.[7]

The main point of this simplification is the reduction of abstract labour to the sphere of circulation, since this is the only way that distribution mediated by circulation can become the central object of the

7. Postone, *Time, Labor, and Social Domination* p8-9 (emphasis in the original)

critique, whereas production, as Postone shows, is only central insofar as it constitutes the *standpoint* (rather than the *object*) of critique.[8] Resulting from this simplified critique comes an equally simplified perspective of a supposed overcoming of capitalism either by means of the paradigm of 'just exchange' or that of state 'planned commodity production' (or a mixture of both), while production as such as commodity forming is explicitly or implicitly regarded in a positivist manner as ontologically given.

Inasmuch as traditional Marxism misunderstood its critique as one of 'production', it referred in consequence not to production in the sense of a social form and activity of real abstraction, but solely to the subjectively and sociologically misunderstood rule 'over' production as a legal property definition. That is to say in the sense of a particular Marxist terminology that merely refers to the 'juridical superstructure' of production, and so production as an activity and in its social substance remains unexamined. Consequently it also refers only to relations of circulation, since only within these do the owners of commodities come into contact with each other as abstractly free atomic individuals with rights and as "keepers of their commodities" (Marx).

If the critique of the fetish form appears here at all, it restricts itself to the sphere of circulation. The fetish form of value overarching the whole process of social reproduction (including 'labour'/production as well as legal, state and political forms) is *reduced in this way to the commodity form in the sense of the mere materiality of circulation.* Paradoxically therefore, "abstract labour" does not appear as the determining moment of production (this is conversely reduced to the concrete and in that way ontologised), it does not even appear in production, but in complete reversal as a mere moment of circulation, as a process of abstraction *ex post* only occurring on the market in exchange. *Consequently, the "Double Character of the Labour Represented in Commodities"[9] that Marx identified is split between two different spheres instead of determining the character of reproduction as a whole. In production there is nothing other than 'concrete' or 'useful' labour, while the product that constitutes the commodity presents itself only in circulation as the representative of abstract labour.*

8.   Ibid. p9
9.   Marx, *Capital I* p131 as emended by Ehrbar p202

The theory of Alfred Sohn-Rethel, who was the first to introduce the concept of real abstraction into the Marxist debate, is prototypical in this regard. However, according to him, socially objectified abstraction is real only as an 'exchange abstraction'.[10] It is only on the market that abstract labour appears as the common substance of commodities, making them compatible at all:

> The abstraction that takes place in exchange arises from the relation of exchange itself. It does not arise from the thinglike nature of commodities, neither their nature as use-values nor as products of labour...[11]

The vulgar materialist misunderstanding that determines the value abstraction and thereby the logic of abstract labour as a thinglike quasi-natural property of production, is here advanced in order to deny every relation of value abstraction to the 'concrete' labour-process at all, even in the sense of a social rather than an natural determination, and to condemn it with the same verdict, whereby production is quietly removed from real abstraction. There is, however, nothing natural about labour itself, and precisely in their form as the products of labour things are already commodities or products of real abstraction, and do not become such only through exchange on the market. Sohn-Rethel has indeed earned the merit of setting down a milestone by developing awareness of the concept of real abstraction as a theoretical problem, but he remains totally and utterly a labour ontologist and for that reason is caught up in circulation with his concept of real abstraction, even more so because of his splitting of the concept of labour into a bad, purely circulatory abstraction *a posteriori* on the one hand and a 'good', supposedly ontologically productive concreteness on the other. He asserts therefore "two forms of social synthesis—one effected by means of exchange, and one by means of labour".[12]

Mainstream labour movement Marxism did not even reach that far and so in its simplification at least remained consistent as the problem

10. Alfred Sohn-Rethel, *Warenform und Denkform* (Frankfurt/Main 1978) p120
11. Ibid. p114
12. Postone, *Time, Labor, and Social Domination* p177

of real abstraction fell by the wayside and production and circulation were both affirmed as forms. Critique referred merely to class-based appropriation (by means of a sociologically simplified understanding of surplus-value) in the sense of the juridical "power of control" and to the "anarchy" of the market. As far as overcoming capitalism was concerned, it appeared on the one hand as the purely external planning of the total commodity forming reproduction process (which was already underway in capitalism itself through concentration of capital, financial control and state regulation) and on the other hand through the appointment of political representatives of the proletariat to the nerve centre of planning. In this simplified understanding there was no place at all for the concepts either of real abstraction or of fetishism.

In a quite naive way the works of academic political economy produced under 'real existing socialism' maintained a grossly positivist and completely unreflective concept of abstract labour that fell far behind the awareness of the problems involved shown by Rubin. To take one example at random, a fat tome put together by an authors' collective under the direction of Günter Mittag, *The Political Economy of Socialism and its Application in the German Democratic Republic*, states:

> Commodity producing labour of socialist producers is on the one hand the planned expenditure of labour in its useful, concrete or use-value creating form. On the other hand it also acts at the same time as abstract, value-forming labour, in its generalised form, abstracted from concrete particularities, that is to say in the value-form, through the overall context of the socialist mode of production. Commodity producing labour has therefore a double character, being at the same time concrete and abstract labour. The concrete labour used in the factory according to plan for the production of material goods always needs to realise itself as abstract, value-forming labour so that it may function as social labour... The double character of commodity producing labour under socialism is fundamentally different from that under capitalism. On the one hand, the commodity producing labour of socialist producers is the planned expenditure of labour in its useful, concrete or use-value creating form, while on

the other hand it appears at the same time in a general form due to the overall conditions of the socialist mode of production, abstracted from its concrete particularities, as abstract value-creating labour, that is to say, in the value-form. Therefore commodity producing labour has a double character, being at the same time concrete and abstract labour. The concrete labour employed in the factories producing material goods according to plan must always realise itself as abstract value-creating labour, in order to function as social labour ... The double character of commodity producing labour under socialism differs fundamentally from that under capitalism. While value-creating labour under capitalist commodity production mediates exploitation and so is a link in the system of capitalist appropriation, the planned process of social appropriation on the part of socialist producers liberated from exploitation expresses itself in value-creating labour under socialism ... Consequently, socialist society puts the labour expended by each production unit engaged in the social division of labour into a relation where socially equal amounts of labour are employed. In this way socialist society reduces that part of total labour to socially necessary labour, or value. Concrete labour is reduced to abstract, socially determined, labour by the realisation of the product of concrete labour, the use-value.[13]

This misses the whole point of the problem of the concept of abstract labour and Marx's critique of it, since right from the beginning what we have is an ideological representation linked to an apology for an unreflected historical process. What Marx presented as an unequivocally negative analysis of the abstraction process here appears merely as a helpful means of optimally 'measuring' social resource outlay in a purely technocratic sense, therefore as a simple 'material aid' to 'realising use-value'. That usefulness (itself merely abstract in the concept of use-value) in general first has to be socially 'realised' through a particular process, causes this

13. Autorenkollektiv, *Politische Ökonomie des Sozialismus und ihre Anwendung in der DDR* (Berlin 1969) p273

ideological thinking no perplexity. Basically, it is nothing other than Adam Smith's mechanism of the 'invisible hand' that is exerting itself; only, paradoxically, this invisible hand which is supposed to steer 'resource allocation' as abstract operation of market processes, is postulated as the visible hand of state socialist planning (and precisely for this reason was bound to fail).

Expressed here is a completely uncritical, positivist and technocratic instrumentalisation of Marx's concept of 'abstract labour', a transparent legitimation of pre-existing and objectified praxis that remains unreflected in its historical constitution; which in the theoretically more demanding Western literature of traditional Marxist origin underwent a secondary ontological grounding. Georg Lukács even managed to formulate an *Ontology of Social Being*[14] founded on 'labour' in which the concept of labour in the sense of a 'teleological positing' of activity in relation to nature and society is granted the usual transhistorical quality.

Now it may be said, and has been since Aristotle, that humanity stepped out of the natural world and animal realm with a relation of teleological positing (ends-means determinations) as, for instance, in the well-known sentence from Marx concerning the difference between the worst architect and the best bee, namely that with the former the whole process has to pass through consciousness. Lukács formulates it ontologically in this way:

> For this lies in a mental plan achieving material realization, in the positing of a desired goal bringing about a change in material reality, in producing a material change in reality which represents something qualitatively and radically new in relation to nature. Aristotle's example of the building of a house shows this very concretely. The house is just as material an existence as the stone, wood, etc., of which it is constructed. Yet the teleological positing gives rise to an objectivity which is completely different from that of its elements. The house, of course, cannot be 'derived' from

14. Georg Lukács, *Zur Ontologie des gesellschaftlichen Seins, Teilband, Die Arbeit* (Neuwied und Darmstadt 1973) Published in English in three volumes as: *Ontology of Social Being, 1: Hegel; 2: Marx; 3: Labour* (London 1978, 1978, 1980) trans. David Fernbach. References to English edition.

the mere being-in-itself of the stone or wood, not from any kind of further development of their properties, the regularities and powers effective in them. What is necessary for the house is the power of human thought and will…[15]

However, it is not at all imperative and not justified by Lukács that the relation of teleological positing as praxis should be identical with the abstraction 'labour', but just axiomatically presupposed. This is the way in which the specific historical form of praxis in Modernity becomes ontologised.

For this reason Lukács extends the concept of *substance* as *labour substance*, which Marx clearly designated as the substance of capital, to an ontological-transhistorical category that just needs to be made more 'dynamic':

Recent insights into being have destroyed the static and unchanging conception of substance; yet this does not mean that it can be dispensed with in ontology, simply that its essentially dynamic character should be recognized. Substance is that which in the perpetual changing of things, while itself changing, is able to maintain itself in its continuity. […] The being of social being is maintained as substance in the reproduction process…[16]

And this substance is defined as 'labour':

Thus labour can be viewed as the original phenomenon, as the model for social being[17]

The specification of the abstraction 'labour' as a real abstraction is obscured through ontologisation; it only appears as "a rational abstraction in the sense used by Marx".[18] Lukács does not even leave out the, in parts unwittingly comic, idea of Engels about *The Part Played by Labour in*

15. Lukács, *Ontology of Social Being 3: Labour* p10
16. Ibid. p94
17. Ibid. pv
18. Ibid. p136

the Transition from Ape to Man; labour as 'original phenomenon' comes ontologically straight after the "the preceding forms of being, the inorganic and organic",[19] constitutes language, etc. so that the 'becoming human being' enjoys both 'upright gait' and 'aptitude for labour'.[20] The realisation of this aptitude for labour is the starting-point "for the extension of his abilities, among which self-mastery (!) is something that can never be forgotten".[21] That sounds a lot more Protestant than an 'original phenomenon' and one cannot help being reminded of the tale told by Locke and Kant with bourgeois ingenuousness whereby the only reason why orang-utans stubbornly refuse to speak is that they do not want to work.

It was inevitable that Lukács (in contrast to Rubin) would have to ontologise not only labour, but also value; in the end the one draws the other after it. The value category is extended and loses focus just like the labour category, while the definition of value found in Adam Smith and other Enlightenment theoreticians of the 18th Century is blurred with ethical 'standards of value', as well as with the concept of 'usefulness'. So the social value abstraction appears to be nested in an ontological process of a labour substance that always maintains itself while in transformation and is likewise an 'original phenomenon':

> First and foremost, the social category of value presents straight away the basic foundation of social existence, i.e. labour. Labour's connection with the social functions of value similarly reveals the fundamental structuring principles of social being that derive from the natural existence of human beings, and also from their metabolism with nature…[22]

It depends on transhistorically determining "the ultimately unitary character of value as a real factor of social being, irrespective of the very

19. Ibid. p20
20. Lukács, *Ontology of Social Being 2: Marx* p88
21. Ibid. p80
22. Ibid. p38

major qualitative changes of structure that it undergoes in the course of social development."[23]

'Economic value' in the narrower sense also receives its ontological consecration as the Labour Theory of Value:

> All other laws that are situated within social being are thus already of a historical character. Marx demonstrated the genesis of the most general of these, the law of value, in the introductory chapter of his master-work. This is indeed immanent to labour itself, in so far as it is linked by labour-time with labour itself as the development of human abilities and is already implicitly present when man has only reached the stage of useful labour, when his products have not yet become values; it remains just as implicitly valid after the sale and purchase of commodities have come to an end.[24]

Lukács shows particularly clearly here that in its historical transformation the understanding of labour movement Marxism relates exclusively to circulation and distribution. 'Sale and purchase' may not yet be present or may have come to an end, but abstract 'labour' and value remain from eternity to eternity. Under socialism, according to Lukács:

> The structure of commodity exchange, the effectiveness of the law of value for individual men as consumers, now ceases. It is evident of course that in production itself, socially necessary labour-time and hence the law of value as regulator of production must remain unchanged in their validity even with the growth of the productive forces.[25]

Ontologising the law of value simply as the 'economy of time' simply in 'production' forgets, however, (as does Marx himself in places) that the *quality of time as such* differs historically and only becomes destructively 'economised' in the modern sense in the functional space of capital.

23. Lukács, *Ontology of Social Being 3: Labour* p79
24. Lukács, *Ontology of Social Being 2: Marx* p93
25. Ibid. p166

'Socialism' in this simplified sense, limiting itself to changing the regulatory relations in law and distribution, but not transcending capitalist ontology, is then forced explicitly, even if unwillingly, to confirm an identical social quality:

> The peculiarity of capitalism is that it produces a social production spontaneously, in the true sense of this term; socialism transforms this spontaneity into conscious regulation.[26]

The qualitative difference, which in the strict sense is none at all, limits itself to the supposed transition from 'spontaneous' regulation ('anarchy of the market') to 'conscious regulation', while the 'what' of this spontaneity or regulation, the basic social content, the 'social production', is ontologically shifted into the "continuity of human development" as the "real substantiality of the process in its continuity".[27] Exactly what needs to be rigorously suppressed in order to rupture the false capitalist ontology ends up being declared to be the 'human condition', which like the idea of a 'human condition' in general, that is of an anthropological 'authenticity' to be summoned up and established in its rights, is characteristic of all fundamentally affirmative thought.

By ontologising abstract labour into a human condition linked to the constitution of a 'second nature' which is represented as insurmountable, Lukács integrates himself into the Enlightenment tradition of a metaphysics of history and ideology of progress, in which the unfolding of the value abstraction is laid down as a metahistorical necessity at the level of a Hegelian 'necessity':

> Socially necessary (and therefore *ipso facto* abstract) labour is also a reality, an aspect of the ontology of social being.[28]

At the same time Lukács knows very well that this history as 'dynamised' ontology was a history of sacrifice:

26. Ibid. p160
27. Ibid. p159
28. Ibid. p40

> In the nineteenth century, millions of independent artisans experienced the effects of this abstraction of socially necessary labour as their own ruin, i.e. they experienced in practice the concrete consequences, without having any suspicion that what they were facing was an achieved abstraction of the social process; this abstraction has the same ontological rigour of facticity as a car that runs you over.[29]

This insight does not lead the labour ontologist towards a radical critique and break with this false ontology, but just to an 'insight into necessity'. That 'rigour of facticity' conceals within itself the "ontological establishment of progress, [...] in which connection it clearly emerges that the essence of the ontological development consists in the economic progress (ultimately affecting the destiny of the human species), and that the ontologically necessary and objective contradictions involved in this are its forms of appearance."[30] Now go ahead and sacrifice yourself nicely to the 'ontological establishment of progress' in the economy of labour and value together with its little risks and side-effects.

Moishe Postone does not discuss the central and late works of Lukács concerning ontology, but what he says about the ultimate inconsistency of his early works that argue rather from the epistemological form of thought, also applies to the *Ontology of Social Being*:

> The identification of the proletariat (or the species) with the historical Subject rests ultimately on the same historically undifferentiated notion of 'labour' as does 'Ricardian Marxism.' 'Labor' is posited as the transhistorical source of social wealth and, as the substance of the Subject, is presumed to be that which constitutes society.[31]

Lukács therefore belongs to that "Western Marxism" (Perry Anderson) that did indeed scratch the surface of the labour movement Marxist paradigm, but never decisively overcame it. 'Real existing socialism' as

29. Ibid. p46-47
30. Ibid. p46-47
31. Postone, *Time, Labor and Social Domination* p82

historical praxis of *recuperative modernisation*, was still totally stuck within the horizons of a capitalist ontology of Modernity, and was supported philosophically rather than being critically decoded.

By way of extenuation we can nonetheless give Lukács credit for writing at a time in which this (transcendentally misunderstood) historical praxis of recuperative modernisation had not yet exhausted itself and only appeared to aspire to its high point as the Russian-Soviet 'model' for a second wave of national liberation movements and development regimes in the global South. However, the unbelievable inertia of ideological patterns of interpretation beyond their real historical basis is shown in the construction of legitimatory theories of an ontologisation of abstract labour that carries on even after the demise of 'real existing socialism' and recuperative modernisation. Just as the toenails of corpses carry on growing for a while, even though the body as a whole is already dead. In a similar manner the weaving of labour ontology by the obsolete and demoralised traditional Western Left is not even taking place any longer in the brain-dead skulls of an already dead history, but only still in the extremities of discontinued models. With these ideological toenails the news of the end of their world has not yet arrived.

Historically speaking this 'toenail' literature of a labour Marxism has already passed away as an epochal formation but will continue to haunt us for a long time and often appears with high theoretical claims. It can nevertheless also bring to bear the whole theoretical wealth of earlier labour-ontological Marx exegesis against the new, embryonic development of value-critical theory with its critique of labour-ontology – only that this once great wealth has now just taken the form of a beautiful funeral. This type of Marxist labour-ontology has a great deal of background and is probably a global phenomenon, but there is no longer any social or historical place for it.

In Germany the work of the Marxist Hegel interpreter Dieter Wolf, with whom value-critical theory has to some extent clashed several times in its evolution since the late 1980s, belongs to this school. It is no accident that Wolf's 1985 book based on labour-ontology, *Commodity and Money*,[32] was reissued in 2002 with the title *The Dialectical Contradiction in Capital.*

32. Dieter Wolf, *Ware und Geld: Der dialektische Widerspruch im Kapital* (Hamburg 1985)

A Contribution to Marx's Value Theory.[33] This new edition should be seen within the context of what is probably the final attempt on the part of a traditional academic Marxism now ripe for retirement in emeritus status to launch a counteroffensive against the new value-critique of capitalism.

Even the way Wolf wants to classify Marx's critique of political economy in terms of the history of theory is already characteristic:

> Marx does not occupy any standpoint independent of the history of theories from which he could turn his predecessors on their heads. As any glance at the genesis of scientific socialism shows, it is rather from within a sociohistorical movement that Marx, in discussion with previous theories and developing socio-economic relations, *advances through these theories to social labour as their common but also unconscious foundation.*[34]

Marx becomes classified in a total movement of the history of theory which remains within the limits of capitalist ontology. It is a typical example of a false concept of 'immanence' as it is mostly implied in the pretensions of so-called 'immanent critique.' The movement out of immanence towards transcendence is bent backwards; transcendence either disappears or a standpoint that essentially remains immanent is passed off as transcending. What had already shown itself in labour movement Marxism as a whole, in respect of the philosophy of the Enlightenment, is repeated in a narrower sense in respect of economic theory: Marx's theory appears as a mere extension to a building, some kind of hall of fame for the history of modern thought, in the construction of which even his 'predecessors' participated and found a place within. Marx's critique thus appears not from the perspective of a *break* with all previous theory, a break which his critique effected in a rudimentary way out of the immanent conflict, but from the perspective of *continuity*, in which it supposedly stands together with the previous theory. From this point of view Marx does not 'break', rather he 'develops further'. It is then axiomatic that the essential concept of this false continuity is grasped as

33. Dieter Wolf, *Der dialektische Widerspruch im Kapital. Ein Beitrag zur Marxschen Werttheorie* (Hamburg 2002)
34. Ibid. p19 (emphasis in the original)

'social labour', as the 'common yet unconscious' foundation not only of the modern continuous history, but also of a transhistorical sociality in general.

From the ideological premise of this false continuous history there now unfolds the legitimatory argumentation of labour-ontology. Wolf has higher standards than the iron-clad technocratic-positivist literature of the dead and forgotten academic activities of 'real existing socialism', in that he does attempt to differentiate the concept of the abstraction 'labour' or 'abstract labour' historically, similarly to Rubin (incidentally without even mentioning him), but in order to save it as transhistorical. To do this he distinguishes three levels of abstraction. The usual circulatory level of the specific labour abstraction of the commodity form derived from the mere 'exchange abstraction' is first of all differentiated from the merely conceptual (nominal) abstraction 'labour' as being supposedly 'rational':

> To make this clear, let us consider a number of stools that are different from one another: the quality of being a stool can be mentally adhered to as their common general quality. In so doing the real facts are taken into account, that each stool, be it a kitchen stool, a living room stool, a garden stool, etc. is accorded the quality of being a stool in general independently of its concrete form aligned to a specific use. Each definite kind of stool, just like each definite kind of labour can, on the one hand, be looked at from the aspect of its particular content, and on the other hand from the aspect of a universal quality abstracted from this particularity.[35]

There is something very odd about equating the labour abstraction with that of the stool. However, precisely because of this the nonsensical aspect is so striking. For with the stools it is obvious what the common quality is that the abstraction refers to and because of which it is actually 'rational'. That is not so with the labour. The completely different qualities of the various fields of human reproduction and life or of the human possibilities of an active 'alienation' can certainly not be merged at the same level in the same way that the stools are 'rationally' merged under a

35. Ibid. p55

common qualitative generic term; on the contrary this merging is in itself quite irrational.

Neither does Wolf save the day when he reduces the question to the transformation of natural materials:

> it only depends on seeing in concrete-useful labour a transformation process of nature which is objectified in a piece of formed matter[36]

The common quality of the various 'concrete-useful' kinds of labour, however, is here quite simplistically determined and ignores the metabolic processes of human beings with each other, that is their activities in social relations, that are not represented in "a piece of formed matter" (therefore that which appears in capitalism under the term 'human services'). If, however, the socially interactive areas of activity are included, then there remains nothing of the abstraction 'labour', apart from the fact that it is a manner of human alienation. However, this quality is so general that it no longer makes any sense at all to say it. Above all at this meaningless height of abstraction it cannot be demarcated any more from such manner of human alienation as play, dream, contemplation, sexuality, promenading, pleasure, etc. Exactly for that reason the concept of abstract labour did not come about as a 'rational' generic term, but originally as a negative social abstraction (whatever the slave does, regardless of its particular content).

Since, however, precisely no *social universality* of the concept of labour can be made through this manner of social abstraction (except in the merely metaphorical sense of negativity, of suffering), this belongs as an abstract concept of 'labour' solely to the modern commodity producing system. The 'universal quality' of the alienation of human energy, calling it 'labour', is not due to any 'rational abstraction', but only makes sense if this 'universality' consists in the potential to posit value; solely by means of this social (negative) common feature can the various activities be subsumed in this way under the concept of labour. The nominal abstraction is therefore merely a consequence of the real abstraction and is not in itself 'rational'.

The situation is no better with the second level of abstraction of the concept of labour where Wolf endeavours to ontologise abstract labour.

36. Ibid. p54

This is supposed not just to be a 'rational' generic term along the lines of the stool, but to represent a social *concept of praxis*. To do this Wolf reaches back to the ontologising line of argument that Marx himself uses, as Lukács and the whole tradition of Marxist labour ontology endeavours to do. Here it is no longer a matter of a mere generic term to designate the "abstract human labour as universal quality of concrete-useful labour",[37] but of the practical-social *relationship* of the various different areas of activity and the single individual 'alienations' to one another.

In this sense of social regulation and mutual 'recognition' a second concept of 'abstract human labour' in a social sense is now introduced:

> Is there, within the social context in which people expend their concrete-useful kinds of labour, a process in which these kinds of labour, abstracting from their concrete-useful character, are also related to each other as human i.e. as abstract-universal? Such a process does exist. It consists in the already mentioned distribution of social labour in definite proportions which all societies have in common. If the reason why the kinds of concrete-useful labour are also related to each other as abstract-human can be explained from this distribution, then it is also a case of an ahistorical fact that is attributable to all communities.[38]

That, however, is precisely the question that was not posed in premodern societies. Wolf confuses here two completely different things. The only self-evident point is that every society implies both a relation to nature and human relationships, that humans effect their reproduction through interaction in order to eat, drink, clothe and house themselves, keep each other company, play, construct a worldview, etc. It in no way follows from this, however, that there is an abstracting process of the 'expenditure of human energy' in the sense of a process of overall regulation. That people know, for instance, that they must sow so that they can reap does not imply any social-universal 'accounting system' of energy expenditure or a corresponding abstract universality. So far as such bookkeeperish regulation occurs in agrarian societies, it only ever relates

37. Ibid. p54
38. Ibid. p48

just to the social abstraction of a particular activity, namely that of the socially dependent persons and precisely not to any 'social universality'; and in certain societies either not at all or not in the first instance to reproductive activities, but to transcendent aims (for instance pyramid building in ancient Egypt).

The whole thing could also be formulated like this: all premodern societies implicitly start from the position that there is in any case always enough time available so that everyone 'has time' and this does not have to be put additionally into some 'shortage relation' of various human activities or alienation generally. Any idea like this would simply appear as quite absurd. Here a particular aspect of the different historical *qualities of time* becomes clear. Marx pointed out several times what absurdity it is that the use of 'timesaving' means in modern capitalism is linked to an eternal lack of time and simultaneously with the conversion of lifetime into 'labour-time'. The reason for this is that the merely technical timesaving (that even at the technical level would often be felt as risible and grotesque by non-capitalist consciousness) is posited through a social relation, that is based on the 'excess' of capital (Marx), namely the excessive incorporation of human energy expenditure in units of abstract time.

So if Wolf maintains that the social "relation of concrete-useful kinds of labour to each other as abstract-human"[39] is a transhistorical 'determination', incidentally (as already noted without acknowledgement) directly following Rubin and his concept of 'social equalisation', and insofar as this relation is "enclosed within the proportional distribution of the total labour available to a community",[40] then he commits an anachronism. The system of tribute, forced payments, etc. in the ancient agrarian societies as expressions of social domination in their determinate fetish constitutions was precisely not based of such a kind of absolute, totalitarian 'accountancy'. Elements of this are found solely in periods of forced labour, for example in the building of pyramids, the Great Wall of China, etc. However, this was in each case a limited affair, and one that in no way covered total social reproduction.

Just the thought of laying hold of the "total labour available to a community" already contains unconsciously capitalist excessiveness and the totalitarianism of the value-form as it was historically prefigured

39. Ibid. p49
40. Ibid. p49

for the first time by Protestantism. That societies based on recuperative modernisation with their logic of state planning always undertook exactly this kind of 'laying hold' and thereby defining the 'population' in general as only an abstract 'total labour-power', was only a repetition of the history of how capitalism constituted its 'sovereignty', which had completed the same process with other ideological clothing.

Although Wolf, contrary to the state socialist ideologues, casually distances himself from transforming "value into an ahistorically valid category",[41] he has to seek to rescue the value determination as transhistorical in a definite sense, very much in the same vein as the labour-ontological passages in Marx or the labour ontology of Lukács by means of the concept of the "proportional distribution of different kinds of labour":

> If the value of the commodity is not an ahistorically valid category and has also not existed in all social formations, it is therefore for this reason not excluded that whatever is at stake here, it is something that all social formations have in common... With this 'something' the issue is... the distribution of the total labour-time available to a society among the individual concrete-useful kinds of labour. This distribution is always executed in a historically determinate social context, which at the same time decides on the social recognition of the individual labours, i.e. on their historically specific form.[42]

'Labour' for Wolf, therefore, only differs historically in the sense of the different 'forms of recognition', whereby the modern, capitalist form is just conditioned by the market, that is to say by the exchange of labour products as commodities. The concept of a 'form of recognition' already includes the possibility of non-recognition, which is likewise ontologised. A relation of recognition and nonrecognition, that needs extra regulation by means of social mediation is, though, a basic element of relations of domination and therefore the fetish.

41. Ibid. p47
42. Ibid. p47

Wolf ontologises the basic relations of reproduction and subjection involved in abstract labour, but wants to detach the market as means of mediation from these relations and declare it alone as what is historically specific to the capitalist mode of production:

> In this way the concrete-useful kinds of labour in a non-capitalist community are to be related to one another in the course of the proportional distribution of the total labour also as abstract-human, but their universal social character considers precisely not in the abstract-human, but rather in the concrete-useful labour in a way that is to be explained from the nature of the social context. As in non-capitalist communities so also in a capitalist community the concrete-useful kinds of labour are related to each other in the proportional distribution of total labour as abstract-human [...] In this question, however, the issue is an *exceptional* social role which the abstract-human labour only plays in a *single* social state.[43]

What is going on here is nothing other than conceptual sophistry. If in a non-capitalist community the socially universal character of different kinds of labour already consists of the concrete-useful labour, then there is simply no longer any place for the concept of abstract-human labour and the concept of labour as such, which in any case represents in itself an abstraction, is no longer applicable in the modern sense or insofar as there is an abstract concept of 'activity in general' this is precisely not related to the society as a whole (slave activities, etc.) That in all forms of alienation in society the issue is something human or social requires no extra abstract concepts, because it is in any case self-evident. Therefore if Wolf operates with a double status of 'abstract-human labour' in which it is to play merely an 'exceptional role' in capitalism as supposedly ontological and transhistorical, while it can specify no meaningful 'role' at all in non-capitalist relations, then this only proves that he is frantically attempting to smuggle the specifically modern labour abstraction into both history and the future.

---

43. Ibid. p49 (emphasis in the original)

His separation of abstract labour into supposedly ontological facts on the one hand, and specifically capitalist facts on the other, just like similar efforts on the part of Lukács, are nothing other than hairsplitting. Western labour movement Marxists can afford such sophistical juggling of concepts since they are not committed to defend a real social reproduction process based on abstract labour and the value-form, while thinkers living under 'real existing socialism' operating in a context of 'planned commodity production' and under the pressure of the contradictions grounded in it had to affirm the category of abstract labour with no ifs and buts quite brutally and openly.

The ideologues of 'real existing socialism' with their affirmative ways of thinking were not more stupid, but in a certain sense cleverer than Western Marxists like Wolf, when from the ontologising of abstract labour they drew the consequence of just such an ontologising of the value-form and ('planned') mediation by the market. For both of them also belong together in reality; the market is nothing other than the indispensable 'sphere of realisation' of the overarching valorisation process. If Wolf is only asserting that mediation by the market is the specifically capitalist 'role' of 'abstract-human labour', but on the other hand ontologising the basic relation of labour-abstraction, then it throws a harsh light on his understanding of a postcapitalist, supposedly emancipated, society.

Any system based on abstract labour without the market mediation that goes with it could only be a monstrously repressive dictatorship of recognition/non-recognition, allocation and rationing, registration and administration of people in the manner of Stalin or even Pol Pot; in other words exactly what traditional Marxists have again and again conjured up as the consequences of value-critique, in order to denounce and guard against it. However, the only thing that is emancipatory is the total overcoming of the system of abstract labour including mediation by the market; but not just the overcoming of the blind operation of market mediation alone (which could not then be an actual overcoming, but only an outside intervention by the state which remained bound to the categorial form of value and therefore the market).

However, it is precisely the supposedly better theorised, Western, critique of abstract labour and fetishism that completely limits its grasp to the sphere of circulation, and this critique is therefore the one that deserves to incur the allegation of implying a system of the Pol Pot kind and not value-critique, that precisely sets itself apart as a radical critique of labour by examining the underlying reproduction relation as a whole and from its roots. Only if the concept of 'abstract-human labour', that haunts Wolf and not only him, is utterly destroyed is an emancipatory perspective to be won that points beyond the capitalist mode of production as a whole and also beyond the paradigm of 'recuperative modernisation' that weighs like a nightmare on the brain of the Left in particular.

5

Critique of Moishe Postone's concept of labour

Without a doubt Moishe Postone deserves credit for being the first to have deconstructed bourgeois labour ontology, transhistorical labour concepts and the positivity of abstract labour in traditional Marxism and to have made a beginning at overcoming them; and in fact doing this to some extent long before the critique of labour developed by the German language approaches to value-critique since the end of the 1980s. Postone's similarly argued theory has its roots in the 1970s, had its elaboration in the course of the 1980s and has been presented in advanced form since the beginning of the 1990s. In Germany the critique of value and labour largely emerged independently of any Postone reception, which may be taken as an indication of the fact that further development and transcendence of Marx's theory in the direction of a radical critique of labour to some extent was in the air as a response to the categorially conceptless bourgeois debate on the 'crisis of the working society' which had already been opened theoretically at the end of the 1950s by Hannah Arendt and had achieved unimagined topicality and urgency in the course of the world crisis of the third industrial revolution (growing structural mass unemployment).

According to Postone:

> [T]he meaning of the category of labor in [Marx's] mature works is different from what traditionally has been assumed: it is historically specific rather than transhistorical. In Marx's mature critique, the notion that labor constitutes the social world and is the source of all wealth does not refer to society in general, but to capitalist, or modern, society alone.[1]

---

1.   Postone, *Time, Labor, and Social Domination* p4

In this respect, Postone breaks definitively with the labour positivism of all previous schools of Marxism and makes the differentiation that:

> This approach to Marx's mature critical theory has important implications which I shall attempt to unfold in the course of this work. I shall begin to do so by distinguishing between two fundamentally different modes of critical analysis: a critique of capitalism *from the standpoint of labor*, on the one hand, and a critique *of* labor in capitalism, on the other. The first, which is based upon a transhistorical understanding of labor, presupposes that a structural tension exists between the aspects of social life that characterize capitalism (for example, the market and private property) and the social sphere constituted by labor. Labor, therefore, forms the basis of the critique of capitalism, the *standpoint* from which that critique is undertaken. According to the second mode of analysis, labor in capitalism is historically specific and constitutes the essential structures of that society. Thus labor is the *object* of the critique of capitalist society.[2]

Work as the standpoint of critique or work as the object of critique, put like this the contrast is brought to a head, as has already been indicated above. Whereby in point of fact the issue is labour as a category or essential determination and not as a mere accidental, categorial, but nonetheless affirmative critique of labour, as for example in Autonomism (namely the character of wage-labour as external dependency, lousy conditions of work, etc.) From this new, negative essential determination of labour Postone is then able to roll out the circulatory or distributional shortcomings of the hitherto Marxist critique of capitalism, and so unfold the (already quoted) critiques of the corresponding theories of Lukács, Sohn-Rethel, et al. Estimation of Postone's achievement increases even more given he has been condemned for over a decade to being a completely solitary figure. Publications in which his approach has been further developed have largely gone without comment; even in diverse collections of articles he has remained an unexpected foreign body who

2.   Ibid. p5-6 (emphasis in the original)

is denied any adequate discussion in the academic community (especially from the German representatives of critical theory) since that would go way beyond the ingrained patterns of thought. What is even more admirable is the tenacity with which Postone has followed his theoretical path and further developed his approach.

It is this isolation from any discourse over such a long period of time that might be responsible for Postone not having thought through his critique of labour, in the sense of the abstraction 'labour', to its logical conclusion. When he speaks, as in the quote above, of "labour in capitalism" this way of expressing it also implies 'labour' outside of capitalism; the problem of abstraction with respect to a concept of 'activity in general' as human alienation and of real abstraction as its unconscious activity is in this way inadequately illuminated and the critique remains incomplete.

Postone's analysis encounters this dilemma every step of the way. He would like to cordon off "labor in capitalism" from a supposedly unproblematic, self-evidently presupposed category of 'labour' that is no longer a theme for discussion by postulating that only in capitalism are "the fundamental categories of social life ... categories of labor." this is by no means self-evident, and it cannot be justified merely by pointing to the obvious importance of labour to human social life in general.[3] Postone therefore accepts without further examination the reference to an allegedly "obvious importance of labor" for social life as such, but does not want to content himself with this in that he emphasises that only in capitalism does labour have its specific role as principle of social synthesis. He does not even pose the question whether or not an abstract-universal concept of labour makes any sense at all outside of this modern constitution of society, or even if it has ever existed.

Postone even has a double concept of the labour-abstraction inasmuch as this supposedly unproblematic concept remains much as ever as a transhistorical category. Accordingly Postone maintains, "that the form of labor and the very fabric of social relations differ in various social formations."[4] Capitalism therefore differentiates itself from other formations not in being the only one to have produced the "form of labor" (to which corresponds the "subject form", likewise only valid for the modern constitution of society), but solely through the "form *of* labor."

3. Ibid. p22
4. Ibid. p25

It is therefore only a difference in form in respect of a transhistorical and thereby ontological issue once again, just as in the aporetic argumentation from Marx. Specifically capitalist, according to Postone, would therefore be the socially synthesising function of labour understood only as the "expenditure of direct labor time"[5] in the production process:

> This social quality, which is historically unique, distinguishes labor in capitalism from labor in other societies.[6]

Naturally, this creates a certain confusion in respect of the transhistorical or specifically historical (only belonging to Modernity) validity of the concept of abstract labour. Postone has an uneasy sense of this when he formulates from time to time the apparently unproblematic ontological-transhistorical concept of labour that now haunts him in ways that nonetheless involuntarily express its problematic nature:

> Various sorts of what we would consider labor exist in all societies.[7]

This formulation already implies that "we" (modern human beings socialised into the category of labour) "normally" also "consider labor" as something existing in other societies that really does not correspond to this abstraction. This becomes clearer when Postone speaks of "laboring activities"[8] in non-capitalist societies. This curious expression clarifies the implicit scruple Postone has in respect of the transhistorical category of labour that has been in a certain sense carried over secondarily, without, however, being made explicit. In this connection Postone returns again to the relation of abstraction to real abstraction in respect of the concept of labour, namely on the basis of Marx's formulation of the double-character of labour as concrete and abstract:

> This initial determination of the double-character of labor in capitalism should not be understood out of context

5. Ibid. p25
6. Ibid. p48
7. Ibid. p150
8. Ibid. p150

as implying simply that all the various forms of concrete labor are forms of labor in general. Such a statement is analytically useless inasmuch as it could be made of laboring activities in all societies, even those in which commodity production is only of marginal significance. After all, all forms of labor have in common that they are labor. But such an indeterminate interpretation does not and cannot contribute to an understanding of capitalism precisely because abstract labour and value, according to Marx, are specific to that social formation. What makes labor general in capitalism is not simply the truism that it is the common denominator of all various specific sorts of labor; rather, *it is the social function of labor which makes it general.* As a socially mediating activity, labor is abstracted from the specificity of its product, hence, from the specificity of its own concrete form. In Marx's analysis, the category of abstract labor expresses this real social process of abstraction; it is not simply based on a conceptual process of abstraction.[9]

Although Postone stresses here the specific way in which labour in capitalism is general, which alone makes sense of such a concept of the general, he nevertheless admits that in itself the purely conceptual abstraction 'labour' in the sense of an apparently straightforward general term is rational, but he then conceives of this abstraction (contrary to Wolf, above) as being "analytically useless" and a "truism", in order to set it against the incompatible capitalist labour-abstraction as the social synthesis. What Postone overlooks is that the mere general term 'labour' is "analytically useless" precisely because it quite simply represents something other than a "truism". As such a "truism" it can only manifest itself within capitalist relations, because the merely conceptually understood abstraction is nothing other than a mental reflex of the real abstraction belonging to Modernity alone and as such not even existing historically in this manner.

Postone's final lack of clarity regarding the abstract concept of labour continues with reference to those statements of Marx concerning

9.   Ibid. p151-152 (emphasis in the original)

a supposedly transhistorical "economy of time" involving a moment of value-determination going beyond capitalism, upon which Rubin, Lukács, Wolf, etc. have emphatically based themselves. Postone takes up this argument as well, assessing it, however, noticeably differently and less affirmatively:

> Marx's statement that considerations of labor time would remain important in a postcapitalist society does not, therefore, mean that the form of wealth itself would be temporal rather than material. [...]
> Although an economy of time would remain important, this time presumably would be descriptive... [H]ence, the relation between considerations of time expenditure and wealth production could be essentially different than in a situation where value is the social form of wealth. [...]
> Marx's notion of a possible postcapitalist economy of time, therefore, and his analysis of capitalism in terms of a temporal form of wealth are not identical and should be distinguished.[10]

However, it is true that Marx himself quite simply did not make this distinction, but rather explicitly characterised the continued effect of an "economy of time" as the continued effect of a moment of the value-form having beyond that an ontological-transhistorical character. In other words: Marx does not see the difference sketched out above between historical time concepts and time-form; what counts for him is just the abstract flow time of Newton, Kant and modern business management. The difference that Postone quite rightly opens up actually forbids us to speak of the "economy of time" remaining "important". Postone wisely speaks of "an" rather than "the" economy of time, but a qualitatively different way of telling the time would simply no longer be abstractly "economic", as if saving time were a value in itself regardless of the content. Postone's insight clashes with his (half hearted) clinging to the letter of the concept in respect to both the abstract concept of time and the abstract concept of labour.

10. Ibid. p379-380

This dilemma is repeated once again in the discussion of the so-called 'necessity' in the sense of 'necessary labour'. As is well-known Marx introduced this determination in a two ways, on the one hand as the socially average necessary labour relative to the expenditure of human energy in capitalism on the basis of a given standard of productivity (that is purely immanent to capitalism), and on the other hand as the transhistorical necessity of labour as such, as the 'realm of necessity', a residual element of which has to remain even after capitalism, beyond which the 'realm of freedom' could arise.

Postone does not criticise the latter determination, although he really ought to given his own argument, but instead doubles the concept of the 'necessity' of 'labour' in a similar way to that of the economy of time by postulating that:

> [O]ne must also, in considering the relation between labor and social necessity, distinguish between transhistorical social necessity and historically determinate social necessity. An example of the former sort of necessity, for Marx, is that some form of concrete labor, however determined, is necessary to mediate the material interactions of humans and nature and, hence, to maintain human social life. Some such activity, according to Marx, is a necessary condition of human existence in all forms of society. [...]
> As a result of its dual character, then, commodity-determined labor, in Marx's analysis, is bound to two different forms of necessity, one transhistorical, and one specific to capitalism.[11]

On the back of the concept of 'necessity' in respect of use-value (whose logical dependence on value-socialisation Postone similarly fails to raise thematically) yet another explicitly ontological concept of labour smuggles itself into the otherwise completely incompatible line of argument. It might be that the blame lies with Postone's attempt to present the critique of labour and value as a new way of reading an intrinsically closed, so to say contradiction free and 'whole' Marx, which can only lead to inconsistencies. What is much more reasonable is to open up the

11. Ibid. p380-381

contradiction in Marx between the ontology of labour on the one side, and the critique of labour and value on the other, corresponding to his historical situation.

The relapse into the ontology of labour becomes quite clear as soon as Postone speaks about the perspectives of a postcapitalist society. For him this implies "the possibility of a different process of production, one based upon a newer, emancipatory structure of social labor".[12] The issue of "nonalienated labor is that it is free of relations of direct and of abstract social domination".[13] This is the way Postone lapses, in this respect, into the jargon of the old labour movement, even if with a paradoxical twist:

> The emancipation of labor requires the emancipation from
> (alienated) labor.[14]

Significantly, the adjective that is supposed to solve the paradox stands in brackets and contributes nothing to the explanation. Leave it out and the paradox stands there in its pure form, uniting only externally the two opposed paradigms: the emancipation *of* labour cannot have the same meaning as the emancipation *from* labour. The very thing that human beings have to emancipate themselves from is already stuck in the abstraction 'labour' as such, as an essential concept of negative social organisation. It is not a matter of a real paradox conceptually reproduced, but of a conceptual contradiction of Postone himself (similar to Marx's aporia in respect of the concept of labour).

This contradiction in Postone's line of argument continues in respect of the totality of capitalist sociability as well. On the one hand he emphasises that it is abstract labour that creates this totality and therefore both of them are to be 'abolished' together. However, at the same time he extends certain moments of this totality beyond capitalism, in the bad Hegelian sense of an affirmative 'sublation' (whereby it is exactly the essence that is maintained); and indeed this is particularly clear in respect of the political sphere, which he obviously does not understand as historically specific, but as ontological. Instead of formulating the critique of labour consistently also as a critique of democracy, Postone would

12. Ibid. p26
13. Ibid. p33 fn48
14. Ibid. p33

like to carry out "a renewed democratic critique of capitalism"[15] and preaches a "postcapitalist democracy";[16] a contradiction in terms which toes the line of the affirmative concept of democracy within traditional Marxism which precisely at this point corresponds to that circulatory and distributive limitation on the concept of capital.

These criticisms should not and cannot, however, detract from Postone's merit as the first to have made the breakthrough to overcoming the modern ontology of labour that is also present in traditional Marxism as self-evidently valid. This groundbreaking achievement cannot be honoured highly enough. Despite the baggage of moments of ontologisation, Postone's decisive difference from labour movement Marxism consists in denying labour under capitalism, including that engaged in the material production process, any transhistorical character whatsoever. He states quite clearly that:

> [T]he labor which constitutes value should not be identified with labor as it may exist transhistorically. Rather, it is a historically specific form that would be abolished, not realized, with the overcoming of capitalism.[17]

The ontological and transhistorical concept of labour that nonetheless remains over in Postone is only an empty embarrassment, the ghost of an actually already overcome understanding; and, by the way, one that is also inconsistent since if there really were 'labour' in a transhistorical sense, it would also have to exist in capitalism which after all does not exist outside of history. Either there exists an ontology of labour, or there does not; but what cannot be is that it exists before and after capitalism, but not in capitalism. That would be too much of the historically specific. If the "labour in capitalism" represents a purely historical, negative relation, there cannot be any "other" transhistorical labour, rather this abstraction belongs as a socially universal relation solely to commodity producing Modernity and its historical formation. Even the mere conceptual abstraction 'labour' is as a concept of social universality bound to this

15. Ibid. p15
16. Ibid. p41
17. Ibid. p29

relation; the concept as a concept is a product of the foregoing real abstraction and is not to be understood apart from this as transhistorical.

6

Abstract labour and value as social a priori

What appears in the value-critical discussion around the value abstraction and is also an issue for Postone, is the problem of the real *a priori* in the constitution of society. Or put more accurately: is abstract labour a concept of production or merely of circulation, the starting-point or merely a transit point? This problem, already sketched out above in the curtailment of the concept of abstract labour to circulation in traditional Marxism, is to be taken up in more detail again here to cast some light on its implications. It is rather odd that classical labour movement Marxism never conceived of this problem, although essentially attributable to its function as an ideology of modernisation. Abstract labour then becomes on the one hand a positivistic, unreflective definition (under 'real existing socialism' treated positively as 'domestic use' by Günther Mittag & Co.), on the other hand it is taken implicitly as a concept of circulation, which becomes explicit, as has been shown, in the more reflective Western theoreticians such as Sohn-Rethel in the concept of abstract labour as 'exchange abstraction' beyond the sphere of production. Likewise, self-evidently, with Dieter Wolf:

> Only in abstraction are the individual labours related to each other as abstract-human labour so that it becomes labour in an historically specific form[1]

Naturally, this corresponds completely to the division of the capitalist reproduction process into an ontological and transhistorical sphere of concrete labour and the material production process on the one hand, and a specifically capitalist sphere of exchange or markets, the 'anarchy' of regulation through markets, on the other, in which the ontologised sphere of production is to be 'liberated' from the specifically capitalist sphere of circulation ('liberation of labour').

1. Wolf, *Der dialektische Widerspruch im Kapital* p79

In this paradoxical way 'labour' does not at all "become labour in historically specific form" in labouring itself and therefore also not as the actual expenditure of labour-power in the real production process, but exclusively outside of labour in its social beyond as the exchange process or market activities where it is no longer a matter of active labour, but only of its fetishistic reflex in the products as commodities.

Postone has broken out of this pattern by explicitly taking abstract labour out of its mere circulatory determination, thereby deontologising capitalist reproduction as a whole. As it is not difficult to see, such an approach was able to emerge not only within the context of a regeneration of the history of Marxist theory, but also had as a field of reference the social and ecological debates of the 1980s. At that time the destruction of the natural basis of life through the economic 'externalisation of costs' was foregrounded in the debates criticising society and slogans such as "work differently, live differently" were in favour. These debates remained quite unreflective in respect of the social form determination by abstract labour and the logic of value; Postone being the first to make a claim for a further development of Marxist theory transformed by the critique of labour and value. This problem is today even more topical and urgent than ever before.

If traditional Marxism had derived the social dimension of the real capitalist production process, the *characteristic social subjugation* of the functional sphere of business management, from the legal property relations understood as merely external, subjective and a question of the will in a way that was always simplified (the means of production do not 'belong' to the producers) and not from the essence of the concrete-abstract logic of production itself as valorisation process, corresponding to the rendering of the supposedly merely 'concrete' sphere of production into something positive and ontological, then it accordingly had to either completely deny (as with some ideologists of 'real existing socialism' in their apologies for the 'socialist' economy that was likewise destroying its natural basis) the ecologically destructive character of the capitalist production process or to simplify this problem in the same way as a legal property question as traditionally understood.

In this way the idea –that actually suggests itself– of harnessing the Marxist concept of abstract labour in the sense of a socio-economic critique of the capitalist production process itself in its material 'logic of production' remained closed. Marxism, with its traditional fixation on circulation (the anarchy of the market), distribution (struggles over distribution in the money-form) and therefore on the externally understood political and juridical dimension (property relations, state intervention), was bound to bypass thinking about socio-ecological problems that had opened up in society. While the socio-ecological movement itself remained conceptless and concretistic, and so quite incapable of any critique of the 'substance of capital'; a state of affairs that only became fixed rather than overcome because the Marxists completely missed the point.

The crucial point is whether the labour abstraction, or real abstraction, can be thought through logically as the logic of production, or whether it remains simplified as circulatory. The question of the priority of abstract labour is therefore equally significant. Does abstract labour constitute the *a priori* of capitalist reproduction as a totality whose validity is therefore already located in the 'concrete' production process itself, or is it merely a matter of a secondary 'exchange abstraction'? Traditional Marxism implicitly accepted the latter for the most part since it could only conceive externally of the capitalist form of the production process, and the logic of abstraction as totalitarian force of destruction had not yet ripened in history; and where the formulation was explicit, as with Sohn-Rethel, a definitional determination was without discursive reference.

Abstract labour as social *a priori* or just an 'exchange abstraction' and so a secondary product of circulation? This alternative, however, is identical with that of whether the *value* of commodities is 'produced' in the production process, or only 'emerges' in the sphere of circulation. For abstract labour as the substance of capital is indeed nothing other than the 'value-constituting substance', that is to say, it is what constitutes value. At first glance the whole problem looks irritating. Naturally, value is produced by labour is it not? Is this not the grave credo of labour movement Marxism, its 'standpoint of labour', its glorification of the 'value-creating' proletariat? What is ironical is that traditional Marxism in its own 'standpoint' is to some extent standing on its head, for although it affirms the 'value-creating class' as productive, it reduces value abstraction at the same time to the sphere of circulation.

On the one hand, production is to be determined only by 'concrete labour' and thus through the manufacture of 'use-values', while supposedly the process of abstraction takes place only secondarily in the sphere of circulation; on the other, the 'production' of value by 'labour' is spoken of completely positively. On the one hand then, the pride of the producers in their sense of how contemptible exchange-value is compared to a would-be exalted creation of use-value that is only externally reshaped by the capitalist value logic (in terms of the superficially understood juridical property determinations). On the other hand, there is the same pride of the producers in terms of 'value-creation' itself whereby it is of all things the capitalist abstract universality that appears as the 'dignity' of labour. It is characteristic that this, its own, hair-raising contradiction no longer caught the attention of Marxism. By moving in such a contradiction this thinking, it could be said, reflects the negative totality or unity of abstract and concrete labour, but quite unconsciously and without any critical concept of this totality.

In the meantime the problem has ripened so far, both objectively in the historical unfolding of the destructive forces of capitalism as well as discursively in the rise of the value-critical approach, that it now has to be explicitly formulated by the traditional Marxist apologetics. For example, the Berlin political scientist Michael Heinrich, who represents some kind of value theoretical mish-mash of half-traditional Marxism and half-postmodern positions, has titled the relevant section of his recently published *An Introduction to the Three Volumes of Karl Marx's Capital*[2] dealing with the 'spectral objectivity' of the commodity form with the question: "A Production or Circulation Theory of Value?".[3] And he self-evidently decides for the circulation theory:

> Accordingly, it is exchange, that consummates the abstraction that underlies abstract labor [...][4]

> Value-objectivity *(Wertgegenständlichkeit)* is not possessed by commodities as objectifications of concrete labor, but rather as objectifications of abstract labor. However, if as we just outlined, abstract labor is a relation of social validation existing only in exchange (where privately expended labor

2. Originally published in German as: Michael Heinrich, *Kritik der politischen Ökonomie, Eine Einführung* (Stuttgart 2004) and subsequently in English as: *An Introduction to the Three Volumes of Karl Marx's Capital* trans. Alexander Locascio (New York 2012). References to English edition.
3. Ibid. p52
4. Ibid. p50

counts as value-constituting, abstract labor) then value also
first exists in exchange.[5]

Heinrich is thus completely in line with traditional Marxism since for
him abstract labour is not a relation of production, but only a secondary
relation of circulation or "relation of social validation". Which implies
that the actual real productive activities in capitalism are determined as
"only concrete" and that "the relations of production" are capitalist solely
because of the purely externally superimposed juridical property question.
In the face of a sophisticated complex of problems Heinrich does not
even hit the bar, instead he leaps far below it. However, in demarcating
himself from the value-critical approach he does do something beneficial
in presenting the supposedly 'authentic' and 'whole' Marx in opposition
to the value-critical historisation of a 'double Marx'. But it is exactly on
this point that Heinrich refutes the authentic Marx.

For a line of argument such as that from Heinrich, *value* or *value-objectivity*
is identical to exchange-value, meaning to the relationship of
commodities one to another in the relation of 'relative value-form' and
'equivalent form' whereby in the latter the exchange-value of the former
'represents' the former in its natural form, right up to the constitution of
money as the 'universal equivalent form' (the 'commodity set apart' that
takes on this form of presentation for all other commodities). If, however,
value, value-objectivity or the 'form of value' are identical with exchange-value,
value does in fact become constituted only in circulation as the
'value-form' in terms of the relationship of commodities to each other.
Then value 'is' nothing other than this relationship, and an individual
commodity cannot exist as such – the products at the end of the production
process, for example in the factory warehouse, would not yet even be
commodities in terms of the value-form, but just simply useful goods that
could actually take on the value-form and therefore also the commodity
form only by sale on the market. Heinrich states this quite explicitly:

[V]alue is not at all a property that an individual thing
possesses in and of itself. The substance of value, that
constitutes the foundation of this objectivity, is not inherent

5.   Ibid. p52-53

to individual commodities, but is bestowed *mutually* in the act of exchange.[6]

But that is absolutely not Marx's line of argument. Neither logically or 'methodologically', since then the *essential determination* 'value' would be identical with the *form of appearance* 'exchange-value'; without mediation essence and appearance collapse into each other. (Which incidentally is typical of postmodern thought that exactly because of this fundamentally loses sight of the problem of social and historical constitution). Marx, in contrast, opens up the difference between essence and appearance where he sees in the first place the necessity of grounding theoretical reflection: "...all science would be superfluous if the form of appearance of things directly coincided with their essence."[7] For this reason Marx refers again and again to the decisive difference between:

> [A]ll forms of appearance and their hidden background...
> The forms of appearance are reproduced directly and
> spontaneously, as current and usual modes of thought; the
> essential relation must first be discovered by science.[8]

Heinrich is quite obviously content to collapse essence and appearance, value and value-objectivity and exchange-value into one, along with that which is "reproduced spontaneously" and with the "current and usual modes of thought." He sticks to the forms of appearance and misses their "hidden background" and consequently outs himself in this point to some extent as a *Marxist vulgar economist*. Marx in contrast reflects clearly in respect of abstract labour and value their difference from the form of appearance of exchange-value. By initially proceeding from the latter he shows precisely the impossibility of explaining the form of appearance for itself:

> Hence exchange-value appears to be something accidental
> and purely relative, and consequently an intrinsic value,
> i.e. an exchange-value that is inseparably connected with

6. Ibid. p53 (emphasis in the original)
7. Karl Marx, *Capital III* trans. David Fernbach (London 1981) p956
8. Marx, *Capital I* p682

the commodity, inherent in it, seems a contradiction in terms.[9]

However, setting the different commodities on the market equal to one another implicitly points to their common substance, that means to their mutual and therefore each for itself common element that must already be there before the commodities are set in relationship to each other:

> What does this equation signify? It signifies that a common element of identical magnitude exists in two different things... Both are therefore equal to a third thing, which in itself is neither the one nor the other. Each of them, so far as it is exchange-value, must therefore be reducible to this third thing.[10]

This is why the commodities 'are' as value-objectivities already a 'congealed mass':

> ...of human labour-power expended without regard to the form of its expenditure. All these things now tell us is that human labour-power has been expended to produce them, human labour is accumulated in them. As crystals of this social substance, which is common to them all, they are values – commodity values [*Warenwert*].[11]

This they are already as values and not only as exchange-values, already as the objects and results of production, not only of circulation. For this reason value and exchange-value are not directly identical; value is the essential determination, exchange-value its form of appearance:

> The common factor in the exchange relation, or in the exchange-value of the commodity, is therefore its value. The progress of the investigation will lead us back to

9.   Ibid. p126
10. Ibid. p127
11. Ibid. p128

exchange-value as the necessary mode of expression, or form of appearance, of value. For the present, however, we must consider the nature of value independently of its form of appearance [*Erscheinungsform*].[12]

Considering the "nature of value" for the present independently of its "form of appearance as exchange-value", is, however, precisely what is just as impossible for Michael Heinrich as for the whole of traditional Marxism and all bourgeois vulgar economics. They consider value only as exchange-value, only as the appearing in the relationship of different commodities to each other. Marx, on the contrary, states expressly that considering things in this way is superficial and downright false:

When, at the beginning of this chapter, we said in the customary manner that a commodity is both a use-value and an exchange-value, this was, strictly speaking, wrong. A commodity is a use-value or object of utility, and a 'value'. It appears as the twofold thing it really is as soon as its value possesses its own particular form of manifestation, which is distinct from its natural form. This form of manifestation is exchange-value, and the commodity never has this form when looked at in isolation, but only when it is in a value-relation or an exchange relation with a second commodity of a different kind. Once we know this, our manner of speaking does no harm; it serves, rather, as an abbreviation.[13]

In itself the commodity, even an individual one, 'is' therefore both a use-objectivity and a value-objectivity; however, the latter 'appears' ('presents itself') only in the exchange relation. Yet, so that something can appear or present itself, it must already be there in itself. This is why Marx states once again as reinforcement:

The internal opposition between use-value and value, hidden within the commodity, is therefore represented

12. Ibid. p129
13. Ibid. p152

> on the surface by an external opposition, i.e. by a relation
> between two commodities[14]

Every single commodity, already contains the internal opposition of use-value and value, but this can be "represented" only in the exchange relationship through an external opposition in the relation of the relative and equivalent forms of value. With Heinrich, on the contrary, there is no internal opposition, but only an external one; he mistakes the "representation" of the thing for the thing itself, the essence for the form of appearance. So he does not know, or does not want to know, what Marx presupposes as known so that this "manner of speaking" about exchange-value "does no harm"; so Heinrich's "manner of speaking" does indeed do harm, namely the corruption of Marx's conceptual analysis.

Value is the social objectivity of the commodity, even the single individual commodity, the commodity before and independently of the secondary relation of exchange where, under capitalist conditions, the appearance of exchange-value in the form of the universal equivalent money is identical with the *realisation of surplus-value*, i.e. the return of capital into its quantitatively expanded money shape. However, value and surplus-value are already essential determinations of the commodity as a value-objectivity before this 'realisation' (insofar as the commodity has always been determined as the specific form of wealth in capitalist societies), and nothing changes here if this realisation fails to take place – the value character of the commodity then expresses itself in its senseless disposal instead of consumption, something that is only even possible because its social essence consists *a priori* in value-objectivity and not in any objectivity of need.

The individual commodity is a value-objectivity, not in an individually attributable quantitative sense which, as shall be shown later, is only determined in the social average, but in the qualitative sense as an individual social thing, a value-thing. That is not a juridical, political or any other external determination of domination, but an internal essential determination of the commodity itself regardless of whether or not it succeeds in being exchanged. (It is only in the understanding of traditional Marxism that legal relations, as a merely subjective relation of wills can appear superficially as something external.) It is precisely for this

14. Ibid. p153

reason that value-objectivity is the spectral, the hidden, the not directly visible thing in the body of the commodity, as Marx clearly states at the beginning of his value-form analysis:

> The objectivity of commodities as values differs from Dame Quickly in the sense that 'a man knows not where to have it'. Not an atom of matter enters into the objectivity of commodities as values; in this it is the direct opposite of the coarsely sensuous objectivity of commodities as physical objects. We may twist and turn a single commodity as we wish; it remains impossible to grasp it as a thing possessing value. However, let us remember that commodities possess an objective character as values only in so far as they are all expressions of an identical social substance, human labour, that their objective character as values is therefore purely social. From this it follows self-evidently that it can only appear in the social relation between commodity and commodity.[15]

Qualitatively, the individual commodity is essentially a value-thing, but as such sensuously 'intangible'. By simplifying the problem of value-objectivity in a vulgar economic way to the apparent 'tangibility' of the "social relation between commodity and commodity", Heinrich skirts the ghostlike character of value-objectivity and flees to the apparent plausibility of the sphere of circulation. He does indeed suspect a hiatus emerges in his line of argument, namely in relation to production, and seeks rather lamely in this respect to withdraw himself from the whole affair after quickly pointing out that according to Marx the value character of things "has already to be taken into consideration during production." Heinrich interprets this in the following way:

> The fact that value is "taken into consideration," the future value of a commodity estimated by the producers, is something different than if this value were something pre-existing.[16]

15. Ibid. p138
16. Heinrich, *Introduction to the Three Volumes of Karl Marx's Capital* p230 fn11

Like this, though, value, or value-objectivity, is located as totally external to production as a merely subjective concern about something "future" that is to take place solely in the sphere of circulation.

The 'authentic' Marx again says the exact opposite. He divides his analysis of the production process into two sub-chapters, namely into the production process as labour process[17] and as valorisation process.[18] In the introduction to the latter it states:

> It must be borne in mind that we are now dealing with the production of commodities, and that up to this point we have considered only one aspect of the process. Just as the commodity itself is a unity formed of use-value and value, so the process of production must be a unity, composed of the labour process and the process of creating value [*Wertbildungsprozess*].[19]

Far from situating value-objectivity only beyond the production process in its form of appearance in the sphere of circulation, Marx grasps the production process itself as the process of creating value. Once again this is made quite clear and explicit in another passage:

> This whole course of events, the transformation of money into capital, both takes place and does not take place in the sphere of circulation. It takes place through the mediation of circulation because it is conditioned by the purchase of the labour-power in the market; it does not take place in circulation because what happens there is only an introduction to the valorization process, which is entirely confined to the sphere of production.[20]

In circulation the creation of value only takes place in so far as circulation has a 'mediating' role through the purchase of the commodity labour-power in the labour market. The relations of production and

17. Marx, *Capital I (Chapter 7.1)* p283
18. Marx, *Capital I (Chapter 7.2)* p293
19. Ibid. p293
20. Ibid. p302

circulation are indeed entwined; every production is preceded by acts of exchange and every circulation by acts of production. Value creation as such quite clearly does not take place in circulation, but in the sphere of production. The process of production is the value-creating process, essentially so as a capitalist production process. That the quantitative 'validation' is executed only as an average of the total social process of production and circulation (realisation) changes nothing in this.

With this determination of the individual commodity as a value-objectivity and the production process as a value-creating process we also have no truck with any so-called 'premonetary value theory' (a term coined by Hans-Georg Backhaus in the debate around the conceptual content of Marx's value-form analysis), that is accepting a value relation existing before and independently from the money relation in an historical sense. Marx begins, as is well known, with the concept of the commodity explicitly as the form of wealth in the modern, capitalist society – his derivations are essentially logical and not historical. This is why money is always presupposed, not only as the universal equivalent, but as a form of capital, as a self-moving end in itself and the form in which surplus-value is realised. The point is to explain this already presupposed thing in step by step derivation and not to deduce the historical genesis of money from some premonetary value relation.

It is precisely the presupposition of capital, in other words of the money-form as valorisation form in a feedback loop, that makes the production process into a value-creating process and the individual product as commodity into a value-objectivity; therefore outside of the capitalist form of reproduction the already fully developed money-form would simply not exist. Only because production is from the outset a valorisation process whose only aim is the realisation of the incorporated surplus-value is the individual commodity already an *a priori* value-objectivity. Just as capitalistically socialised human beings are always *a priori* subjects of money, quite independently of whether they are taking out their wallets or flipping open their cheque books, so too is the capitalistically produced commodity always a value-objectivity, quite independently of whether it is being sold on the market at that moment.

This means that Heinrich cannot invoke Marx in any way whatsoever. What matters here is not the letter of an orthodoxy, but the thing itself. And here Marx is right against Heinrich: value is produced, it is a relation of production and no mere circulatory "relation of validation" (we shall see in Part II of this study that this aspect plays a decisive role in the determination of abstract labour as a quantitative relation and therefore also in crisis theory).

If value is produced the commodity is already a 'value-objectivity' before entering the market, i.e. into circulation, in other words it is a 'spectral objectivity' inasmuch as it is 'intangible' as such in its sensuous shape. However, in order to grasp value at all, determining it in this not directly tangible ghostlike form is exactly what must be done, and not in the form of appearance of exchange-value.

I made this problem the theme of an essay as *The Two Levels of the Value-form Concept*[21] and described the exchange-value that appears in the relation between two commodities, that is in the relation of the relative form of value to the equivalent form, as 'the form of a form'. The social form as such is the value-form in the sense of the value-objectivity of each individual commodity, whose value is 'manufactured' in the sphere of production. This essential form, 'intangible' in the individual commodity, the 'nature of value', 'appears' in the secondary form of exchange-value inasmuch as (an appearing) 'form of a form' (of the essential form 'value'). In other words, in reality just as Marx presents it, even if the problem in the sense of the discussion with postmodern-influenced neo-Marxists such as Heinrich is not explicit; because it might be that he cannot imagine such a thing as a Marxist vulgar economist.

This determination of the 'form of a form' also appears as utterly incomprehensible to a traditional Marxist, opposed to value-critique, such as Alexander Gallas: "the 'form of a form'… this nonsense is obviously no product of sloppiness, but a symptom of a problem of critical peculiarity."[22] Such a lack of conceptual thinking, that also extends to anti-critique, indicates that in crass opposition to Marx for both the traditional and neo-Marxists (particularly those enriched with postmodernism) there is no difference between essential form and form of appearance, between value and exchange-value. They remain fixed to the surface of the circulatory concept of exchange-value, because they insist

21. Robert Kurz, *Abstrakte Arbeit und Sozialismus* in *Marxistische Kritik 4* (Erlangen 1987) p62
22. Alexander Gallas, *Marx als Monist? Versuch einer Kritik der Wertkritik [Masters dissertation]* (Berlin 2003) p23

on understanding the concept of abstract labour not as the *a priori* of the reproduction process, but only as a secondary 'exchange abstraction'.

Abstract labour not only comes first in the sense that the exchange abstraction appearing in circulation would be a preliminary as moment of the production process itself in the sense of a real value-creating process, that is merely as the priority of a determinate particular sphere, namely production, as opposed to another particular sphere, namely circulation. The determination of abstract labour as social *a priori* is rather a determination of the totality (here meaning the reproduction of the capitalist form in the narrow sense as a whole, which is not identical, however, with the actual total reproduction that always includes other, disassociated moments). This means that abstract labour extends over the total capitalist reproduction process as the moving force of the value abstraction. What 'appears' in the exchange-value of the sphere of circulation is the antecedent value-objectivity of the commodities in which the abstract labour determining the production process manifests itself. Abstract labour and value-objectivity are only different aggregate states of one and the same real abstraction in which moves the capitalistically form determined reproduction process and its history; and exchange-value is its everyday form of appearance apparently without history.

7

What is really abstract about abstract labour?

Naturally, the traditional Marxists have in the meantime smelled the coffee and understood through their dispute with value-critique that they could be convicted of limiting their critique of capitalism to the sphere of circulation, whereas they have always supposed themselves to have a clear concept of capitalism as a 'relation of production'. In their desperation they attempt to hide yet again behind the "labour movement Marxist" Marx, that is the labour ontologist Marx caught up in an aporia. Gallas, for example, attempts to evade the critique of labour ontology by undertaking a displacement. There is indeed a transhistorical, 'anthropological' dimension to labour, but by no means is the capitalist production process therefore made ontologically positive in opposition to the sphere of circulation; such an assumption would prove itself:

> ...as unjustified in the face of the existence of a Marx in *Capital* who thinks the concept of labour in transhistorical and historically specific dimensions together. This Marx draws a distinction between the 'social form' and the 'material', that is the anthropological 'content'[1] of phenomena of human coexistence. Thus he notes that "Labour... is a condition of human existence which is independent of all forms of society"[2] in order at the same time to work out its specific nature under capitalism: "the worker works under the control of the capitalist to whom his labour belongs"[3] Marx shows like this the functional interlocking between natural factors and relations due to

1. Marx, *Capital I* p126
2. Ibid. p133
3. Ibid. p291

historical contexts: production in capitalism also has an anthropological function...[4]

According to Gallas value-critique throws everything together; it assumes the traditional position, because this attributes an anthropological status to labour:

> ...a dualist understanding of the object. But this is not compatible with the concept of labour from Marx as quoted above. Capitalist form and anthropological content of labour do not, following Marx, stand independently from one another. This then rules out comprehending labour and capital as self-contradictory structuring principles of society[5]

Consequently, the outlook of value-critics is inaccurate, "with their attacks on a dualistic understanding they have struck at all ways of reading the critique of political economy whose concept of labour does not correspond to that of value-critique";[6] thereby merely creating "a 'cardboard cutout' called 'traditional Marxism'..."[7]

According to Gallas one can hold an ontological and transhistorical or 'anthropological' concept of labour and yet still conceive of 'labour under capitalism' along with Marx as historically specific; the 'anthropological' and the historically specific moments are just to be 'thought together' in their interlocking. And that is then simply supposed to be no 'dualistic understanding' in the sense of an ontology of production or concrete labour on the one hand and an historically specific nature of circulation or abstract labour, on the other.

What has now been shown is firstly, that not only has the especially crude labour movement Marxism, for example from social-democratic or Leninist provenance, such a 'dualist' understanding, but so too does the more demanding Western Marxism right up to today's academic Marxists such as Heinrich with his explicit circulation theory of abstract labour

4. Gallas, *Marx als Monist?* p15
5. Ibid. p16
6. Ibid. p16
7. Ibid. p17

and value. Secondly, Gallas's line of argument with which he seeks to ground a non-dualist understanding of the ontology of labour and its specific historical nature, is rather the proof of the opposite. Namely, when Gallas states that Marx makes a division between the 'social form' and the 'material', that is anthropological 'content' of the 'phenomena of human coexistence', it is just exactly that dualism since if the material content of production and reproduction is 'anthropological', then the historically specific moment of 'social form' only refers to the method of distribution and sphere of circulation.

The only thing that Gallas actually specifies in relation to Marx as historically specific in production is the reference to the fact that labourers work "under the control of the capitalist" to whom "their labour belongs." However, he thereby describes exactly no inner logic of material production itself, but only an externally understood, subjective volitional relation of domination and juridical appropriation. Hence everything remains pretty much the same; the allegedly non-dualist interlocking of 'anthropological' and specifically historical moments in the production process itself evaporates into thin air and what remains is exactly that 'dualist' understanding of a merely external and subjective domination of the capitalist class, in this superficial sense mediated by law and circulation, over a production that is 'eternal', the 'material content' given positive expression. It is therefore deceptive packaging to do this with such a superficial understanding, as if it implied a critique of labour in the sense of an historically specific relation.

Typical in this respect, incidentally, is Autonomism that has completely detached labour from abstract form determination and fetishisation and in an extremely superficial way dissolved it into the merely external control requirements of the 'capitalist class', all the way to a total renunciation of the critique of political economy in favour of a supposedly 'non-political' relation of domination over production (particularly clear in the case of Negri).

Naturally, the question is in what way does abstract labour as social *a priori* represent itself *practically* in the production process. As an abstraction that is not merely conceptual, but as practical social activity it is the disregarding of the material and sensuous character of commodities in the process of exchange, their practical treatment as value-things in purchase and sale which amounts to the real abstraction. How does this real abstraction now represent itself in the process of production itself? Here there is apparently nothing other than concrete labour, the determinate modification of natural matter; whereby the concept, admittedly as has been shown, is a paradox and self-contradiction.

Marx refers to this material and sensuous aspect of the 'form' of labour as the labour of carpentry or weaving. However, this material form is other than the social form. Concrete labour as 'form', say of cabinet making, relates to the manufacture of wooden furniture, for example. But the social form of labour there is abstract, i.e. labour expended in the concrete, material form of cabinet making only counts socially as a definite mass of abstract labour, expended human energy as such (of "nerves, muscles, brains"). This 'validation', however, does not take place first of all in circulation, but is as the overarching determination also decisive for the process of production; and it is also not just an issue of 'validation' in the sense of a formal execution (as in circulation), but of a practical intervention.

The ghostlike nature of value-objectivity is already to be found in the process of its manufacture as the ghostlike nature of the production process itself. Just as the value-objectivity of the finished commodity is not directly 'tangible' to the senses, because it is an abstract social form determination, so also in the production process as such its function is as a value-creating process not directly 'tangible to' the senses, at least that is, not at first glance and not for an individual socialised into this social form. To all appearances there 'is' only concrete labour, the material, sensuous modification of matter. But this is not what it seems to be, instead it is merely the expression or form of appearance of something else. What is at issue here is not essentially the manufacture of furniture for domestic purposes, but the creation of value for valorisation purposes.

In this respect, labour in the production process does not 'count' as it seems to do, namely as the concrete manufacturing process of furniture, but as the expenditure of abstract labour-power as such, as the (managerially optimised) expenditure of nerves, muscles and brains. That is a thoroughly practical point of view that affects and in the end completely dominates the total organisation of production. For this reason even the criteria for the operational flow and managerial direction are abstract and universal, utterly independent of the concrete content of production. In the name of the abstract social form determination (value) abstraction also occurs in practice from the concrete form of the production process in the sense of material content (the content of furniture production equals 'labour' in the form of cabinet making, etc.) The concrete activity, cabinet making, here counts practically as 'labour', as mere expression of the expenditure of human energy as such. And this real abstraction also rubs off onto the concrete modification of the material just as it does onto its result, and very much destructively.

In capital, as has already been pointed out, the relation of abstract and concrete has been turned on its head; the concrete, the really sensuous, varied world only counts as the form of appearance of the abstract, of a totalitarian essential determination called value. *Regardless of what it is, it is always value – or it should become such.* When valorisation as a subject casts a glance at humans and nature it only sees them as objects for valorisation, and this determines its practical activity. Concrete labour and abstract labour are one and the same labour, bound together in the abstraction 'labour' as a real abstraction:

> On the one hand, all labour is an expenditure of human labour-power, in the physiological sense, and it is in this quality of being equal, or abstract, human labour that it forms the value of commodities. On the other hand, all labour is an expenditure of human labour-power in a particular form and with a definite aim, and it is in this quality of being concrete useful labour that it produces use-values.[8]

But first, "all labour" here is only that determined in capitalist Modernity and not "all labour" in a transhistorical sense (as is clear from Marx's context). Secondly, the "on the one hand – on the other hand" are by no means of equal weight. Not only can the concrete side not be separated from the abstract, but the former is subordinated to the latter. In other words: use-value is only a form of representation or appearance of value, the concrete labour only a form of representation or appearance of abstract labour. Overarching both is the abstraction 'labour' as a real abstraction (and it is only within the context of such a real relationship, to emphasise the point once again, that the conceptual nominal abstraction 'labour' as the concept of a social universality makes any sense at all).

8.   Marx, *Capital I* p133

This is to say that concrete labour 'is' according to its social essence in actual fact abstract labour, although not directly 'tangible' as such, just as the sensuous shape of the commodity is actually a value-objectivity, although as such just as little directly 'tangible'. However, this concept of 'intangibility', only describes the appearance as appearance; everything depends on 'grasping' the underlying, hidden element by analytical efforts and decoding it right through its mediation. That does not just hold good in the sense of a theoretical reconstruction, but at the same time as the designation of facts that are really experienced as taking place in practice but whose character does not, however, appear. Critique as a result of analysis is nothing other than the conscious determination of something that has been really experienced and practically known for a long time and is now bathed in a revealing light by reflection in which its mediations become visible.

In what, then, do the practical mediations consist that allow concrete labour to be decoded as the mere form of appearance of abstract labour? In the first instance this concerns the *space* in which the process of production takes place. Just as we are apparently dealing with wholly innocent concrete, material modification processes, so in this space, as a factory for instance, we have it seems a wholly innocent functional building. But the space of production is not merely material in the sense of this functional building, but a social space whose character is just as little directly 'tangible' as that of value-objectivity.

The social space of capitalist production is the *functional space for business,* a special social place determined not essentially by its material form, but through its social function as the space where valorisation takes place (its material form follows from this and not the other way round). The functional determination of this space 'puts aside' (abstracts from) all other areas of daily life and needs outside economic determination, being the location of the value-creating process; and in this respect this space constitutes an element of real abstraction. It is a space 'disembedded' from the total life process, roughly in the sense that Karl Polanyi spoke of with his auspiciously chosen concept of a 'disembedded economy' (even if with a somewhat different connotation and not related to the problem of abstract labour).

This 'disembedding' was also an historical process closely bound up with the military revolution of early modern times, firearms innovation and the resulting 'disembedding' of the military machine from society (standing army, absolutism, bureaucratic territorial state, etc.). In early military despotisms, having firearms at their disposal, this in turn brings about the insatiable hunger for money, the monetisation of feudal dues and finally via various intermediary steps (state manufacturing, slave agricultural industries, etc.) the transformation of the population into an homogeneous mass of material available for the valorisation of abstract labour (that 'total national labour' ontologised and made positive by Marxists in the context of recuperative modernisation). The history of discipline including workhouses, reformatories and lunatic asylums, or even 'camps', as described by Marx in the chapter on "So-called Primitive Accumulation" or in the writings of Foucault and Agamben, also belongs to the constitution of the disembedded functional space for business.

What in Marx's words applies to money, also applies for the constitution of this disembedded space: "The movement which mediated this process vanishes in its own result, leaving no trace behind."[9] Modern humans come upon the space of business as a finished shape whose disembedded character they feel, but can no longer name. It is the space in which the individual, as the young Marx states, "feels himself only when he is not working; when he is working he does not feel himself;"[10] and precisely not in the external juridical sense of the property concept, but as the specific functionality of this space for the value-creating process. The division of production from all other areas of life (for instance housing, community, childcare, play, culture, etc.) is by no means given *per se* in that it is a question of production for others and not for one's own needs, that is as social production. The dissolution of the life-world that included production is not to be blamed on the transition to social production as such, but on the transition to the valorisation of value. Only the usurpation of the social by the real abstraction of value and abstract labour has created the disembedded functional space of business as a ghostlike social realm beyond all sociability.

Abstract labour's constituting of itself as abstract, disembedded functional space also indicates a gendered connotation. The dissociation of all other areas of life and relationships (personal care, feelings, etc.)

9.   Karl Marx, *Capital II* trans. David Fernbach (London 1978) p187
10. Karl Marx, *Economic and Philosophic Manuscripts (1844)* in *Early Writings* trans. Rodney Livingstone and Gregor Benton (London 1975) p326

from production as a process of value-creation and valorisation connotes the disassociated moments just as much as nature abandoned to economic normalisation as 'feminine', which has led to corresponding practical attributions and 'responsibilities' of women (detailed presentation in Roswitha Scholz, *Das Geschlecht des Kapitalismus*, Bad Honnef 2000). The dissociation of the feminine therefore belongs essentially, and not just accidentally, to the real abstraction of abstract labour in the production process. This corresponds to the historical roots of abstract labour, that is the interlocking of the 'disembedded economy' with the 'disembedded' military machine based on firearms in the early process of constituting Modernity.

Abstract labour *per se* is structurally determined as masculine, even if women were definitely active in the production process from the very beginning. That women are consistently worse paid, seldom attain leadership positions, must put in considerably more effort than men, etc., are mainstream facts still significant today and should not be hived off to the historical and empirical level of appearances and where possible declared to be a mere hangover from premodern conditions, or as their merely subjective and regressive return. Instead they are an expression *of dissociation relations as an essential mark of abstract labour itself* and its economically functional space.

The opposite conception, misinterpreting the relation of dissociation to gender asymmetry in Modernity as a merely historical, empirical and tendentially dwindling moment, is fundamentally bound up with the misinterpretation of real abstraction as a mere 'exchange abstraction' that, nonetheless, appears for a change as a positive and progressive relation. For in fact, in circulation looked at for itself, there is no dissociation as a moment of real abstraction; here the only thing that counts is the ability to pay regardless of gender, age, skin colour, etc. Circulation, therefore, is indeed known as the El Dorado of bourgeois progress and ideologies of freedom, even though it implies competition and the dehumanising of those unable to pay. But yet again, destructive competition and the dehumanising of the loser is executed in the specifics of the sphere of circulation in the form of abstract universality: silently, without consideration of persons and with polite 'recognition' in the sense of the legal equality of commodity owners. Persons who cannot compete and cannot pay simply do not exist for the logic of circulation. The apparent dwindling of gender determination also falls under this.

Naturally though, the sphere of circulation and law cannot be looked at alone, and with respect to this the abstract freedom ruling here is mere appearance in a double sense: it is first of all founded on the repressive determinations of reproductive activities in the metabolic process of society with nature and with itself; second, it is therefore also in the circulative sense 'freedom' only in an Orwellian sense, that is as a self-repressive relation, as the formal self-subjugation under the logic of abstract labour. When considered in connection with the abstract labour of the sphere of production, together with its determinations of gender and subjugation, and from the standpoint of the total process, the circulation sphere with its 'exchange abstraction' is itself something quite other than superficial. Considered for itself, it is objectively *the sphere of surplus-value realisation* and subjectively *the sphere where social coercion is executed* on the formal level of bourgeois exchange relations.

A further glaring contradiction of traditional Marxism shows itself in this respect: on the one hand it reduces the historically specific relation of capital to regulation by the sphere of circulation (market mediation), abstract labour to a mere 'exchange abstraction', relations of domination to relations of commodity distribution and the 'relations of production' to the external juridical property concept. As the specifically capitalist mediation form the sphere of circulation or the 'exchange abstraction' would have to be abolished. On the other hand it swears by the idealism of the sphere of circulation, taking recourse to the 'heritage of the Enlightenment' from which originates the postulate of equality that in some way (such as through 'democratisation') ought to be extended to production. Incidentally, this aporia is particularly pronounced in Adorno who on this point remains totally imprisoned in the traditional Marxist way of thought.

What is fundamentally missing is the inner connection of real abstraction as a mediating relation between abstract labour in the production process and its realisation or 'representation' as value-form or 'exchange abstraction' in the circulation process, together with its attendant juridical determinations of an apparently gender-neutral 'abstract individuality.' The one conditions the other. Neither can circulation be abolished without abolishing abstract labour as the logic of production, nor on the contrary, can the formal and ideal equality of abstract subjects be extended from circulation to production and reproduction. Since there the very same process of abstraction necessarily presents itself in another way: as the high command over labour-power with its gender connotations. The same also holds, having rubbed off from the 'disembedded' functional sphere of business, for all social institutions in the overall structure of value socialisation and the world of everyday life.

Soldiers as civilians are a similar case (corresponding in turn to the historical roots of the 'disembedded economy'). As the latter they are free subjects of law and circulation like everyone else. On the other hand, as the former they are objects of the high command, parts of a machine, killers and if need be, cannon fodder. The structurally masculine character of the entire performance is more strongly marked here since women figure far less than in the production process, not to mention the (merely functional) management positions, etc. This example, pointing to capital's historical constitution, shows at the same time how senseless it would be to want to force, for instance in respect of gender, the abstract equality of the sphere of circulation onto the yet unconquered spheres of capitalist reproduction (including, where possible, even the army). Such an intention cannot have anything emancipatory about it as it is to a much greater extent a matter of overcoming the total conditions of abstract labour/gender dissociation/circulation.

Often felt and complained of is the ghostlike character of the disembedded space of business activities as a really abstract functional sphere beyond the remaining life contexts, and there have been repeated attempts, both in the history of the trade unions as well as in the more recent social ecology movement, to re-establish a lost life context by propagating a 'life-work' unity or (more narrowly) one of 'living and producing'. However, such thoughts remained undefined in respect of the underlying connection of abstract labour and value. Integration of the life-world is supposed to happen on the basis of the undisputed categories of value-socialisation including circulation; an undertaking doomed to failure right from the beginning.

The same also holds for administrative attempts 'from above' to sneak other moments of the life-world into the disembedded functional space of business, or to forge links to it, either from ideological or disciplinary grounds. We know from the history of the major corporations about the institutionalising of 'company communities' where they tried to bind and motivate a privileged core labour force to the company logo with a life-world of company housing, nursery schools, clubs, etc. Quite apart from the functionalist character of such measures, with regard to making workers fit even more tightly into the real abstraction of the production process and squeezing out higher performance, these arrangements always remained marginal and transitory experiencing a sharp decline in times of crisis. Today they are fast disappearing in the wake of rationalisation and globalisation (a shining example with respect to this being Germany's Siemens Corporation).

The same is true of the state cocooned works communities under 'real existing socialism' in which the integration of moments of the life-world was considerably more strongly and deeply anchored; definitely an advantage in terms of quality of life and self-determination in comparison to the West, even if it was moulded by bureaucratic imposition. It was precisely these emancipatory moments where the abstract functional space of business fragments that had to clash with the real basis of abstract labour, leading to their failure at the hands of the retained value socialisation. In the end these integrative moments were not consciously conceived as alternative mediations for overcoming abstract labour; on the contrary, they underlay their affirmation. It was thus just a matter of a mere niche formed under the conditions of a system of recuperative modernisation, whereby the (ultimately unsustainable) bureaucratic direction of market processes opened up the functional space of business in part unwillingly, in part ideologically to the terrain of the life-world. For instance, the consequence drawn from this failure was not to make abstract labour responsible and arrive at a perspective of its overcoming, but, on the contrary, to supply the functional space of business in practice with its logical determination and to 'purge' it of all those life-world moments that are dysfunctional in the economic sense.

As long as abstract labour constitutes the *a priori* of social mediation and reproduction, it will repeatedly posit from itself the functional space of business as "disembedded" and divided from all other life moments, as simply real abstract space. That is actually the problem that Marx speaks of at the end of chapter 6 in the first volume of *Capital*, when he determines the relation between the spheres of circulation and production of capital in respect of the 'commodity labour-power':

> The sphere of circulation or commodity exchange, within whose boundaries the sale and purchase of labour-power goes on, is in fact a very Eden of the innate rights of man. It is the exclusive realm of Freedom, Equality, Property

and Bentham. Freedom, because both buyer and seller of a modality, let us say of labour-power, are determined only by their own free will. They contract as free persons, who are equal before the law. Their contract is the final result in which their joint will finds a common legal expression. Equality, because each enters into relation with the other, as with a simple owner of commodities, and they exchange equivalent for equivalent. Property, because each disposes only of what is his own. And Bentham, because each looks only to his own advantage. The only force bringing them together, and putting them into relation with each other, is the selfishness, the gain and the private interest of each. Each pays heed to himself only, and no one worries about the others. And precisely for that reason, either in accordance with the pre-established harmony of things, or under the auspices of an omniscient providence, they all work together to their mutual advantage, for the common weal, and in the common interest.[11]

So much for the sphere of circulation together with its idealism of equal and free legal subjects. However, it is time to take leave of it and follow the progress of the total reproduction process. Marx continues:

When we leave this sphere of simple circulation or the exchange of commodities, which provides the 'free-trader *vulgaris*' with his views, his concepts and the standard by which he judges the society of capital and wage-labour, a certain change takes place, or so it appears, in the physiognomy of our *dramatis personae*. He who was previously the money-owner now strides out in front as a capitalist; the possessor of labour-power follows as his worker. The one smirks self-importantly and is intent on business; the other is timid and holds back, like someone who has brought his own hide to market and now has nothing else to expect but – a tanning.[12]

11. Marx, *Capital I* p280
12. Ibid. p280

From the course of the argument up till now it must be clear how traditional Marxism has to read this presentation, that is simply not as the relation of abstract labour as "exchange abstraction" on the one hand and the logic of production as real abstraction on the other, but merely as an external and juridical relation of the capitalist (as owner of the means of production) and the wage-labourer (as owner of labour-power) that does not even touch the concept of abstract labour as a real abstraction. This way of reading may definitely appear in Marx's diction, but he limited the juridical relation here to the sphere of circulation. What now follows as the 'tanning' is not in any way to be understood as merely the subjective, external and distributive exploitation of one juridical will by another, but the entrance to the real abstract, 'disembedded' functional sphere of the ghostlike space of business. In a certain way this is also true for the capitalists themselves, or for the functionaries commanding valorisation (management, etc.).

Since the traditional understanding of the 'exploitative character' of the capitalist *mode of production* stays within the limits of the crude appropriation of the determination of juridical subjects of volition, it completely misses the character of the functional space of business. However, by doing so the dissociation of the modern commodity producing system into separate spheres of reproduction and functionality must also be missed. For this dissociation is indeed only posited through the constituting of the disembedded functional space of business for the self-expansion of value, implying in itself the separation of all other areas of life as special spheres, but at the same time becoming the centre that dominates all these other 'spheres', making them appear as 'derived'. On the other hand, everything that is not absorbed into the logic of the central, disembedded functional space and its 'departments' (above all particular activities of reproduction) is assigned to the gendered dissociation relation and thereby socially an occupation for the 'feminine'.

This relationship also presents itself as an historical development: "Value-dissociation is… not a rigid structure as sometimes encountered, for instance, in the structural models of sociology, but a process. It cannot, therefore, be grasped as static and always the same."[13] This process appears to be culminating in the crisis of the third industrial revolution. On the one hand, the logic of the originally disembedded functional space of

13. Roswitha Scholz, *Das Geschlecht des Kapitalismus* (Bad Honnef 2000) p118

business, afflicted by a crisis of accumulation and finance, forces itself onto all of the derived, secondary spheres of social reproduction: politics, culture, healthcare, education, etc. They lose their own logic and are treated according to the criteria of economic functionality, that is directly subsumed under the logic of abstract labour, something that up to now only occurred indirectly and in derived forms.

On the other hand, this expansion of economic functional logic beyond its proper, specific space cannot contain the crisis and certainly not replace the dissociated 'feminine' sphere of reproductive activities: "Instead there is a brutalisation of the commodity producing patriarchy, in that it works itself loose from its institutional support."[14] The break-up of the traditional family and demolition of welfare state structures do not make the gendered dissociation pointless, but sharpen it even more. To the same extent as the real abstract, dissociated space of the valorisation process attempts to totalise itself and must necessarily fail, the dissociated, 'feminine' moments are subjected to a hopeless overloading. That as a result social reproduction breaks up altogether is precisely the practical proof that the functional logic of economic space is utterly hostile and misanthropic, that is to say this space represents everything but a neutral, innocent, transhistorical and ontological location for the 'concrete' material production of 'useful' goods that just receives an unkosher determination from an external, juridical 'control' by exploiters.

What corresponds to the 'disembedded', real abstracted economic functional space is a similarly 'disembedded' and abstracted time, to some extent the specific *functional time* of abstract labour. The issue is a *specific historical form of time or time determination*, belonging solely to the modern commodity producing system. This form of time or time determination is the abstract astronomical flow of time of the mechanical Newtonian universe, analogous to the similar physical-reductionist atomic components of this universe.

Socially, it is the time form of the measureless, that is an unlimited, indeterminate time that is bound to nothing (the astronomical dimension serves solely as an external and arbitrary measure); a time flowing endlessly, serving only the boundless demands of the 'automatic subject' for an endless incorporation of expended abstract human energy measured by

14. Ibid. p133

similarly abstract units of time (seconds, minutes, hours of 'labour' detached from all content), therefore the transformation of all lifetime into labour-time. Hence, the astronomical flow of time is the paradoxical measure of the measureless, an insatiable time no longer bound to any (always limited, determined) need; the time measure of an irrational self-sufficient purpose, no longer measuring any limited movement in time for a definite purpose or process, but running as an endless time band feeding back into itself, as the time form of the endless valorisation movement of value feeding back into itself. The 'concrete labour' of the capitalist production process does not just take place in the 'disembedded' functional space; it also runs in reality by the measureless measure of the 'disembedded' abstract flow of time, not according to the measure of a temporally determinate (and essentially limited) modification of matter.

Moishe Postone has concerned himself less with the specific character of 'disembedded' space than with the specific character of the capitalist time form and has made groundbreaking discoveries. The uncanny character of 'abstract time' has been discussed either explicitly or implicitly again and again in the history of modernisation, but without ever relating it to abstract labour and the categorial mediations of value-socialisation. Postone, basing himself on social historians such as Thompson, Gurjevich, Needham, etc., initially differentiates 'concrete time' in the way it was determinative as time quality in premodern time (and in another way must also be essential for a postcapitalist society) from the 'abstract time' of modern commodity production:

> I shall term 'concrete' the various sorts of time that are functions of events: They are referred to, and understood through, natural cycles and the periodicities of human life as well as particular tasks or processes, for example, the time required to cook rice or to say one paternoster. Before the rise and development of modern, capitalist society in Western Europe, dominant conceptions of time were of various forms of concrete time: time was not an autonomous category, independent of events, hence, it could be determined qualitatively, as good or bad, sacred or profane. Concrete time is a broader category than is cyclical time, for there are linear conceptions of time which are essentially concrete, [...] Concrete time is characterized

less by its direction than the fact that it is a dependent variable.[15]

The current idea of premodern time as merely cyclical (bound to seasons and rhythms of life, etc.), seemingly limited to the agrarian mode of reproduction and its fetish forms, offers something to a critique of commodity-producing Modernity only in a reactionary sense for the most part. On the contrary, Postone's broader concept of concrete time as a "task-oriented notation of time",[16] dependent upon events and not separate from what are finite processes in time (regardless of whether they are cyclical or linear). Over against this stands the other, negative time quality of Modernity, namely the disembedded economic functional space:

> 'Abstract time', on the other hand, by which I mean uniform, continuous, homogeneous, 'empty' time, is independent of events. The conception of abstract time, which became increasingly dominant in Western Europe between the fourteenth and seventeenth centuries, was expressed most emphatically in Newton's formulation of "absolute, true and mathematical time [which] flows equably without relation to anything external." Abstract time is an independent variable; it constitutes an independent framework within which motion, events, and action occur. Such time is divisible into equal, constant, nonqualitative units.[17]

The "independent framework" of this time of which Postone speaks here, can also be understood as an 'independent space', precisely as the 'disembedded' economic functional space. The abstract, astronomical flow of time of the valorisation process constitutes this ghostlike space, just as this flow of time is conversely constituted as ghostlike time by this space. Postone indicates that:

15. Postone, *Time, Labor, and Social Domination* p201
16. Ibid. p216
17. Ibid. p202

[T]his form of temporal alienation involves a transformation of the nature of time itself. Not only is socially necessary labor time constituted as an 'objective' temporal norm, which exerts an external compulsion on the producers, but time itself has been constituted as absolute and abstract. The amount of time that determines a single commodity's magnitude of value is a dependent variable. The time itself, however, has become independent of activity— whether individual, social, or natural. It has become an independent variable, measured in constant, continuous, commensurable, and interchangeable conventional units (hours, minutes, seconds), which serves as an absolute measure of motion and of labor qua expenditure. Events and action in general, labor and production in particular, now take place within and are determined by time—a time that has become abstract, absolute, and homogeneous.[18]

However, time initially only became abstract, independent and absolute in a determinate social space, precisely that disembedded economic functional space in which it no longer depends on the time 'for something', but on time plain and simple in the sense of 'labour' or the expenditure of human energy plain and simple. The disembedded space and the time within it that has become absolute together constitute *a specific social space-time*, a *space-time continuum* beyond all human needs and the whole social life-world. In the historical process where capital enforces itself space-time rubs off onto the derived spheres and finally even on the world of everyday life itself; it is the usurpatory space-time grasp of the "alien god" (Marx), of the "automatic subject" (Marx). That totalitarian demand for valorisation as it emerged from the hunger for money of the early modern firearms economy and military revolution, and further developed itself into a *social machine*.

However, the origin and centre is and remains the specific space-time of the economic valorisation process, of abstract labour, allowing it to extend itself over the whole life-process at the cost of total social self-destruction. It is increasingly clear that the process of the current global crisis of the third industrial revolution is approaching this state of disintegration.

18. Ibid. p215

Once the character of the abstract social space-time of the economy has been elaborated, it becomes clear how crude the idea is that this whole relation could be reducible to the juridical 'power of disposal' in the hands of mere volitional subjects of exploitation. It is not the case that 'private property in the means of production' constitutes the system of abstract labour and its space-time constitution, but precisely the reverse it is the mode of production of abstract labour, the self-sufficient purpose of the 'automatic subject' through which the juridical form of private property in the means of production is constituted (along with the self-mediating movement of abstract labour/value through the sphere of circulation). Merely posing the (juridical) 'property question' is therefore anything but radical, instead it puts the cart before the horse: it touches neither the space-time character of the social reproduction process, nor the subject form of its bearers. If, for instance, subjects of abstract labour, that is subjects of the economic space-time (and consequently of competition in the mediation through the sphere of circulation) 'democratically vote' on questions of reproduction, they can in this way only reproduce, express and bring into play the contradictions of their social way of life, but not emancipate themselves from the functional laws of this abstract space-time, that is from the fundamental fetish relations.

Emancipatory intervention must delve deeper and burst open and destroy the space-time of abstract labour itself, while the elimination of private property in the means of production would merely be a logical consequence of this revolution, but not the revolution itself. The opposite conception, held by traditional Marxism, can only ever lead to the reproduction of the juridical form of private property, something that is in no way bound to individuals or families, in some sort of institutional form (state bureaucracy, dictatorship of the party, works councils, co-operatives, etc.) Private property in the means of production (and likewise in labour-power as a commodity) is not a subjective or even arbitrary 'power of disposal' in the sense of mere 'enrichment', but nothing other than the juridical form of the system of abstract labour and its specific abstract space-time. More exactly: it is the necessary juridical form of the functional subjects of this space-time, but not the social ground of the whole performance.

A threefold real, practical process of abstraction takes place paradoxically in the abstract space-time of the economy. Firstly, although it is they themselves that 'labour', the functional subjects must first abstract from themselves, extinguishing themselves in a certain way as human beings, to obey the imperatives of abstract labour. This does not follow from the material character in itself, for instance from (social) production for others rather than for one's own needs, but from the fundamentally 'alien' fact of the capitalist self-sufficient purpose, the valorisation of value. The point is not to produce useful objects, either for oneself or for others, but it is essentially to produce value and surplus-value, that is to burn up a maximum of one's own abstract human energy within the functional space of economic space-time, to turn oneself as a human being into a social combustion engine.

It is for this reason that the subjects of abstract labour as functionaries of the 'automatic subject' (management included) have neither any influence on the concrete content of production (predefined by the self-sufficient purpose of valorisation) whose meaningfulness or meaninglessness is outside of their authority, nor are they able to plan the course of the production process or its ambience according to their wishes and needs. The abstract space-time of the economy does not allow its activities to be made 'nice'; it is not a matter of our own lifetime and our own living environment in which we set up our lives, but of an alien space-time – not 'alien' in the sense of the alien private property of another volitional subject (of the capitalist), but 'alien' in the sense of the functional logic of abstract labour as such. The abstract flow of time should be interrupted as little as possible, precisely because the whole purpose is the maximum human expenditure of energy per unit of time; not consumer articles, and not the needs of the producers. For instance, rules on work break times are not at the discretion of the producers themselves and tend to be minimised (up to the question of whether someone may even go for a piss).

Producers can just as little use the means of production, tools, etc. for their own purposes on the side, as they remain reserved by strict rules for the purpose of valorisation. Here, too, the reference to juridical private property falls way short, since the absence of a power of disposal on the part of the producers does not follow an external relation of personal wills, but the inner logic of economic space-time itself. Where this logic is violated, for instance by the incompleteness and 'slackness' of the economic regime in the state socialist bureaucracies, this is always punished by loss of function. As long as the logic of abstract labour and its specific space-time itself is not consciously abolished, it can only lead to functional defects and setbacks if the producers assert themselves in the production process as having human needs.

Secondly, the functional subjects of abstract labour must also abstract themselves from each other in practice, even though at the same time they have to co-operate with each other in the concrete production process. However, this co-operation, as Marx described it many times, is not their own and nor is it merely under the external command of the private owner/capitalist as volitional subject, rather it is structured by the abstract space-time of the valorisation process itself. What the producers cannot do as individuals, they can also not do when co-operating, and that is to determine the content and course of the production process. Throughout their co-operation they remain isolated from each other as units of the expenditure of abstract human energy, since although their co-operation follows the demands of the concrete material transformation of natural products, this is merely the 'expression' of something else, namely the valorisation process. And the capitalist production process is *essentially* the valorisation process, to which 'concrete labour' remains subordinated. Therefore, the co-operative aspect at the level of concrete labour is inessential; what is essential is the non-co-operative aspect of the quasi-autistic expenditure of abstract human energy at the level of abstract labour.

In this sense the producers are posited even in the production process itself as monadic competitors and not only in circulation on the labour market as competing sellers of the commodity labour-power. *Abstract economic space-time reduces the co-operative moment strictly to the instrumental character of the technical processes, while all social co-operation is presented as systematically dysfunctional and "dangerous".* The basic logic of abstract labour tends towards the elimination of every moment of non-functional co-operation; time and again even the corners for coffee and chatting are presented as 'distracting' and are torn out. This also fractures the oft praised 'teamwork' and 'social competence' that themselves can only lead to their functionalist reduction to the absurd. It is economic space-time itself, where the producers remain separated by glass walls from each other, that paralyses every kind of horizontal communication and as if by itself repeatedly reproduces vertical structures of command.

The same is true of the architectonic structure of the functional buildings of abstract labour, their spatial divisions and the connections between them. The abstraction of 'working' individuals and their co-operation then becomes quite plain. The de-aestheticised functionalism of buildings, industrial estates and business parks (something that has for a long time rubbed off onto the life-world, housing and cultural buildings) hurts the eye as well as spatial feelings and follows just as little from any objective requirements of 'concrete labour' as do all the other moments of economic space-time, but results solely from the character of the production process as a valorisation process. That the producers must disregard themselves as human beings, that economic functional space is not their own living space and that economic functional time is not their own living time, is also reflected in the ambience of their activity that is as little subject to their self-determination as the sense, purpose and course of production itself.

Thirdly, in the end producers under the spell of economic space-time must in a certain way also disregard (abstract from) the concrete material objects of their activity, even though it is just these things that have been shaped in a technical sense by concrete labour. However, in the operation of production itself the producers' concrete activity counts only as abstract, indifferent combustion of their energy. Accordingly, the 'material' to be worked on as well as its concrete modification remains for them essentially indifferent and alien so that they can no longer identify with it in economic space-time as premodern handicraft workers could identify with their object. Identification with the activity follows only secondarily, for the most part as merely socially competitive points of view detached from their object. For example, one's position in the 'militaristic management' hierarchy, the command over others, or sales success, abstract pride in performance counted in units of time/quantity, the purely functionalistic, materially detached know-how qualification and its recognition, the 'aura' of a logo, etc. Only in remote branches not dominated through and through by economic space-time, such as art, are there still to be found elements of identification with the material and its qualitative modification, despite mediation by money and therefore at least circulatory real abstraction; but even here the indifference of abstract labour rubs off in the process of commercialisation.

The 'productive real abstraction' of the objects of apparently mere concrete labour is in no way only conditioned by the largely subjective indifference of individual producers towards the matter they act upon, activity that represents for those engaged in the production process itself essentially an abstract combustion process of their energy. The production process itself, in its inner logic as real abstract labour, is much more what posits this indifference *a priori*. It is therefore social objectivity that enforces the character of the abstract combustion of human energy on subjects indifferent to content as bearers of the processes, and not the other way round (certainly not some sort of subjective 'greed for profit' on the part of property owners).

This social objectivity of the indifference to material content follows from the essential character of the production process as valorisation process. It occurs in a curious inversion of the relation of value abstraction and so-called use-value; put more precisely the famous use-value exposes itself, as already indicated, as a mere form determination of value-objectivity itself and its realisation as exchange-value.

The inversion where use-value presents itself directly as a function of the constitution of value and exchange-value is initially determined by the specific character of the commodity labour-power. It is the commodity character of labour-power that makes possible the generalisation of commodity production into the social form of reproduction by capitalism. With this commodity, being both constitutive as well as specific, however, the determinations of the commodity form stand to some extent upside down. With all other commodities the so-called use-value consists at least at first glance in its material usefulness. Not so with the commodity labour-power. Its use-value for the capitalist production process is precisely not its ability to manufacture certain material or immaterial articles of need. Quite the opposite:

> In order to extract value out of the consumption of a commodity, our friend the money-owner must be lucky enough to find within the sphere of circulation, on the market, a commodity whose use-value possesses the peculiar property of being a source of value, whose actual consumption is therefore itself an objectification of labour, hence a creation of value. The possessor of money does find such a special commodity on the market: the capacity for labour, in other words labour-power.[19]

19. Marx, *Capital I* p270

What is therefore decisive is "the specific use-value which this commodity possesses of being a source not only of value, but of more value than it has itself."[20]

Production and its result do not depend on the apparent (material) use-value of the products, but on this specific social use-value of the commodity labour-power, consisting solely in the positing of value and surplus-value. However, the use-value of the commodity labour-power actually constitutes the concept of use-value in the formal interrelationship of universal capitalist commodity production. Marx himself thereby repudiated his ontological and anthropological determination of a transhistorical 'use-value production' which should also eternalise the abstraction 'labour'. Just as the use-value of the commodity labour-power consists in socially producing value over and above its own reproduction costs, so *the social use-value* of the products consists in 'representing' this surplus-value as a self-moving end in itself and then realising it through sale. The one is not to be separated from the other. *The social use-value in this sense dissociates itself from the material or immaterial concrete usefulness.*

That this usefulness in the concrete, tangible sense of an object of need also represents for capitalist production a necessary evil and a kind of residual condition, does not grant it, however, any transhistorical and ontological character as such, not even in this dissociation from the social use-value. To a greater extent the abstract, destructive, negative qualitative determination of the social use-value as the end in itself of valorisation affects the dissociated object of need and its production

Initially, this concerns the 'what' of production, its objective content. As is well-known, both owners of capital and management, as well as wage-labourers must be indifferent, for reasons of competition and the constraints of profitability, towards what they produce, regardless of whether it is apples or parts for an atom bomb. The main thing about the negative social use-value of abstract wealth, of surplus-value as an end in itself, is that it be produced and realised. There is absolutely no social entity that could consciously determine, according to some criteria of the reasonableness of needs, the objective content of production. Pointing to the supposed 'consumer power' is nothing but ideology. In truth the *a priori* of abstract labour and value also determine the structure of social

20. Ibid. p301

needs, subordinating them to the constraints of their specific abstract use-value logic of surplus-value production.

Subject to the dictates of this production and realisation of abstract wealth, production facilities even for elementary needs are closed down every day as unprofitable and insolvent, while pushing ahead with the production of destructive products for destructive needs (not only in the weapons industry). But not only in this sense does the abstraction from the needs-based content assert itself massively in the production process. Even the apparently non-destructive contents of production are destructively mangled by abstract labour. Whether it is tomatoes being grown without regard for taste to meet the packaging norms for continental distribution, apples being irradiated for longer shelf-life or groceries more generally being denatured for valorisation purposes and the loss of a whole historically accumulated wealth of diversity in useful plants and farm animals in favour of a stripped-down range aimed at economic rationalisation, whether in housing construction where the dictates of cost reduction lead to using building materials dangerous to health and where a dysfunctional layout of the rooms and an aesthetic outrage arises: the material content is aligned to the determinations of valorisation, and not the other way round; and indeed to an historically growing extent with advancing capitalist development.

The 'automatic subject' of valorisation virtually breeds human material for abstract labour also in the sense of shaping their needs. The logics of production and consumption intertwine under the dictates of the social a priori of abstract labour. While on the one hand elementary needs (and precisely those that in a certain sense can be determined transhistorically, for instance the need for clean drinking water, sufficient domestic space, etc.) are brutally neglected, the same real abstraction awakens destructive, purely compensatory, aggressive or simply stupid and childish needs even deep into everyday life. *The system of abstract labour virtually inverts the relation of needs and production: it is no longer the needs that generate production as its purpose, but the end in itself of a disembedded production increasingly generates negative needs as its mere means.* Even in the wealthiest capitalist countries ever more people have to go hungry while at the same time the barely imaginable 'need' should be aroused for watching a film on a postage-stamp sized display while jogging.

The social *a priori* of abstract labour as the logic of production itself therefore implies the neglect of elementary needs, the production of purely destructive goods and the qualitative reduction of all goods (to a stripped-down range, 'factory rubbish', throw-away production, aesthetic norming and de-aestheticising, etc.), in the end the shaping of needs generally to the imperative of the valorisation process up to and including the reduction or even destruction of their ability to bring us pleasure. Shaping production to the logic of abstract labour concerns not merely the 'what', the determination of the content of goods whose material character is subjugated to and adapted to a ghostlike value-objectivity, but also the 'how' of the labour process itself, the approach to the activities modifying natural materials or their human counterparts (service provision).

The abstract economic space-time demands, through the optimisation of valorisation logic, an adaptation of 'concrete labour' to the abstract space and time of the endless flow of the production line: "Time is money". This means that everything in the concrete labour process as a flow process of economic space-time must be negated and eliminated that in any way bars this flow of optimal combustion of human energy and causes frictional losses. The flow process runs at its smoothest, however, with objects of dead, physical matter (symbolically represented by, for instance, the 'classical' assembly line in the car industry). The economic space-time implies thereby a specific *reductionism*, very similar to the one corresponding to modern natural science.

We can speak of a physical reductionism of modern natural science that strives for a monistic explanation of the world from the elementary particles of the mechanistic Newtonian universe. That necessarily means a twofold reduction. In the first step the social, cultural and historical human must be reduced to its biological functional mechanisms; a commonplace of bourgeois ideology since the 18th Century. This biological reductionism spans the range from the pseudo-naturalness of the capitalist relations of production and distribution in economics since Adam Smith (expanded in more recent times to the pseudo-scientificity and 'mathematisation' of economics) through the biologisation of the social (social Darwinism) and up to the supposed genetic programming and determination of 'human nature'. In a second step the biological world must then be reduced to chemical and physical functional mechanisms, reducing living matter to dead. The hubris of searching for a total 'world formula' from which all being could be monistically 'derived' is still today based on this reductionist way of thinking and therefore in a mechanistic world view, although quantum mechanics seems actually to stand in contradiction to it.

The physical reductionism of modern natural science in *theory* is, however, represented in economic space-time as abstract-universal *praxis*, as the actual treatment of the world of objects in the sense of a reductionism of this kind. This approach makes possible in the first place an abstract-universal access logic, independent of its object, of the labour process as a valorisation process. The negation of the inner logic and inner time of qualitatively different universes of discourse and areas of life is only traversed along the route of physical reduction. Human beings are treated like animals and plants, but then animals and plants are treated like stone and metal. In economic praxis this takes place as a comprehensive reduction of social matters and living matter in general to dead physical objectivity. The ghostlike value-objectivity of the commodity appears in its process of production as the physical reduction of its materiality. The production process as valorisation process is essentially the process of killing off its objects.

The most outward consequences of this reductive logic have become visible for a long time, for instance in the monistic agro-industries, in the brutal continental transport of animals for slaughter, but also in the practices of social-care businesses, for instance when elderly and ill people are treated according to the pattern of carwash facilities or the 'tender loving care' for the dying is subordinated to the time-management of economic rationalisation. In the practices of suchlike agro-industrial factories, hospitals and 'care-gulags', as they have become known worldwide in rapid succession, in the meantime only leading to scandals everyone is weary of, but which show themselves to be no more than the tip of the iceberg of the logic of physical reduction as it dominates the whole economic space-time through and through right into the pores of the social reproduction process.

Also belonging to this reductionism is the secondary destruction of the planetary biosphere by the physical "refuse of production" (Marx) and the quite similar secondary destruction of the social relationships by to some extent mental "refuse of production". Indifference towards the directly qualitative content of 'labour' implies a similar such indifference to the 'environment' of the valorisation process, both in respect of the biological as well as the social. The 'disembedded' space-time of the economy only knows and tolerates its own intrinsic logic; it has no feelings for anything outside of its own field that is subordinate to another quality of space and time. This is the reason for the failure of all the climate treaties and other attempts made by a helpless ecologism to some extent to price in the 'externalised costs' of the economy again according to its own logic and without breaking with this logic as such. Just as helpless remains the appeal to compassion, social responsibility, 'civil society', etc. that calls for non-reductionist behaviour in social relationships without fundamentally questioning economic space-time as the core of reductionism.

As in a war of annihilation where utterly brutalised people are no longer able to reintegrate into 'civil' life, individuals conditioned to a reductionist pattern of behaviour inside economic space-time are just as little able to behave 'socio-ecologically' outside of it. This is quite apart from the fact that this 'outside' or 'beyond' of economic space-time is increasingly being chewed up and absorbed – not that economic space-time could really totalise itself and incorporate the dissociated moments; in fact these are 'neglected'. It is just absurd when the official authorities of global crisis capitalism on the one hand invoke a socio-ecological 'ethics', while on the other hand in the same breath they push for the extension of economic space-time and its reductionist logic to all areas of life. Reason as respect for the intrinsic logic of the biosphere and social relationships is situated in a noncommittal way like a Sunday sermon in the personal responsibility of atomised individuals and to some extent in their 'freetime activities', while at the same time the negative social reason of abstract economic space-time determines the real social reproduction process in all its breadth and depth, even accelerating thereby the associated reductionist intervention.

The foreseeable result consists in the transformation of the mundane world of the biosphere and human social culture into a physical desert. Science-fiction in popular literature has long anticipated this result in the topos of the robot-world where a self-replicating mechanical 'intelligence' of dead machines rules over a chemically and physically reduced world. This love of physical reduction, both theoretical and practical, might also explain why the capitalist anticulture is so fascinated by the planet Mars that it forms the favourite goal of space exploration by means of rockets and robot vehicles. Mars is precisely the physical desert into which the earth still has to be made by abstract labour and its space-time. Poking around in this desert for at least bacterial life symbolises unwittingly the desperate self-destructive logic of a humanity ruled by the social *a priori* of abstract labour.

{8}

The concrete-historical time of capitalism

What is evident is the real destruction of the world by abstract labour as a process of production. If traditional Marxism as the immanent ideology of modernisation wants to limit the concepts of abstract labour and real abstraction to the sphere of circulation, this does not only show its contamination by the Protestant ethic, capitalist productivism and a false historical ontology of labour, but overall its limitation to the inner space of the modern commodity producing system and its abstract space-time. However, it also completely misses the concept of capitalist historicity. For capitalism is indeed on the one hand the return of the eternal, the ahistorical abstract time of the disembedded economic continuum; on the other hand, however, it is a blind concrete-historical process, an irreversible history of its own constitution, enforcement and crises represented in qualitatively different stages of development.

Moishe Postone consequently distinguishes two different, in a certain sense contrary kinds of time determination in the capitalist reproduction process; according to Postone this means "that the dialectic of capitalist development is, on one level, a dialectic of the two sorts of time constituted in capitalist society and, therefore, cannot be understood adequately in terms of the supersession by abstract time of all forms of concrete time."[1] The replacement of the earlier concrete time of the everyday as an always conditioned, limited time "of something" or "for something", as a task-oriented idea of time, by the abstract, disembedded space-time of economics is one kind. This metamorphosis, however, generates at the same time a new type of concrete-historical time at another, second level, a blind, historical dynamic of "development" and crisis.

Alongside the abstract, homogeneous, ahistorical space-time of economics, and emerging from it, capitalism as value-socialisation also posits therefore a completely determined concrete-historical time. Postone derives the relation of both these time-forms in a quite straightforward

1. Postone, *Time, Labor, and Social Domination* p216

way from the relation of the two dimensions of materiality and value-objectivity of the commodity: "...the interaction between the two dimensions of the commodity form can also be analyzed in temporal terms, with reference to an opposition between abstract time and a form of concrete time peculiar to capitalism."[2] It could also be put like this: the abstract, ahistorical time of value-socialisation is the temporal logic of the valorisation process; the concrete-historical time of value-socialisation, on the contrary, is the temporal logic of the materiality mobilised by this valorisation process, both in the sense of modified natural materials as well as in that of the connected social development.

The problem that appears here is once again the "use-value dimension" (Postone) of abstract labour, now regarded from the standpoint of the time-form. The determination of the use-value of the commodity labour-power as the production of surplus-value posits a social determination of use-value as merely materialisation of value/surplus-value and its 'realisation', while the material concreteness, and with it the material quality, is dissociated and remains secondary, a mere (indifferent) appendage to valorisation. Nevertheless, capitalism cannot free itself from this concrete materiality, the social use-value of surplus-value production and its realisation must 'incarnate' itself at ever higher levels of productivity, as is forced upon it by universal competition, ever renewed and in ever new, further developed concrete forms of the transformation of nature and sociality.

Precisely within this tension between indifference of content and abstractness of 'labour' and value on the one hand, and the material-content 'development' driven by the valorisation process itself on the other, is the dialectic of the two time-forms grounded. The abstract space-time of the economy knows no 'development'; one hour here is always one hour of homogeneous, autonomous time, without quality or content. This time corresponds to the value dimension of reproduction, abstract time and with it the value-objectivity of matter, that is the social fetish-use-value of production and the realisation of surplus-value. The indifferent, material content transported by this does undergo change, on the other hand and is continually redetermined, and not just simply in ever changing randomness, but with advances in the application of science and productivity in a concrete historical process. In this relation, in terms of a content to which valorisation as an end in itself is indifferent, but

2. Ibid. p292

which nonetheless asserts itself in practice, an hour is not always the same hour, but is increasingly filled anew, becoming the time of something else, 'development time'.

Postone indicated the logical level of opposition and intertwining of these two time-forms:

> The abstract temporal constant, then, is both constant and nonconstant. In abstract temporal terms, the social labor hour remains constant as a measure of the total value produced; in concrete terms, it changes as productivity does. Yet because the measure of value remains the abstract temporal unit, its concrete redetermination is not expressed in this unit as such. [...]
>
> That the abstract time frame remains constant despite being redetermined substantively is an apparent paradox... This paradox cannot be resolved within the framework of abstract Newtonian time. Rather, it implies another sort of time as a superordinate frame of reference. [...]
>
> This movement resulting from the substantive redetermination of abstract time cannot be expressed in abstract temporal terms; it requires another frame of reference. That frame can be conceived as a mode of concrete time. [...] Hence, this movement of time is a function of the use value dimension of labor as it interacts with the value frame, and can be understood as a sort of concrete time.[3]

The meaning of the use-value dimension here is the dissociated, concrete materiality that, incidentally, does not have to be 'useful' in any strong sense, but above all contains the development of the forces of production as forces of destruction. On the one hand, that is, we are dealing with "an abstract, homogeneous, temporal frame that is unchanging and serves as the measure of motion."[4] On the other hand, the concrete-historical time of a dynamic, irreversible process of social development is being driven

3. Ibid. pp292/293
4. Ibid. p293

by just this economic space-time at the concrete material level of the development of the forces of production and destruction:

> It involves ongoing changes in the nature of work, production, technology, and the accumulation of related forms of knowledge. More generally, the historical movement of the social totality entails ongoing, massive transformations in the mode of social life of the majority of the population—in social patterns of work and living, in the structure and distribution of classes, the nature of the state and politics, the form of the family, the nature of learning and education, the modes of transportation and communication, and so on ... Historical time in capitalism, then, can be considered as a form of concrete time that is socially constituted and expresses an ongoing qualitative transformation of work and production, of social life more generally, and of forms of consciousness, values, and needs. Unlike the 'flow' of abstract time, this movement of time is not equable, but changes and can even accelerate.[5]

Abstract, homogeneous, autonomous time as the measure of what claims to be the infinite combustion of human energy corresponds to and collides with a concrete-historical time of development made blindly dynamic and autonomous, in which not only is the face of the world changed historically, but also where the real categories of value-socialisation qualitatively mutate. Not only is it the development from the stagecoach by way of the railway to the 'automobilisation' of society, but also from the traditional family structure of production by way of the concentration of 'labour armies' up to abstract individualisation. At the same time it is the development of the connected relations of gender dissociation; it is the process of moving from the formal subsumption of structures of production already existing to the real subsumption of the processes of life and production under capital standing on its own foundations. Again it is the history of modern science intertwined with the dynamic of capitalism, the relations of industrial accumulation and a growing demand for an overall social framework (infrastructure), etc.

5. Ibid. p294

Regarding the two time-forms as concerns the social consciousness of subjects, individuals and institutions, the abstract economic space-time could be identified as the subjectively determining time-form and the concrete-historical time of capitalist development as the time-form that manifests itself objectively. This is because the intrinsic social activity of subjects only takes place in the abstract, homogeneous time frame of the disembedded economy and under the pressure of its imperatives, or (somewhat to the side of state and politics) in relation to this pre-given time frame. This time is autonomous, but it posits the direct conditions of the subjects' activity. Concrete-historical time, on the contrary, is a blind result, the objectified dynamic of a history of the 'automatic subject' and only indirectly made by human beings themselves, that is absolutely not under their collective control. It is a paradoxical time relation: subjective, conscious time is empty and abstract, the combustion time of human energy indifferent to every content; on the other hand, the concrete-historical time of the development of the real material content is unconscious, objective time and therefore historical destiny.

What follows from this is that social emancipation can only consist in the collective control over concrete-historical time to win the conscious destruction and abolition of the disembedded economic space-time, and thereby overcoming the logic of valorisation. Only the inclusion of reproduction in the life-world, the dissolution of abstract time and therefore gender dissociation, can also end dissociation and increasing indifference towards the material content of the production process. This would be the end of the division between life and production, content and form, production and circulation, economics and politics. The capitalist process of world destruction may only be stopped, that is, if social integration is brought about in which members of society for the first time in history consciously organise the use of their common resources (for instance in a differentiated, comprehensive organisation of councils) and in this way for the first time determine their own concrete-historical time – social development thus ceases to be a blind process of destiny.

Traditional Marxism cannot even think this task, let alone fight for a way to solve it. If the concrete-historical time of capitalism did not appear to past theoreticians of labour movement Marxism according to its concept, it did at least indirectly appear in the more or less positivist discussions about 'stages of development' in capitalism, and in this way today's remaining representatives of this thinking have completely banished from their reflection the problem of concrete-historical time and therefore the historicity of capitalism. The reason for this is that the intrinsic history of capitalism, the history of its development and crises is today hitting at its limits. Therefore, concrete-historical time as the result of abstract economic space-time is also no longer categorially immanent in the sense of a 'critical' interpretation of the next push for development. Concrete-historical time can now only be thought in the sense of a categorial critique of the disembedded space-time of abstract labour itself.

The remnants of traditional Marxism, being totally and utterly incapable of this categorial critique, withdraw in respect of the concept of capital into an idea of 'the eternal recurrence of the same', turning into some kind of 'Buddhist Marxism'. This characterisation is not even polemically over-exaggerated. Just to take one significant example, in what is for good measure a particularly demanding treatise that nevertheless cannot hide the asses ears of obsolete old-Marxist thinking, it states that: "It shows… how difficult it is to come across something substantially new, even original, in capitalist reality above and beyond what Marx had already thought long ago… This is not to pay homage to Marx: the issue is nothing other than the ascertaining that… at its core capital represents the eternal return of the same."[6] Explicitly or implicitly this hostile thinking towards an historical development in the value relation is found today almost without exception in the stranded survivors of a bygone era of categorial immanent critique of capitalism.

In other words: this thinking now limits itself completely to the time frame of abstract and homogeneous economic flow-time. In this time frame there occur changing events, but no development and no history. This corresponds to the structural reduction of the concept of capital to the level of individual capital and its supposedly eternal capacity to reproduce itself ('there's always some winners'). The total social dimension of value-socialisation disappears together with concrete-historical time from the field of vision. In this way traditional Marxism in its own final stages fuses with the bourgeois historical and economic approach (end of history, 'microeconomic' point of view). Since traditional Marxism cannot think of any new developmental stage of capitalism that the 'Left'

6. Initiative sozialistisches Forum, *Der Theoretiker ist der Wert [The Theoretician is Value]* (Freiburg 2000) p79

can occupy, because it no longer exists, it ceases to think about concrete-historical time at all. Traditional Marxism proves in this way only its own categorial immanence in the value-socialisation that it has specified as the ontologisation of abstract labour. Thus it, together with its object, comes unavoidably up against an historical limit.

This already indicates the problem of the categorial crisis. The concrete-historical time of capitalism, set free as a blind process from the results of abstract economic space-time onto the concrete-material and social level, does not just constitute a developmental, but also a crisis history. The irreversibility of this process flows into a 'stage of development' that already no longer exists, but by which an absolute historical limit manifests itself. Categorial critique and categorial crisis are mutually conditioning. Grounding this connection at the level of concrete-historical time requires an analysis of abstract labour in respect of its quantitative relations. The historical desubstantialisation of value, or devaluation of value, presents itself as a quantitative problem of abstract labour, forming the core of Marx's crisis theory. This quantitative relation of abstract labour in the sense of an inner limit to disembedded economic space-time is to be discussed in Part II of this study.

Part II

The failure of labour-ontological Marxist theory of crisis and the ideological barriers against the further development of the radical critique of capitalism

'Breakdown theory' as loaded term and counterfeit concept in the history of Marxist theory

There is just one thing that might raise the hackles of traditional Marxism more than the critique of 'labour', and that is breakdown theory. There is a direct connection between the two. A radical critique of the labour abstraction and a radical theory of crisis condition each other. If abstract labour forms the substance of capital, excluding thereby every ontology of labour, because the labour abstraction as a 'social universal' is only valid in this way for the one historically specific social formation, then crisis and an absolute historical limit to capital can only consist of a contradictory inner mechanism of the process of capitalist valorisation within which removes labour from itself, making it 'superfluous'. In this way capital 'desubstantialises' itself, value is devalued, positing thereby an absolute inner limit not only logically, but also as a necessary historical-empirical appearance.

However, before the problem of desubstantialisation as such can be developed, firstly the ideological barriers must be broken down that commonplace Marxism in all its variants (from traditional or labour movement Marxism to the Western New Left since the '60s, from the orthodox to the 'undogmatic' and postmodern positions) has erected against the theory of such an objective and inner limit to the self-expansion of capital. What is the bone of contention that leads again and again to hefty defensive reactions against this thinking, even though today this defensiveness amounts at the same time to a rejection of reality?

A rumour going about says that the old orthodox Marxism either of social-democratic or of Leninist stamp has itself fallen victim to an 'objectivist breakdown theory' and one that has been refuted both theoretically and also historically-empirically. So it is no longer necessary to seriously concern oneself with it, and anyone professing such a thing today must expect to be accused of untenable speculation, being 'esoteric' and downright dubious. Typical of this are the omissions made by Michael Heinrich in his *Introduction to the Three Volumes of Karl Marx's Capital* (already mentioned in Part I) . There he maintains without evidence or even indications:

> In the history of the workers' movement, the notion that economic crises would ultimately lead to the collapse of capitalism, that capitalism was marching toward its 'final crisis,' was widespread. *Capital* was interpreted as providing a 'Marxian theory of collapse.'[1]

This claim is simply false and there is no evidence for it from the history of the old labour movement. The positivistically misunderstood concept of the 'natural laws' of the capitalist mode of production and the movement or development of the categories does indeed always form a general background to traditional Marxist notions; but the idea of an objective economic breakdown plays no role, in any case not a *theoretical* one in the sense of a systematic justification. The objectivity of the crisis only appeared at all at the historical-empirical level, but not at the categorial; at the most, that is, in the sense of a background experience, connected to Marx's critique of political economy only in the form of vague, rather associative metaphors ('crash', 'unholy mess', etc.) A significant role was played by the experience of the Long Depression from 1873 to 1879 (crisis of German industrialisation) that petered out into a long period of stagnation until about 1895. However, nowhere did the connected labour movement Marxist debate and imagery solidify into a decided 'breakdown theory' that "*Capital* was interpreted as providing".

This is also confirmed by the investigation (itself not motivated by crisis theory) of Rudolf Walther, despite its limitations, of the relevant ideas in Social-democracy at that time:

> The often relatively clear distancing of the theoreticians from breakdown theories does not lead to the obvious conclusion that these theories played absolutely no role at all... For the theoreticians there definitely did exist the temptation to freeze the fluctuating development of capitalism between 1890 and 1914 once and for all into a breakdown theory and this is why breakdown theory

1. Heinrich, *Introduction to the Three Volumes of Karl Marx's Capital* p175

forms a permanent problem that the theoreticians of the labour movement consciously or unconsciously attempted to handle. That only very few of them fell for a breakdown theory and that their conceptions can be explained without reference to them is the main result of this study.[2]

Walther's way of expressing himself is indeed somewhat inexact, since here he equates the concept of a 'breakdown theory' as synonymous with vague notions and even 'unconscious' and unresolved problems, etc. But the conclusion is unambiguous: a fully worked out breakdown theory did not exist in the classical Marxist labour movement before the turn of the 20th Century. It remained in the virtual status of an unclear 'temptation' as it resulted from the contradictions in the history of Marx's theoretical reception; but it did not come to the realisation that Heinrich maintains.

The term 'breakdown theory' as such never had any positive status, but from the beginning a negative one; it was introduced in fact with polemical intent by Eduard Bernstein, the promoter of so-called 'revisionism', to discredit the opposed positions of the 'Orthodox'. In his series of articles that appeared in 1896-1898 in *Die Neue Zeit* under the heading *Problems of Socialism* there is also an essay *The Struggle of Social Democracy and the Social Revolution* with the subheading *Breakdown Theory and Colonial Policy*.[3] But there is nothing that could even distantly be a referred to as a 'theory' that would be an 'interpretation' of Marx's works, but just a single resolution from the International Socialist Workers and Trade Union Congress in London 1896. There it states:

Economic development is currently so far advanced that a crisis can soon set in. Congress therefore calls on workers of all countries to learn the command of production in

2. Rudolf Walther, *"...aber nach der Sündflut kommen wir und nur wir". "Zusammenbruchstheorie", Marxismus und politisches Defizit in der SPD, 1890-1914* (Frankfurt/Main 1981) p28ff

3. Eduard Bernstein, *Die Zusammenbruchstheorie und die Kolonialpolitick* in *Die Neue Zeit* (19 Jan 1898) quoted in Peter Friedemann (Ed.), *Materialien zum politischen Richtungsstreit in der deutschen Sozialdemokratie 1890-1917* (Frankfurt/Main 1977) p377

order to be able to take over the command of production as class-conscious workers to the common good of all.[4]

It was from these two sentences that Bernstein derived the claim:

This means that the conviction had established itself in Social-democracy that this course of development was an unavoidable law of nature, the great, comprehensive, economic crisis of the inevitable road to the socialist society.[5]

Bernstein, however, disavows the concept of 'breakdown theory' itself when he wants to demarcate it from the generally accepted concept of crisis and exaggerate it:

It could now be replied that, when speaking of the breakdown of the existing society, more is meant than a generalised crisis of society, even deeper than before, that is a total breakdown of the capitalist system from its own contradictions. But this idea is utterly misty (!) and totally ignores the great differences in the nature and course of development of different industries and their very different capabilities of taking on the stature of public servants. Any nearly simultaneous total breakdown of the current system of production, given the advancing development of society, is becoming less not more likely...[6]

By criticising this (imputed) position as "utterly misty", Bernstein unwillingly denies its character as justified, and in its justification, refutable, theory.

In fact since then those having recourse to the supposed breakdown theory of traditional Marxism have only ever uttered catchphrases, to which from time to time the term 'breakdown' belongs as well; but in no other way than in academic theory and in the press, that is, always

4. Ibid. p377
5. Ibid. p379
6. Ibid. p387

and only with reference to temporary commercial crises as cyclical sales crises (as with Heinrich Cunow) or individual banking crashes, etc., but not with reference to an objective and absolute inner limit to the mode of production as such. The term 'theory' was only stuck on by Bernstein, because he needed a straw man.

Karl Kautsky, the representative of the then 'orthodoxy', rubbed his nose in it: "A particular 'breakdown theory' was never constructed by Marx and Engels. The word comes from Bernstein..."[7] Its attribution to the Marxism of Social-democracy was likewise rejected:

> Bernstein will look in vain in the official statements of German Social-democracy for a claim that in some way expresses what he means by breakdown theory. In the passage from the Erfurt Programme that deals with crises there is no word about breakdown. However, there are probably hardly any speeches or newspaper articles by German party comrades to be found in which it would be maintained that a commercial crisis will initiate the social revolution, or the proletariat could only seize political power during a commercial crisis.[8]

The matter is clear: there had been absolutely no breakdown theory 'interpreted' from the works of Marx and Engels in the whole of Marxism before 1900, neither in speeches nor in newspaper articles was such a theory maintained, it was certainly not formulated and justified as such by anyone at all. The result is intriguing: the phantom of breakdown theory, concocted by Bernstein for the purposes of denunciation, has been mobilised for more than a century of Marxist theoretical history by the most diverse positions for the same purposes of denunciation against whoever is the current enemy; from revisionists just as much as from orthodox, from Leninists, ultralefts, spontaneists, etc. right up the postmodern Left. The corner that Michael Heinrich has installed on this ghost train is relatively modest and only one of many. The Left, however,

7. Karl Kautsky, *Bernstein und das Sozialdemokratische Programm*; (Berlin 1979, first pub. 1899) p42
8. Ibid. p43

feels spooked by it, even though the ghost has worn so thin already that it is just a joke.

It is obvious that there can be no labour movement Marxist breakdown theory. For such a theory would have to be *substantial,* and according to Marx the substance of capital is as a matter of fact labour. For traditional Marxism, founded on an ontology of labour, labour does not represent the substance of capital, but the (ontological) basis of emancipation. The inconsistency resulting from this can only be ostensibly overcome with much hairsplitting by differentiating Marx's term 'abstract labour' from 'labour in general', even though this term only contains the nominal reappearance of the modern real abstraction of labour. Nonetheless, the terrain is enough of a conceptual swamp for traditional Marxism to want to walk around it, preferring to avoid the problem (compare the discussion in Part I).

This position renders a substantial crisis theory a logical impossibility, and a breakdown theory farfetched. The concept of crisis is thereby as limited as the concept of critique: both can only refer in the last instance to the level of *circulation*. The critique remains stuck at the level of distribution within the form of abstract wealth (claims to the 'withheld surplus-value', etc.), the crisis appears merely as a result of the 'anarchy of the market'. And yet going as far beyond this as may be, these timid efforts draw attention for not stepping over the limits of labour ontology.

10

Reductive breakdown theories as Marxist minority position in the era of the world wars, part one: Rosa Luxemburg

Elaborated breakdown theories only emerged on the horizon of labour movement Marxism very late, that is within the context of the era of the world wars and Great Depression in the 20th Century, and even then only from an extremely small minority against the mainstream of Marxist thought. In fact the sole issue was the approach to crisis theory of Rosa Luxemburg and Henryk Grossman, which was thoroughly dismissed by the overwhelming majority of their Marxist contemporaries. Neither come close to a substantial crisis theory and therefore offer their detractors ample targets for their critique.

With Rosa Luxemburg it is clear from the beginning that her reflections on the inner limits of the capitalist *mode of production* only refer to the capitalist *mode of circulation*. What she puts forward is a crisis theory not of production, but of the 'realisation' of surplus-value, which indeed has to happen in circulation (by sale of the commodities on the market). Luxemburg takes up an argument that Heinrich Cunow briefly and vaguely sketched out in 1898 in the context of the Bernstein debate, without however, constructing a breakdown theory. The production of surplus-value was even expressly described in her book *The Accumulation of Capital* as unproblematic: "With the development of the process, which expresses itself through a falling tendency of the rate of profit, the mass of surplus-value thus produced is swelled to immense dimensions."[1]

The limits of capital, as she continues, lie at another level:

> Now comes the second act of the process. The entire mass of commodities, the total product, which contains a portion which is to reproduce the constant and variable capital as well as a portion representing surplus-value, must be sold. If this is not done, or only partly accomplished, or

1.   Rosa Luxemburg, *The Accumulation of Capital* trans. Agnes Schwarzschild (London 1951, New York 2003, first German edition 1912) p323

only at prices which are below the prices of production, the labourer has been none the less exploited, but his exploitation does not realise as much for the capitalist. It may yield no surplus-value at all for him, or only realise a portion of the produced surplus-value, or it may even mean a partial or complete loss of his capital. The conditions of direct exploitation and those of the realisation of surplus-value are not identical. They are separated logically as well as by time and space. The first are only limited by the productive power of society, the last by the proportional relations of the various lines of production and by the consuming power of society. This last-named power is not determined either by the absolute productive power or by the absolute consuming power, but by the consuming power based on antagonistic conditions of distribution, which reduces the consumption of the great mass of the population to a variable minimum within more or less narrow limits.[2]

Just like the rest of traditional Marxism, then, Rosa Luxemburg sees the evil not in the form of abstract wealth itself, in the commodity form or value-socialisation, but only in the 'antagonistic distribution' within this form that is not explicitly questioned. In the light of crisis theory this emerges as the problem of the realisation of the apparently inexhaustible surplus-value that comes from production into circulation, because the capitalist relations of distribution systematically limit the purchasing power of the masses. Capital's self-contradiction, according to Luxemburg, was to lead in the end to a tendency to breakdown, and therefore for her was to be found not within the production of value and surplus-value, but in the disproportion between the unlimited production of surplus-value on the one hand, and limited possibilities for realisation in circulation on the other.

This argument becomes more sophisticated by linking it to the connected disproportionality in the relation between the two major departments of capitalist reproduction, that is Department I (means of production), and Department II (means of subsistence). Here, Luxemburg

2. Ibid. p323

picks up the analysis by Marx in *Capital III,* where the application of science to industry and permanent raising of productivity dislocates the relation between capital equipment (constant capital) and labour-power (variable capital), the so-called 'organic composition of capital', to the benefit of the former: "...it is clear that a quicker growth of constant as compared with variable capital, i.e. the progressive metamorphosis of the organic composition of capital, must take the material form of faster expansion of production in Department I as against production in Department II."[3]

However, ultimately both departments depend upon the social capacity for consumption and purchasing power, according to Luxemburg, because the means of production have in the end to be deployed in the production of means of subsistence whose sale, though, is limited by this limited social purchasing power. This means that the realisation of the total mass of surplus-value fails not only because of weak purchasing power as such, but also due to the linked disproportionality between the two departments of capitalist reproduction. Therefore, she criticised Marx's reproduction schemas in *Capital II* in which the reproduction of the relation between the two departments comes into equilibrium and "adds up", by opposing it to the development of Marx's own analysis in *Capital III* where: "This eternal contradiction seeks to balance itself by an expansion of the outlying fields of production. But to the extent that the productive power develops, it finds itself at variance with the narrow basis on which the conditions of consumption rest."[4] It must, therefore, reach the point where the production of surplus-value, "swelled to immense dimensions," can no longer be realised (returned to the money-form), because circulation in relation to production has become the eye of a too narrow needle.

Luxemburg asks why it is that this point has not yet been reached until now. The reason, she maintains, is that capitalism can for the time being compensate for the limits of its inner capacities to realise surplus-value with external expansion, by, to a certain extent tapping into and overrunning the non-capitalist layers within the capitalist countries and the regions of the world not organised by capital. In other words: capitalism needs money coming in from external, non-capitalist 'simple

3. Ibid. p320
4. Ibid. p324

commodity production'. Rosa Luxemburg, that is, begins with a global social empirical analysis in which global reproduction has not yet been made thoroughly capitalist.

However, in the same way that capital uses its superior productivity to siphon off the money incomes of non-capitalist 'simple commodity production' in order to realise surplus-value, it also at the same time destroys this external production and therewith its own condition of existence, as Luxemburg describes in her *Anti-critique* against her Marxian critics:

> Accumulation is impossible in an exclusively capitalist environment. Therefore, we find that capital has been driven since its very inception to expand into non-capitalist strata and nations, ruin artisans and peasantry, proletarianize the intermediate strata, the politics of colonialism, the politics of 'opening-up' and the export of capital. The development of capitalism has been possible only through constant expansion into new domains of production and new countries. But the global drive to expand leads to a collision between capital and pre-capitalist forms of society, resulting in violence, war, revolution: in brief, catastrophes from start to finish, the vital element of capitalism.
>
> Capital accumulation progresses and expands at the expense of non-capitalist strata and countries, squeezing them out at an ever faster rate. The general tendency and final result of this process is the exclusive world rule of capitalist production. Once this is reached, Marx's model becomes valid: accumulation, i.e. further expansion of capital, becomes impossible. Capitalism comes to a dead end, it cannot function any more as the historical vehicle for the unfolding of the productive forces, it reaches its objective economic limit. [...] Marx's model of accumulation – when properly understood – is precisely in its insolubility the exact prognosis of the economically unavoidable downfall of capitalism as a result of the imperialist process of expansion whose specific task it is to

realize Marx's assumption: the general and undivided rule of capital.[5]

An explicit and fully-formed breakdown theory had up to then been so unfamiliar that a downright wave of indignation and criticism broke against Rosa Luxemburg's arguments. Against her 'catastrophe theory', as it was also called, positions were taken up in the course of time by social-democratic, Leninist and council communist theoreticians. In his work on the main currents of Marxism Leszek Kolakowski finds that: "It is noteworthy that although Rosa Luxemburg's intention was to establish once and for all the economic inevitability of the collapse of capitalism, none of the Marxist theoreticians who believed in the historical necessity of socialism endorsed her argument, and the most important of them opposed it..."[6] From the social-democratic party newspapers there were even administrative efforts to make her toe the line, as she complained in her *Anti-critique*: "Against those who had published a positive view of the book a high-handed action was taken by the central organ. A quite unique and somehow funny event … Such a fate had happened to no other party publication as far as I know..."[7] Traditional Marxists, both academic and political, as well as the postmodern Left would just love to take this line even today against any kind of breakdown theory.

The critique of Rosa Luxemburg's breakdown theory naturally highlighted exactly that point which was both her weakness and the common reference of the whole of labour movement Marxism, including Luxemburg herself, and that point was the shared idea of a constantly growing working-class producing surplus-value. Precisely that which Luxemburg criticised in Marx's reproduction tables, that is the thesis that the means of consumption additionally produced by additional means of

---

5. Rosa Luxemburg, *The Accumulation of Capital - An Anti-critique: The Accumulation of Capital, or What the Epigones Have Made of Marx's Theory* In: *The Accumulation of Capital - An Anti-critique and Imperialism and the Accumulation of Capital* by Rosa Luxemburg and Nikolai Bukharin respectively trans. Rudolf Wichman (London/New York 1972) p145-146

6. Leszek Kolakowski, *Main Currents of Marxism, Vol. 2: The Golden Age* trans. PS Falla (London 1981) p70

7. Luxemburg, *The Accumulation of Capital - An Anti-critique* p47-48 (In: Luxemburg/Bukharin 1972)

production would be purchased by the additional workers employed in industries making means of production, so that in respect of realisation problems, capitalism, through its own dynamic, could pull itself out of the swamp by the scruff of its neck, was presented as a proven reality and used as a weapon against her line of argument. What she was putting forward as an impossibility, according to the Austromarxist Gustav Eckstein in one of the first negative reviews of her book, "corresponds to Marx's model, but also to reality".[8]

Moreover, according to Eckstein, the armaments industry could compensate for weak demand, so that: "In Department II, where means of consumption are manufactured, now more uniforms, barracks and battle fleets are produced, and fewer workers' clothes, and less means of subsistence and rented accommodation."[9] An argument that Kolakowski also believed valid decades later; according to him "...Rosa Luxemburg's theory that compound reproduction depends wholly on non-capitalist markets has been refuted by our experience of the state's power to create, in the form of arms production, a huge market that may have a decisive effect on economic growth."[10] That government spending on the military is logically dependent upon surplus-value production can be disregarded since she also considers this to be a virtually 'limitless' possibility.

Otto Bauer, similarly from the Austromarxist position of Austrian Social-democracy, argued in the *Neue Zeit* against Rosa Luxemburg, assuming a constantly growing population from which he derived a supra-historical 'natural law' of accumulation in *material* form and identified this with a similarly constant increase in variable capital, that is with the surplus-value creating working class. He also sees capitalist reproduction working out 'by itself' even in expanded form:

> The workers' consuming power grows as quickly as their numbers. The capitalists' consuming power grows first as rapidly, since with the number of workers the mass of surplus value also increases. The consuming power of the

8. Gustav Eckstein, review of *Rosa Luxemburg, Die Akkumulation des Kapitals. Eine Besprechung,* from: *Vorwärts* (1913) quoted in Luxemburg/Bukharin, *Anti-critique* p86

9. Ibid.

10. Kolakowski, *Main Currents of Marxism, Vol. 2: The Golden Age* p74

whole society thus grows as rapidly as the value product. Accumulation alters nothing in this; it means only that fewer consumer goods and more production goods are required than with simple reproduction. *The extension of the domain of production*, which is a presupposition of accumulation, is here made possible by the growth of the population.[11]

This equilibrium between the production and realisation of surplus-value, according to Bauer also immanent in a pure capitalist system, asserts itself, however, not directly but mediated by the cyclical movement of prosperity and crisis, overaccumulation and underaccumulation:

Prosperity is overaccumulation. It provides its own counteraction in the crisis. The depression that follows is a period of underaccumulation. It resolves itself by creating out of itself the conditions of a return to prosperity. The periodic return of prosperity, crisis, and depression is the empirical expression of the fact that the mechanism of the capitalist mode of production by itself overcomes overaccumulation and underaccumulation, perpetually adapting the accumulation of capital to the growth of the population.[12]

Apart from the quasi-biologistic argument about 'continuous population growth' which has nothing to do with the political-economic analysis, Bauer's way of reasoning is exactly the topos of crisis theory as it has been 'picked out' again and again by Marxists up to Michael Heinrich & Co. The crisis is nothing but the cyclical inner 'cleaning mechanism' of the valorisation process, belonging to the 'functioning' of capital and therefore not to be regarded as the inner limit of the production process, but on the contrary as its positive operating mechanism.

11. Otto Bauer, review of *Die Akkumulation des Kapitals,* from: *Die Neue Zeit* (1912) quoted in: Paul Mattick, *Economic Crisis and Crisis Theory* (1974) See: www.marxists.org/archive/mattick-paul/1974/crisis/ch03.htm, (emphasis in the original)
12. Ibid.

That there was no difference at all between Social-democrats and Communists on this point, and that the Great Schism played no role here, is shown by the continuation of the outraged debate around Rosa Luxemburg's breakdown theory after the interruption of World War I, when the author herself could no longer express herself having been murdered in the counterrevolution with which her former party comrades were associated. Nikolai Bukharin's critique appearing in the mid-1920s followed wholeheartedly the line of the Social-democratic reviewers of 1912/13. In his essay *Imperialism and the Accumulation of Capital* that appeared in the theoretical journal *Under the Banner of Marxism*, he claimed of the realisation problem that: "...in the last analysis the matter is extremely simple. The employment of additional workers produces an additional demand, which realizes precisely that part of the surplus-value which is to be accumulated, to be exact, that part which must of necessity convert itself into functioning, additional variable capital."[13] His explanation of the reproduction tables was just as succinct: "The capitalists themselves buy the additional means of production, the additional workers, who receive money from the capitalists who buy the labour-power of these additional workers, buy the additional means of consumption."[14]

In a line of argument analogous to that of Otto Bauer, Bukharin also reduces the crisis problem to mere friction in the process of realisation due to ever-returning disproportionalities between the different aggregate states, amounts and forms of appearance of accumulation that are, however, just as regularly overcome. At issue here is a "process... which takes place by stages",[15] "*all these amounts on no account overlap each other*"[16] but realisation takes place right through the friction:

> The accumulated surplus value is obliged to pass through the money phase in its movement, yet it is not realized at once, but bit by bit, not as a compact heap of commodities to which is counterposed a compact heap of money, but by

13. Bukharin, *Imperialism and the Accumulation of Capital* p166 (In: Luxemburg/Bukharin, 1972)
14. Ibid. p177
15. Ibid. p180
16. Ibid. p186 (emphasis in the original)

> way of innumerable commercial operations, in which one
> and the same money unit successively realizes, out of the
> amount of commodity proportions, one proportion after
> the other; each individual portion, according to its value,
> is equal to this money unit.[17]

Bukharin's line of argument is not totally coherent: one time what enables the expanded realisation process is the additional workers realising the additional surplus-value with their additional money (wages), then again it is the increased velocity of circulation of the same sum of money. Nonetheless, the preponderance of reasoning is on the side of the additional workers, since this is a matter, not just of realisation, but also of the production of the additional surplus-value. In this respect all participants are unanimous – the premise of their entire debate is accumulation as expanded reproduction by means of the employment of additional workers. So it is not just in Bauer that we find the biologistic fallback onto a 'continuous increase in population' as the actual premise of accumulation, out of which a transhistorical lawlike regularity of sociality is actually made.

Bukharin, in repudiation of Rosa Luxemburg's theory, also arrives at that concept of mere cleansing crises, or the crisis as indispensable condition for the functioning of capital that dances on through his contradictions as the process of accumulation:

> Indeed, does the possibility of realization mean 'undisturbed'
> growth of the productive forces? Not at all. In Part 4 we
> have seen what confusions Rosa Luxemburg has caused.
> 'Undisturbed' growth means to her growth without
> contradictions, but even in 'pure capitalism' the whole
> development is full of contradictions. If there is no
> continual over-production, there is a periodic one. If
> there is no continual impossibility of realization, there are
> periodic crises instead. If there is no final solution to the
> contradictions, there is instead temporary postponement,
> hence a conditioned solution'. If there is no continual

17. Ibid. p186

possibility for capitalism to exist, there is instead expanded reproduction. And so on and so forth.[18]

As may be seen the line of argument from Michael Heinrich today, despite its critical claims, can, as regards crisis theory, be classified as belonging to the essentials of traditional Marxism, including its Leninist variant.

Reflections on crisis theory from the council communist side also belong to this tradition in which Rosa Luxemburg's breakdown theory is rejected because of its simplification into a theory of circulation. For instance, for Anton Pannekoek "it is clear that Rosa Luxemburg has herself made a mistake here."[19]

The accumulated surplus-value in the shape of additional means of consumption are "in fact bought by the additional workers",[20] and thereby realised. This same line of argument has been repeated since World War II by Paul Mattick:

> And at the turn of the century, the Marxist Rosa Luxemburg saw in the difficulties of surplus-value realization the objective reasons for crises and wars and for capitalism's eventual demise. All this has little to do with Marx, who saw that the actual world of capitalism was at once a production and a circulation process, to be sure, but who held nevertheless that nothing circulates unless it is first produced, and for that reason gave priority to the problems of the production process. If the production of surplus-value is adequate to assure an accelerated capital expansion, there is little reason to assume that capitalism will falter in the sphere of circulation.[21]

18. Ibid. p186 (emphasis in the original)
19. Anton Pannekoek, *The Theory of the Collapse of Capitalism* (first published in *Rätekommunist Nr.1* 1934) trans. Adam Buick in *Capital and Class* (Spring, 1977) See: www.marxists.org/archive/pannekoe/1934/collapse.htm
20. Ibid.
21. Paul Mattick, *Marx and Keynes: The Limits of the Mixed Economy* (Boston 1969) p92 See: www.marxists.org/archive/mattick-paul/1969/marx-keynes/ch09.htm

In general, sporadic engagements with Rosa Luxemburg's theory of the capitalist dynamic have not led to any new insights since World War II; an exception of sorts was the findings of Roman Rosdolsky in his work *The Making of Marx's Capital*, which is, however, essentially methodological in nature and does not belong here. As a rule, however, Rosa Luxemburg's breakdown theory, reductive as it was along the lines of circulation theory, was only taken as an occasion to reject any idea at all of an objective and absolute inner limit to the movement of valorisation. Ironically, in this way the idea, in itself correct, of returning to the sphere where surplus-value is produced, leads completely away from crisis theory. Indeed, in traditional Marxism (as shown in Part I) production is partly determined ontologically and transhistorically in respect of the substance of labour, which is outside of any crisis theory of capital, and partly through a detour by the plain question of distribution and the juridical power of disposition, so that the decisive posing of the question is completely closed off. In the latest approaches, for instance from Michael Heinrich, value and surplus-value are even explicitly determined in the manner of circulation theory as mere insubstantial 'validation relations', so that in struggling against the thought of an absolute inner limit to valorisation no recourse has to be taken to 'giving priority' to the production process.

11

Reductive breakdown theories as Marxist minority position in the era of the world wars, part two: Henryk Grossman

In contrast to that of Rosa Luxemburg, the other solitary remaining breakdown theory of the first half of the 20th Century, that of Henryk Grossman, came closer to a 'production theory' of crisis. For this reason alone Grossman has been stamped as a theoretical *persona non grata*, even more than Rosa Luxemburg, by mainstream Marxism right up to postmodernist interpretations. Most of those who pass him by, assuming that they are condemning him, have not even read him.

Grossman shares the one common premise of all the variations on traditional or labour movement Marxism, that is the ontology of labour. For him too the abstraction of labour and the substance of labour are eternal conditions for the existence of the human "metabolism with nature" (Marx). Grossman does indeed refer to the production of surplus-value in his explication of the 'law of breakdown', and not just to its realisation, but he does not base his line of argumentation at the level of the value substance as such. Instead, he superficially follows the complex problem already discussed in the classics of bourgeois political economy (Smith, Ricardo, Mill) of a logically necessary growth in the disproportion between the increasing upfront costs of production (constantly increasing application of science, machinery, etc.), and yields which are decreasing relative to these costs; Marx, as is well-known, characterised this as the relation of rising organic composition of capital and tendentially falling rate of profit.

Since Grossman cannot decode the historical process of desubstantialisation immanent to the logic of capital, that is the obsolescence of labour, because of his premise of an ontology of labour that is in the truest sense of the word the substantial background to this complex of problems, he proceeds blindly from the assumption of a constant increase in the element of capital v (wage-labour), just as did Luxemburg, Bauer, Bukharin, etc., that is from ever more additional human labour being sucked in; a process that at the most could be adversely affected externally by the problem of perhaps not having sufficient available labour-power (population growth). Since v (wage-labour) can increase infinitely and only its relative size in relation to c (real capital) falls, Grossman's theory of breakdown and crisis can only refer to relative proportions of the value substance that itself is not open to question.

With this purpose Grossman insists upon one aspect that seems downright curious. That is, he emphasises the difference within the concept of surplus-value between the portion destined for further accumulation (reinvestment) on the one hand, and on the other the portion destined for the personal consumption of the capitalists. Surplus-value, then, falls into into k (capitalist consumption) and a (accumulation fund), the latter further dividing into a_c (accumulated constant capital) and a_v (accumulated variable capital). One may already guess where this argument is leading: from the growing disproportion between c and v, that is the growing organic composition of capital, there follows not the loss of substance and with it the end of any valorisation at all, but simply a problem for the proportion k, the capitalists' own consumption; to which falls the burden of this shift within the proportional parts of capitalist reproduction.

At first, according to Grossman, this problem of calculation in the model (taken over from Otto Bauer, in order to criticise it immanently) was not visible: "...the portion of surplus-value reserved for the individual consumption of the capitalists (k) represents a continuously declining percentage of surplus value. But it grows absolutely despite increasing accumulation from year to year, thereby providing the motive that drives capitalists to expand production."[1]

"The motive" of capital accumulation is determined here in a way that is at the same time vulgar materialist, subjective and 'coincidentally' psychological; that is the greed of the capitalists for luxury consumption and the like. For Marx, on the contrary, capital accumulation or the

1. Henryk Grossman, *Das Akkumulations – und Zusammenbruchsgesetz des kapitalistischen Systems (Zugleich eine Krisentheorie)* (First pub. Leipzig 1929; reprint: Frankfurt/Main 1967)
    Incomplete translation published as: *The Law of Accumulation and Breakdown of the Capitalist System (Being also a theory of crises)* translated and abridged by Jairus Banaji (1979) See: www.marxists.org/archive/grossman/1929/breakdown/ch02.htm References to online translation and original German as indicated.

valorisation of value is an irrational end in itself that has made itself independent, the capitalist only figuring as its functionary. For this reason he is no glutton like the feudal lord (whose "motive" was also not completely absorbed by luxury consumption, but was determined by the constitution of the fetish at that time); instead, he has to be: "Fanatically bent on making value expand itself" (Marx). The entire level of the "automatic subject" (Marx) is erased in Grossman, as in the rest of traditional Marxism, so that he can arrive at his reductive determination of the inner limits of capital.

So at first the portion of surplus-value reserved for the capitalists' personal consumption k grows absolutely in the composition of surplus-value and diminishes only relatively to a, the accumulation fund, analogous to the organic composition of capital where v (wage-labour) grows absolutely and only declines relatively to c (constant capital). Grossman extends the calculations in Bauer's model in time and establishes that the proportional relations must gradually change:

> If we follow Bauer's system into year 36, holding firm to all the conditions postulated by him, we see that the portion of surplus value reserved for capitalist consumption *(k)* which amounts to 86,213 in the fifth year and grows over the following years, can only expand up to a definite high-point. After this it must necessarily decline because it is swallowed up by the portion of surplus value required for capitalisation.[2]

According to Grossman, this reversal is effected by the rapid increase in real capital in the organic composition of total capital, because in the end such an overwhelming portion of surplus-value is required for additional machines, etc., that the capitalists themselves have nothing more to eat:

> The constant capital grows rapidly, it rises from 50 per cent of the total product in the first year to 82.9 per cent of the annual product by year 35. Capitalist consumption *(k)* reaches a peak in year 20 and from the following year on declines both relatively and absolutely.

2. Ibid.

In year 34 it reaches its lowest level only to disappear completely in year 35.[3]

This is how Grossman manages the sleight of hand of an objective logic of breakdown with a well-nigh absurd argument and without having to take recourse to any process of desubstantialisation, or to the reduction of the substance of labour, or to the devaluation of value:

> ...the system breaks down. From year 35 on any further accumulation of capital under the conditions postulated would be quite meaningless. The capitalist would be wasting effort over the management of a productive system whose fruits are entirely absorbed by the share of workers. If this state persisted it would mean a destruction of the capitalist mechanism, its economic end.[4]

Capital accumulation as such could substantially continue infinitely – only the capitalists "would be wasting effort"! In one of the first critical reviews of Grossman's book the Social-democrat Alfred Braunthal derided this way of thinking as a theory of the "impoverishment of the capitalists".[5] Even the material premises of this grotesque construct are incorrect. Grossman makes out as if the equivalent of *v* were a fixed quantity. But, as is well-known, Marx had already indicated that the value of labour-power contains "a historical and moral element". The value of the means of subsistence that are needed for the reproduction of labour-power is not fixed, but actually determines itself through standards of civilisation, that is through the quantity and quality of the means of subsistence considered as the minimum necessary for the reproduction of labour-power. Society's own history shows the struggles there have been over determining this amount. The systemic immanence of the labour movement and class struggle consisted precisely in being a 'struggle for recognition' on the ground of abstract labour, something that was not questioned at all. Also belonging to this struggle was the one around

3. Ibid.
4. Ibid.
5. Alfred Braunthal, *Der Zusammenbruch der Zusammenbruchstheorie*, in: *Die Gesellschaft. Internationale Revue für Sozialismus und Politik* (Berlin 1929)

reproduction costs at a given level of civilisation. However, just as this 'struggle for recognition' is always at the same time a trap of obligation and self-imposed duty towards the systemic laws of the valorisation of value. In regard to this self-imposed duty, as happens regularly in times of major crises, it is competition among the workers themselves that ensures a fall in the historical and moral element in the value of labour-power and in their average reproduction costs being bombed back to levels below those already reached. In the current world crisis of the third industrial revolution this appearance is showing itself again, and raised to a higher power. In the USA already the historical and moral element of the reproduction costs of labour-power do not include an apartment as a matter of course ('homeless employment'); and this condition is spreading rapidly throughout the Western world, not to mention the periphery. So there is always enough scope to preserve the darling capitalist class from ignominious starvation because of lack of "the portion of surplus-value earmarked for capitalist consumption".

Grossman needs his seriously flimsy construct to pull off the feat of determining an absolute inner limit to the self-expansion of value from the side of the production of surplus-value, without having to start from a desubstantialisation in the shape of the obsolescence of labour. Massive redundancy of labour-power is, then, for him not, for instance, the decisive *cause*, but merely a *consequence* of the inner limit that has been constructed in another way. Accordingly, "...the failing rate of profit is accompanied by a fall in the surplus value earmarked for capitalist consumption (in our scheme this appears in year 21) and soon afterwards of the portions of surplus value destined for accumulation."[6]

This turns the causal connection on its head. Capital accumulation, according to Grossman, does not break down because the continuous development of productivity brings about an historical situation where it is impossible to take up sufficient living labour at the standard level of productivity and profitability, but solely because supposedly there is not enough surplus-value for the consumption of the capitalists. It is only as a secondary appearance of this supposedly real reason and the connected slackening of accumulation (the capitalists have ceased to have a 'motive') that there also arises in the end a continuously growing reserve army of no longer usable labour-power. To some extent it is the cunning of labour-

6.   Grossman, www.marxists.org/archive/grossman/1929/breakdown/ch02.htm

ontological 'reason' that forces such hairsplitting contortions in this line of argument.

Initially, according to Grossman, things are even the other way round. In the beginning the crisis, or inner limit, exists just as Bauer & Co. maintain, in a lack of labour-power:

> Imperfect valorisation due to overaccumulation is, however, only one side of the accumulation process; we have to look at its second side. Imperfect valorisation due to overaccumulation means that capital grows faster than the surplus-value extortable from the given population, or that the working population is too small in relation to the swollen capital.[7]

Only after the capitalists, for want of their own means of consumption, have lost their zest, does the situation change:

> From this point [year 35] onwards valorisation no longer suffices to enable accumulation to proceed in step with the growth of population. Accumulation has become too small, which means that a reserve army is inevitably formed and grows larger year by year.[8]

Grossman excludes expressly, and not merely implicitly, the obsolescence of labour by development of productivity and thereby the desubstantialisation of capital or devaluation of value as the ground of the 'law of breakdown' that he has set up:

> The displacement of workers by machinery [...] is a technical fact [...] All technological advance rests on the fact that labour becomes more productive, that it is economised – or set free – in relation to a given product. That machinery sets free labour is an incontrovertible fact that needs no proof; it belongs to the very concept of machinery as a labour saving means of production.

7. Ibid.
8. Ibid.

This process of the setting free of workers will occur in any mode of production, including the planned economy of socialism. From this it follows that Marx could not possibly have deduced the breakdown of capitalism from this technical fact.[9]

This supporting line of argument is just as hairsplitting as the actual and higher-level one about the 'breakdown in capitalist consumption'. That there may also be technical development of productivity independently of capitalism at the purely material, 'natural' level does not mean that such a development of productivity under capitalist conditions could not have an effect on valorisation, as Grossman claims. He separates the value, or valorisation, level completely from the technical material level and makes out that the one would have nothing to do with the other. In so doing he misses totally the dynamic unique to capitalism that is precisely characterised by the development of productivity and desubstantialisation through the dialectic of matter and form or of their substance. The substance of the value-form is not transformed natural matter, but rather past abstract labour, the mass of burned up human energy. Since he cannot proceed to this decisive, deeper level of the problem of crisis, because of his labour-ontological premises, Grossman must turn the matter on its head by maintaining that in respect of economics:

> [T]he process of setting free labour that Marx describes in the chapter on accumulation, and which is reflected in the formation of the reserve army, is not rooted in the technical fact of the introduction of machinery, but in the imperfect valorisation of capital specific to advanced stages of accumulation. It is a cause that flows strictly from the specifically capitalist form of production. Workers are made redundant not because they are displaced by machinery, but because, at a specific level of the accumulation of capital, profits become too small and consequently it does not pay to purchase new machinery and soon.[10]

9. Ibid.
10. Ibid.

Grossman's reversal of cause and effect is also crass insofar as with Marx it is precisely the rising organic composition of capital that underlies those internal movements in the value relations of capitalist reproduction, to which Grossman himself lays claim, and from which the material and technical development of productivity is derived, but which suddenly now no longer condition the "lack of possibility of capital valorisation", indeed they play no further economic role whatsoever. It is the *horror vacui,* abhorrence of emptiness, as in the very thought of the obsolescence of the substance of labour, which causes the whole of labour-ontological Marxism to back away. This abhorrence also plagues Grossman and leads his line of argument into hopeless eccentricity. This is why he has to declare an "absolute (independent of the trade cycle) unemployment" as absurd, or explain it as an insignificant phenomenon caused by frictional forces connected with "changing jobs", even at the height of a boom; and this has "nothing to do either with displacement by machinery, or with the accumulation of capital".[11]

Reducing the logic of breakdown to the internal movements within substantial surplus-value creation, which itself is not open to question, makes Grossman's construction of a theory on the basis of Bauer's Platonist model into a dull, totally conceptless arithmetical calculation, one, as he says himself, of "arithmetical and logical proofs"[12] without recourse to the underlying problem of substance. Against this background it is understandable that he should drive his reversal of crisis logic even further, and as regards the development of productivity fall back utterly into Social-democratic and Leninist thought about a supposed obstacle to the productive forces in the shape of a stagnant, parasitic, etc. capitalism. Grossman even maintains that: "...under the conditions of the capitalist mode of production at a given level of capital accumulation, technical development must slow down, because the *valorisation* of capital is not sufficient to fulfil this function".[13] Accordingly, there is a "senility... of capitalism",[14] that proves "...that in capitalism an unlimited expansion

11. Ibid.
12. Ibid.
13. Henryk Grossman, *Das Akkumulations – und Zusammenbruchsgesetz des kapitalistischen Systems* p265 (emphasis in the original)
14. Ibid. p275

of productive forces is impossible, because it finds a limit precisely in the possibilities for valorisation".[15]

However, in real crisis capitalism and at the real absolute limit of valorisation, it is exactly the opposite that happens: up to its last historical breath, so to say, capitalism develops the productive forces without limit through universal competition – and exactly by doing so it is brought to its fall; full of a dynamic of destruction and not resting comfortably in senility. The infamous "contradiction between the development of the productive forces and the development of the capitalist mode of production"[16] is solved exactly the wrong way round by Grossman who was thinking within the horizon of traditional Marxism. The closer that capitalism approaches to its absolute limit, the more capitalism accelerates technical and scientific development which then collides with the value-form, because it makes the substance of this form, labour, to an ever greater extent obsolete while at the same time destroying the earthly natural foundations of life.

The development of a productivity indifferent to content and quality as the blind development of destructive forces must be stopped if society ever wants to be master of its own reproduction. Only to the extent that this is done will that contradiction between productive forces and the capitalist mode of production ripen; not in the way that labour movement Marxism along with Grossman meant it, that is that weak profitability i.e. stagnation of valorisation with low growth rates would also bring technical innovation to a standstill and the 'working-class' would have to take on the job of a further limitless (i.e. but also aimless, a self-moving end in itself) development of the productive forces. This formula, just as ingrained as it is false, only shows how much the underlying thinking itself owes to the logic of capital.

Grossman did indeed have the courage to take up in a positive way what was already at that time the perjoratively loaded term 'breakdown theory', and to take it up seriously, but because his theory worked with essential simplifications, he finally had to take fright at his own courage and grasp at relativisations which all look so similar to the arguments of Bauer, Bukharin and today's Michael Heinrich that they could be confused. In this sense he emphasises that:

15. Ibid. p278
16. Ibid. p278

> Obviously, as Lenin correctly remarks, there are no absolutely hopeless situations. In the description I have proposed the breakdown does not necessarily have to work itself out directly. Its absolute realisation may be interrupted by counteracting tendencies. In that case the absolute breakdown would be converted into a temporary crisis, after which the accumulation process picks up again on a new basis.[17]

So after all, is it the endless reproduction of 'contradictions' and the eternal recurrence of the same? Then all that effort of more than 600 pages would have been a waste of time. Grossman even relativises, it is true, his own relativisation by remarking somewhat lamely "...these solutions would have a purely temporary impact."[18] But in the end he is caught up in the snares of his own line of argument, firstly because he does not begin theoretically from the logic of a desubstantialisation of capital and so from a categorial critique of labour, and secondly because simply for this reason he does not reflect the concrete historical process of the contradiction between development of productivity and the value-form/valorisation. In the manner of Otto Bauer he succumbs to an abstract, ahistorical Platonic model. The 'arithmetical proof' within the framework of this reductive approach remains conceptless, or it makes itself conceptually foolish with its reduction to the supposedly insufficient possibilities for 'capitalist consumption.'

17. Grossman, www.marxists.org/archive/grossman/1929/breakdown/ch02.htm
18. Ibid.

13

From Grossman's demonisation to the passing away of the Marxist debate on crisis and breakdown theory

Contrary to Rosa Luxemburg's breakdown theory, Henryk Grossman's contribution did not spark any more wide-ranging Marxist debate. At first glance this is astounding. For the year that Grossman's book was published, 1929, is well-known as marking the beginning of the greatest and deepest world crisis of capitalism to date, in the wake of which even many otherwise ignorant and professionally optimistic bourgeois economists such as, for example, Schumpeter began to doubt the further existence of this mode of production. Even theoreticians who engaged more intensively with the Great Depression 1929-1933 long after World War II, and who were ill-disposed to breakdown theory, such as Christel Neusüß in the 1970s, when faced with this tremendous slump had to register quiet doubts about the simple *function* of crises as an immanent cleansing mechanism aimed at regaining the capacity to accumulate. A function that has once again been generalised by Michael Heinrich today. The Great Depression, according to Neusüß, contrary to the superficial world market crises of the 19th Century, was not subsumed into this 'cleansing function':

> If these crises had in fact the *function* of bringing pent-up contradictions to a temporary resolution, so as to drive forward the accumulation process on an expanded scale, then the Great Depression in the years after 1929 had initially no *function* at all for capital, namely in the sense of cleansing (as bourgeois economics calls this exercise). The result was much more of an open backsliding into barbarity in one of the most developed capitalist countries, a long-lasting stagnation in the other capitalist countries and finally World War II, which dwarfed by far the barbarity of World War I. Only after a twenty-year phase of crisis,

war and postwar crisis did capital renew the accumulation process on the world market.[1]

This insight should serve as a reminder of how frivolous it is to subsume the destructive dynamic of capitalism under the bourgeois concept of 'cleansing function'. The Great Depression of 1929-1933 may have been the harbinger of a far greater historical disaster in the wake of the third industrial revolution, whereas the phase of prosperity after World War II seems today to have only been a short-lived intermezzo. But insight is at the same time a warning, and the fate of Grossman's theory is implied in that warning. It is characteristic, how, for instance in the 1950s, Martin Trottmann (supervised by Edgar Salin) in his dissertation on Grossman formulated this fate bluntly:

> Grossman's work forms the final and most extensive, but not crowning contribution to the controversies over breakdown theory which Marxist theory, German above all, dominated over three decades, without finding a conclusive solution to the problem. The discussion cannot be considered as concluded; it was only broken off in the 1930s by the disfavourable times that struck the Marxist theory native to Germany particularly hard.[2]

"Disfavourable times": one could not redefine the catastrophe with greater understatement. According to the laws of the 'market in opinions' in the bourgeois circulation of ideas (to which the circulation of radical critique is to a certain extent subjected since it cannot jump out of the existing society), Grossman's book ought to have been a bestseller that heated up the debate. The opposite was the case. That did not lie so much on the weaknesses of Grossman's line of argument as on the irruption of barbarity in which critical reflection was completely absorbed by the struggle for immediate existence, critique was generally paralysed and the sphere of theory was subjected to the same brutal restrictions as the sphere

1. Christel Neusüß, *Imperialismus und Weltmarktbewegung des Kapitals;* (Erlangen 1972) p202 (emphasis in the original)
2. Martin Trottmann, *Zur Interpretation und Kritik der Zusammenbruchstheorie von Henryk Grossmann* (Zürich 1956) p7

of socio-economic reproduction. This fate, not only of Grossman's theory, but of a whole historical debate could be the writing on the wall for today's situation. The dramatic aggravation of crisis phenomena, although they are a strong indication for the correctness of the radical crisis theory critique of labour and value, could at first lead to the opposite of an adequate debate, that is to another thinning out and minoritisation of theoretical reflection generally, and what follows is flight into neo-utopian constructs, subjectivisms and ideologies of immediacy.

As far as Grossman's breakdown theory is concerned, it only found relatively weak critical resonance in the whirlpool of events of the early 1930s. Standing in the tradition of Rosa Luxemburg, Fritz Sternberg, who further developed her theory of the realisation problem, turned to a polemic against Grossman[3] in which, however, he again essentially only defends the complex problem of realisation as being decisive.

The polemic of Leninist Eugene Varga against Grossman turned out to be even more furious. In his essay *Accumulation and Breakdown of Capitalism*, appearing in the journal *Under the Banner of Marxism*, the theoretical organ of the Third International, he attempted to give Grossman a downright chastising, as Bukharin had previously done to Luxemburg. His critical economic and crisis theoretical arguments remain, however, just as weak. For example he accuses Grossman, because of his Platonic model building, of following Otto Bauer in assuming "quite arbitrarily a population increase of 5%"[4] and "just as unreal" is "the presupposition of an annual increase in the constant capital of the whole capitalist society as the Bauer-Grossman schema assumes. This leads the schema's fantastic result, that constant capital has increased twenty-five fold in 35 years! One only need remember the numbers in the business census from various countries to see that such a rise in constant capital stands in blatant contradiction to reality."[5]

There is certainly something crude about wanting a theoretically constructed model to answer directly to the empirical world of the 'business census'! Varga's assignment would have been to criticise the Platonic

3. Fritz Sternberg, *Eine Umwälzung der Wissenschaft?* (Berlin 1930)
4. Eugen Varga, *Akkumulation und Zusammenbruch des Kapitalismus*; in: *Unter dem Banner des Marxismus*, 4. Jhg. (Wien 1930; Reprint: Erlangen 1970) p74
5. Ibid. p75

model construction at its own theoretical level, instead of locating 'reality' with false immediacy in the 'empirical'. Had he done that he would have uncovered Grossman's merely internal movements within surplus-value production which make the crude Platonic model construction explicable at all. But Varga shared with all other Marxists at the time the same labour-ontological limitations as Grossman that made impossible right from the beginning any adequate theoretical determination either of temporary crises, or of the absolute inner limit of capital's underlying complex of desubstantialisation problems.

Varga did no better with Grossman's false argument that the displacement of workers had nothing to do with the supposedly merely 'technical' development of productivity:

> Therefore it is not the machines that supplant workers, making them unemployed, but the low rate of profit at a given level of accumulation. But why has the profit rate fallen? Because someone had put machines in the place of workers! *High organic composition of capital, low rate of profit and replacement of workers by machines are different sides of one and the same process* that in Marx is already contained in the definition of the concept of organic composition.[6]

Varga, nevertheless, stalls at this correct discovery, which in respect of Marxist theory is little more than a philological point, and does not even engage with a theoretical discussion of the underlying complex of problems – for this would surely lead to the taboo zone of a concept of desubstantialisation!

In crisis theory Varga largely retreats to the problem of realisation:

> Grossman only knows the failure of valorisation by overaccumulation that he himself has constructed: *only the value-form exists for him*. He wants to explain crises given the premise that there is no problem of realisation, no problem of exchange between Departments I and II. That the overaccumulation process must necessarily create a disproportionality between Departments I and II, forming

6. Ibid. p89

the basis for periodic crises, that the masses' limited ability to consume forms an element of this disproportion, all this is rejected by Grossman as false or incidental, in flagrant contradiction to the views of Marx and Lenin.[7]

Now it is Varga who himself falls back upon the mere internal movements within capitalist value relations that, if in another way, had led Grossman precisely to his Platonic model building! By reducing everything to the realisation question and the disproportionality between Departments I and II, he takes a step back from Grossman's move to a theory of production, and not merely of circulation, to explain crises and the absolute limit. That at this level, to which Varga has stepped back, no breakdown at all can be derived, was indeed fortunately the result of the sweeping criticism made of Rosa Luxemburg. Varga believed himself to have finished not only with Grossman, but with every breakdown theory as well.

Just as inadequate is the critique of Grossman that Anton Pannekoek published in 1934 in the same article in the journal *Council Communist* where he had also rejected Rosa Luxemburg's theory of breakdown. In a similar manner to Varga, Pannekoek complains about the Platonic model building based on Bauer's reproduction schemas, so that Grossman "sees his schema as a correct representation of capitalist development".[8]

Here, the critics indeed sensed a weakness of Grossman's; Alfred Braunthal had already spoken of the "method of that schema fetishism". But it always stayed at that same unclear sensing. Even Pannekoek does not make the least attempt to look into the theoretical approach laid out by Marx into this complex of problems with the aid of the relation between the development of productivity and the substance of value. For him, too, there is no approach, but nothing other than a smooth impenetrable wall made out of the labour ontological theoretical basis of traditional Marxism in all its variants.

What Pannekoek has still to say about the problem of the relation between 'technical progress' and the reproduction of capital rivals Grossman's own argument about the breakdown in 'capitalist consumption' in its scurrilousness:

7. Ibid. p78 (emphasis in the original)
8. Pannekoek, www.marxists.org/archive/pannekoe/1934/collapse.htm

Let us consider a little closer the basis of this collapse. On what is the necessary growth of constant capital by 10 per cent each time based? In the quotation given above it was stated that technical progress (the rate of population growth being given) prescribes a given annual growth of constant capital. So it could then be said, without the detour of the production schema: when the rate of profit becomes less than the rate of growth demanded by technical progress then capitalism must break down. Leaving aside the fact that this has nothing to do with Marx, what is this growth of capital demanded by technology? Technical improvements are introduced, in the context of mutual competition, in order to obtain an extra profit (relative surplus value); the introduction of technical improvements is however limited by the financial resources available. And everybody knows that dozens of inventions and technical improvements are not introduced and are often deliberately suppressed by the entrepreneurs so as not to devalue the existing technical apparatus. The necessity of technical progress does not act as an external force; it works through men, and for them necessity is not valid beyond possibility.[9]

It really is a paradox: Grossman, along with Bauer, allows constant capital to grow every time by 10%, without reflecting upon the development of productivity that underlies this growth (even though for Marx this is the decisive moment), and if he adds to this a 'purely technical' process having absolutely nothing to do with the value relations, then Pannekoek introduces the development of productivity in turn only to retract it immediately as the foundation of the value problem. This same supposed stagnation in the development of productivity that Grossman himself, quite without reflection, sneaks into the internal movements of value relations, should, independently of this, come up against an absolute limit, and in Pannekoek it becomes the argument against every immanent tendency to breakdown. If, for Grossman, capitalism breaks down because the capitalists have nothing left to eat, for Pannekoek it does not break down, just because the capitalists no longer have enough

9. Ibid.

money to finance the development of productivity. It is enough to drive one to despair. The labour-ontological basis shared by both sides distorts their vision of the decisive connection, so that the one line of argument is just as confused as its contrary.

It cannot be denied: the offshoots of the Marxist debate on theories of crisis and breakdown since the turn of the 20th Century have involuntarily gone beyond an immanent tendency for capitalism to eternalise itself, and have become more Catholic than the Pope, since in the face of the Great Depression bourgeois economists doubt it is possible that the system of valorisation could be maintained. Even the economist Natalie Moszkowska, to whom we shall return in the context of the law of the tendency of the rate of profit to fall, rejects the thought of any absolute inner limit to the capitalist dynamic, even though she does take recourse to a 'production theory' of crisis.[10] For her the production of relative surplus-value and the linked increase in the rate of surplus-value cancels out every tendency to breakdown (this is not the appropriate place for the presentation and critique of this line of argument, which is to be provided in Part III[11] of this study in the context of a value and labour critical theory of the substance of the absolute inner limit of the capitalist dynamic).

The whole debate ran into the sand, because Marxist reflections upon the critique of political economy were largely paralysed as a result of the victory of National Socialist barbarity, the historical consequences of World War II and the subsequent era of postwar prosperity (*pax americana*, economic miracle). In this context, no stringent further development of the disputes of the first half of the century could be generated. With Grossman's student Paul Mattick, just to quote one example of postwar Marxist thinking, nothing remains but helpless perplexity:

> The interpretation of the great crisis between the two world wars as a possible final crisis of capital made the wish the father to the thought. But this could only be known afterwards. In principle in developed capitalism any great

10. Natalie Moszkowska, *Zur Kritik moderner Krisentheorien* (Prague 1935)
11. Although Kurz makes reference to a planned Part III and IV of *The Substance of Capital* in the course of the text these were never completed. (T.N.)

crisis can become the final crisis. If it does not, it remains a presupposition of further accumulation. This is not to say that there cannot arise a situation of "permanent" crisis, since this concept must also be construed not as referring to eternity but only in contrast to temporary, quickly surmounted crises. In this sense the "permanent" crisis is just as conceivable within the Marxian system as surmountable crises. When Marx denied that there are permanent crises, he was referring only to the business cycle of the previous century and to Adam Smith's theory of accumulation, in which the profit rate must always fall. That under the present-day conditions of world capital a state of persistent economic and political crisis can arise is just as possible as that the crisis will give capital a chance to begin a new expansion.[12]

The line of argument crumbles completely here and can only say that in principle "everything is possible", but we can never exactly know. As little as theoreticians need be prophets (this attribution is generally polemical and pejorative if the findings and logical predictions of theories fail to suit preconceptions), just as little can they forego clear conceptual and analytical determinations that permit general predictions, i.e. predictions not about concrete processes and events, but about the inner logic and results of a development. Mattick's helplessness, his obvious 'wavering about', indicates the definitive end of the Marxist debate on crisis and breakdown, which seemed in any case to have become irrelevant along with the 'economic miracle' of postwar prosperity.

Rosa Luxemburg was made into the icon of a traditional Marxism whose Social-democratic strand had even assisted in her murder (here radical critique must always keep its unforgiving memory), while her breakdown theory tended be regarded as a lapse and a forgivable theoretical sin. Grossman, a figure hard to make into an icon, was, on the contrary, positively demonised and treated as a prime example of a totally and utterly failed theoretical approach. He appeared more and more only as a theoretical phantom, usually being slapped down, without anyone

12. Paul Mattick, *Economic Crisis and Crisis Theory* (1974)
   See: www.marxists.org/archive/mattick-paul/1974/crisis/ch03

still making the effort of a closer theoretical dispute: a kind of gymnastics for Marxist beginners and wiseacres of polished reasoning.

Only with the occurrence of a new, at first still undetermined, cycle of crises at the end of the 1960s whose quality differed from all earlier ones and that has led since the 1980s to a new type of world crisis of the third industrial revolution, brought Marxist crisis theory to life once again in the New Left after the movement of 1968. But the Marxism of the 1970s, which had a short lifespan and whose academic luminaries are today's emeritus professors, was still in no position to come up with any decisive innovation. The theoretical debate on crisis and breakdown in labour movement Marxism was dead, and it was not remoulded or overcome, but merely reproduced. It was just the same with the debates on reform and revolution. It was the era of reprints and excavations, restagings and revivals, while personal theoretical efforts were rather more broad than deep, i.e. mostly imitative, at least as concerns the completely overflowing politico-economic literature, which today is being gradually sorted and removed from libraries by the yard, just as those who had delivered it are being sent to the retirement home.

While this was occurring, the question of desubstantialisation was posed again and again that could have illuminated a new horizon of the problem. This is how it is put by Christoph Deutschmann:

> The Marxist theory of history finds its greatest concreteness in the law of the tendency of the rate of profit to fall as developed in *Capital III*. Here unfolds the fundamental Marxist thought of the historical, i.e. transhistorical character of capitalist form of production. Precisely *in order* to realise its immanent principle, the production of surplus-value, capital is forced to raise continuously the productivity of social labour and the organic composition of capital, whereby it undermines its own foundations in abstract labour.[13]

13. Christoph Deutschmann, *Die Weltwirtschaftskrise als Problem der marxistischen Krisentheorie*, in: *Krisen und Krisentheorien* (Frankfurt/Main 1974) p163 (emphasis in the original)

This example may stand for many. But the flash of thought was not held tight and formulated to the point where it could break the dead discourse open, mainly for the reason that the concept of abstract labour was not developed into a radical critique of the Marxist ontology of labour. The failure of the New Left and the Marxism of the 1970s was due to the critique of labour-ontology and value-form (see the discussion in Part 1 of this study). So Deutschmann can only fall back on the immanence of the old debate on crisis theory, by once again invoking Rosa Luxemburg against Grossman:

> If Grossman had endeavoured to achieve an adequate reception of the realisation problem that she had highlighted in his dispute with Rosa Luxemburg, instead of engaging in a largely irrelevant polemic that missed her arguments, he might have come a step closer to the theoretical elucidation of the problem of crisis.[14]

This means that Deutschmann is criticising precisely the progress Grossman made over Rosa Luxemburg's breakdown theory, limited as it was to circulation, with the recourse he made to the production of surplus-value. This turning back does not, however, lead to a reconstruction of Luxemburg's version of a reductive breakdown theory, but to something quite different. The problem of realisation already appears in the context of his handling of 'economic policy':

> A reanimation of Marxism as a theory of capitalist development presupposes proof of how precisely the *success of Keynesian remedies* can be integrated into Marx's crisis theory. As long as this success is minimised or flatly denied, the crisis of Marxist theory cannot be overcome.[15]

This shows the weight that the experience of the historically short period of prosperity after World War II still has, an experience that still limits discourse on crisis theory, and a short period that is falsely attributed to the 'success of Keynesian policies'. Naturally, the result was

14. Ibid. p177
15. Ibid. p177

not the integration of Keynesian concepts into Marxist crisis theory, but exactly the opposite, the silent integration of large parts of leftover 1970s Marxism into the Keynesian world of discourse. It is not even necessary to scratch the surface today to see the still merely 'unhappy consciousness' of a Keynesian nostalgia peeping through under the anyway peeling varnish of Marxism, a nostalgia that labours away with fatigue at the neo-liberal paradigm.

It is to Grossman's credit that he was not just the only one apart from Rosa Luxemburg to have the courage to develop a theory of the absolute inner limit of capitalist valorisation, but that he went beyond the reductive circulation theory of Luxemburg's breakdown theory to open a way to a production theory reformulating the problem of crisis and breakdown. If he fails due to an unresolved labour-ontology and has to take refuge in a somewhat grotesque set of arguments, this certainly remains a reason to subject him to unrelenting criticism. However, Grossman must be defended against his demonisation by those who imagine themselves superior, because unlike him, they have never advanced onto 'dangerous' terrain. Far more stupid than Grossman's fall is the complacency of a kind of Marxist reasoning that never even reaches high enough to fall, and from this frog's-eye view believes itself capable of disqualifying every breakdown theory without making any effort of its own.

14

***Subject and object in crisis theory. The apparent solution
to the problem in mere relations of will and force.***

Summarising the whole historical dispute two things stand out. One
is that the phobia of the idea of an absolute inner limit to valorisation
is not really linked to the social cycles of economy and politics, crisis
and prosperity. The scandal of so-called breakdown theory enraged just
as much during the sedate times of Marxist notability in the Wilhelmine
German Empire as in the catastrophic era of the world wars and Great
Depression, and even more so in the era of postwar prosperity – and
finally today too in the world crisis of the third industrial revolution. The
scandal existed, and still exists, independently of any specific historical
experience; even in the middle of the worst catastrophe in world history,
the thought of an immanent absolute limit could not become hegemonic
in mainstream Marxist discourse.

The other thing that stands out is how shallow theoretical reflection is
in the whole debate, how quickly the conceptual question of the capitalist
dynamic comes to be disregarded, and how little is seen in this of the
whole conceptual array of instruments laid out by Marx. Critique is not
so much developed of the object itself, that is the inner contradictions
of capitalist reproduction in a dynamic historical process, but in fact the
object is bypassed as fast as possible to come to a quite different matter.
The great scandal is not even the threatened break with Marxist labour-
ontology, from which there is in any case nothing to be seen far and wide,
since Luxemburg and Bukharin never left this territory in their breakdown
theories. At best this problem may be vaguely intuited and that *horror
vacui*, abhorrence of emptiness, that labour movement Marxism has in
the face of the loss of substance, made into the ulterior motive.

To begin with there is quite obviously something else going on, and it
occupies a broad space in the debate: and that something is felt as a threat
and an impertinence, namely that an objective breakdown in valorisation
from its own inner contradictions could remove from the proletariat,
the wonderful working-class, its vocation, making it unemployed not
only in the sense of direct reproduction, but also as the *subject of history*.

That is the deeper reason for the phobia against thoughts of breakdown. Essentially, it is not a question of critical economic reflection in the context of Marxist crisis theory, but on a fundamental ideological connection that has to be understood through the critique of ideology and not through crisis theory.

Otto Bauer had, in fact, to some extent used the proletarian subject as principal witness against the logic of breakdown in the debate over Rosa Luxemburg's theory of accumulation:

> Capitalism will not collapse from the mechanical impossibility of realizing surplus value. It will be defeated by the rebellion to which it drives the masses. Not only then, when the last peasant and the last petty-bourgeois change into wage-workers, thus no longer providing a surplus market, will capitalism disintegrate: it will be cut down much earlier by the growing rebellion of the ever-rising working class, educated, united and organized by the mechanism of the capitalist mode of production itself.[1]

The argument about the proletarian will, as *deus ex machina,* is supposed to decide the dispute over crisis theory, which it does by denouncing as 'objectivist and deterministic' the culmination of the theory in breakdown. Making this accusation against Rosa Luxemburg of all people really is a tasteless joke, for at the same time she is the one who stepped forward as theoretician of proletarian spontaneity, of the mass strike and revolutionary activism against the reformist inertia of Social-democracy. Rosa Luxemburg then at the same time threw Otto Bauer's opportunism in the catastrophe of the world war directly in his face. Exactly a theoretician like that who made the vilest affirmation of capitalist rule had to bother the 'revolutionary class subject'! Nonetheless, there is hidden here an unresolved problem of the subject-object relation in modern bourgeois society.

Rosa Luxemburg clearly makes rather defensive arguments as soon as she comes to speak of this problem in her *Anti-critique*:

1. Luxemburg, *The Accumulation of Capital - An Anti-critique* (in: Luxemburg/ Bukharin, 1972) p149

Marx's model of accumulation – when properly understood
– is precisely in its insolubility the exact prognosis of the
economically unavoidable downfall of capitalism as a result
of the imperialist process of expansion whose specific task it
is to realize Marx's assumption: the general and undivided
rule of capital.

Can this ever really happen? That is, of course, theoretical
fiction, precisely because capital accumulation is not just
an economic but also a political process. [...]

Here, as elsewhere in history, theory is performing its duty
if it shows us the tendency of development, the logical
conclusion to which it is objectively heading. There is
as little chance of this conclusion being reached as there
was for any other previous period of social development
to unfold itself completely. The need for it to be reached
becomes less as social consciousness, embodied this time
in the socialist proletariat, becomes more involved as an
active factor in the blind game of forces. In this case, too,
a correct conception of Marx's theory offers the most
fruitful suggestions and the most powerful stimulus for
this consciousness.[2]

Naturally, this clue does not solve the problem. Might not the
tendency to breakdown anticipate the proletariat, taking away its task,
before it was able to realise its 'active intervention'? On the other hand:
can the proletariat only intervene, because this objective tendency has its
back? Could it not also achieve social emancipation quite independently
of this kind of tendency? The relation of subject and object remains
unexplained; all that is clear is that some such relation has to exist,
and that it is precisely due to its unexplained nature that it can be
instrumentalised against breakdown theory. This also has something to
do with the often discussed slight to human self-confidence occasioned
by the great scientific and social theories of Modernity. If, on the one
hand, the Enlightenment raised the autonomous subject onto the throne
as creator of its own self, then, on the other, critical reflection cast it down
once again, and even more painfully. Copernicus, as is well known, had

2.   Ibid. p146-147

already banished humanity from the centre of the world; Freud denied it full psychic consciousness of itself; and with Marx it is the fetishism of the commodity producing system that cancels out even politico-economic subjectivity as the final reason for socio-economic development. These references has long become a topos of discourse in social theory. It is well-known how this yarn was spun further and affirmatively in structuralism and systems theory, where the subject is but a shadow of itself, or merely the 'environment' of a self-referential systemic context.

Coming down from this level, which could not yet play any role in the Marxist debate on breakdown theory, the problems seems at first to be of somewhat smaller dimensions. For its own 'action of the subject', Social-democracy certainly did not need a breakdown, a social cataclysm. The idea was just that the continually higher level of organisation of capital itself only needed to be carried over into state hands, and these in turn into proletarian hands (as, for instance, in Hilferding), in order to arrive serenely at socialism through parliamentary channels. The reformist wish as father of the idea was peeping around the corner, when Gustav Eckstein concludes with clear relief his polemic against Rosa Luxemburg:

> The practical conclusion which Comrade Luxemburg constructs on the theory of necessity of non-capitalist consumers, especially the catastrophe theory, falls with the theoretical assumption.[3]

Rosa Luxemburg's reaction was all the more fierce in her *Anti-critique* after the veritable catastrophe of the world war had already broken out; now she spoke of "catastrophe as a mode of existence" of imperialist capitalism.[4] But the dispute was not taken up entirely by the opposition of 'reformist' and 'revolutionary' theories of subjective activity. Even the communist and other revolutionary-activist positions that did not actually need to fear a cataclysm, attacked the theory of breakdown even more strongly because of its 'objectivism and determinism'. Bukharin, for example, accuses Rosa Luxemburg of 'economic determinism', while he himself seems to lapse into it only two pages further on, when he says, however, concerning the periodic, eternally recurring instabilities and

3. Ibid. p148n
4. Ibid. p147

crises, and their 'conditioned solution': "Its increasing size and growing intensity will unavoidably lead to the collapse of capitalist rule."[5]

The notion of 'unavoidability' is naturally itself deterministic, but this is meant paradoxically in a purely subjective sense, when Bukharin reveals in what follows what he understands by it as opposed to 'economic determinism':

> Today we are able to watch the process of capitalist collapse not merely on the basis of abstract constructions and theoretical perspectives. The collapse of capitalism has started. The October Revolution is the most convincing and living expression of that. The revolutionization of the proletariat was doubtless connected to the economic decline, this to the war, the war to the struggle for markets, raw materials and spheres of investment, in short with imperialist politics in general.[6]

It is clear cut that Bukharin has turned the problem on its head. The objective inner limit that valorisation has because of its own contradictions is transformed into a purely subjective, political limit, into the limit of a mere relation of wills. Crisis comes from politics, and emancipation or revolution also come from politics, while the so-called economy, which in reality is the basic logic of valorisation, overarching over all official spheres, only forms a low background noise and as a matter of fact remains more or less irrelevant for the course of events. In this context the concept of breakdown is a sham. For a breakdown is, in its very essence, something objective, suffered passively, contingent on the laws of nature or of the system, and not an act of will or relation between wills. It is a breakdown when someone faints or suffers a heart attack, or when an overladen bridge collapses, an engine seizes up, a star collapses into itself forming a black hole, or just when an entire system (e.g. a computer program) becomes unstable and 'crashes', etc. The concept is inappropriate if it is used for an act of will in a conscious conflict. Even more important, though, is that in his misrepresentation Bukharin makes yet another leap and unwillingly

5. Bukharin, *Imperialism and the Accumulation of Capital* (in: Luxemburg/Bukharin, 1972) p265
6. Ibid. p266

makes a revelation. For, even though he turns the objectivity of breakdown into something subjective, dissolving it into politics, in the same breath he does the reverse and turns this subject itself into something objective, by declaring its actions to be 'unavoidable', that is to say, determined. Once again we here come up against the unsolved subject-object problem of Modernity.

And this problem repeats itself and is dragged right through the whole debate on crisis and breakdown. It may also be found in the sorties Varga launched against Grossman some years later. Varga likewise pulls the (class) subject out of the box as *deus ex machina*:

> He [i.e. Grossman] divides the economy from the class struggle; that is why *his* 'breakdown' is not the collapse of the capitalist social order, but a purely economic phantasy.[7]

And just as with Bukharin this 'determinate will' condenses into a Soviet power that makes redundant all crisis theory in the sense of blind systemic mechanisms.

> Whoever has the courage in 1929 to publish a six hundred page book on 'the law of breakdown' of capitalism, without saying a word about the already successful breakdown of capitalism in Russia, may pile up as many quotes from Marx and make as many scholarly explanations of Marx's method as he wants – but he has not comprehended the alphabet of the Marxist research method! [...] He keeps his silence about the collapse of capitalism in Russia so obstinately because it is *blatantly obvious that the cause which is supposed to lead to the breakdown of capitalism, according to Grossman, played absolutely no role in the actually successful breakdown of capitalism in Russia.* The fact is that it would be ridiculous to claim that capitalism in Russia – known as a country very poor in capital, which constantly imported large sums of foreign capital – broke down from

7. Varga, *Akkumulation und Zusammenbruch des Kapitalismus* p65 (emphasis in the original)

> the overaccumulation of capital! [...] For us, *fighting
> communists*, it is of great reassurance the real breakdown of
> capitalism is not connected to the causal mechanism that
> Herr Grossman has proclaimed with much publicity.[8]

Consequently, just three years before the National Socialist seizure of power the reassured Varga looked forward to the worldwide "collapse of capitalism... long before a worldwide 'overaccumulation' of capital could succeed".[9]

Looked at from the standpoint of today the grandiose blunder of this line of argument can be grasped tangibly: what Varga, like the majority of people at this time, thinks he understands by the 'breakdown of capitalism' in Russia was in reality a 'recuperative modernisation', a social and historical implementation of the abstract labour system under state communist direction in a zone at the periphery of the world market left underdeveloped by capital. It was a regime of primitive accumulation out of its time historically that broke down by itself after seventy years under the conditions of the third industrial revolution. But Varga's line of argument does not just go nowhere historically and in terms of political economy, in the sense of the limit to capitalist socialisation on the basis of abstract labour and its value-form. He also unwillingly throws a harsh light, similar to Bukharin, on the subject-object structure of Modernity that is connected to the problem of crisis and breakdown, and that can only be paradoxically dissolved into the subjectivity of the political – and just for that reason brings forth temper tantrums against the 'economic determinism' of breakdown theories.

It is no surprise that, just as the lines of argument from the Social-democrat Otto Bauer and the Bolshevik Nikolai Bukharin against Rosa Luxemburg's 'economic determinism' are confusingly similar, so are the respective arguments of the Communist Eugene Varga and the Social-democrat Alfred Braunthal against Henryk Grossman, even if Braunthal straightaway wants to give the Communists a good whacking in the process:

8. Varga p62 (emphasis in the original)
9. Varga p63

But not only in this are Communists and breakdown theorists unrealistic, or rather estranged from reality, that their theories are not taken from living reality, and they also neglect the real data inasmuch as they close their eyes to transformational powers of society already operating today. Putting these powers into the calculation makes one conscious of the importance of the growing organisational tendencies in industry, the growing influence of the working-class and the growing pressure coming from it for democratisation of the economy so that society may be reshaped from capitalist to socialist. It becomes clear from this that the working-class does not need to wait in dull resignation for a distant future in which, after a terrible transitional period filled with misery and poverty, the breakdown tendencies of capitalism automatically assert themselves, but through this awareness the working-class will be fired into mobilising all its powers, not indeed to force the breakdown of capitalism, but rather its reshaping into a socialist system of society.[10]

It is impossible to ward off the feeling of dread in the face of such naivety directly on the eve of the Great Depression, National Socialist barbarity and consequently World War II. However, at the same time it becomes clear how little separates reform and revolution in their defence against breakdown theory when it comes to the problem of the subject. What is actually at issue is an historically disjointed situation, where the difference is between an already developed Western capitalism and a capitalistically still underdeveloped society undergoing 'recuperative modernisation' at the periphery. Now, whether the (Western) working-class is to exercise a supposed 'growing pressure coming from it for democratisation of the economy', or the proletarian revolution is to bring about the supposed 'breakdown of capitalism' in the shape of a state communist dictatorship of abstract labour, the subject-object structure and its apparent dissolution in the direction of political subjectivity against 'economic determinism' remains the same.

10. Braunthal, *Der Zusammenbruch der Zusammenbruchstheorie* p304

That there is an unresolved problem hidden here, and one that cannot be resolved on the ground of value-socialisation, might be shown at its clearest if the left and council communist positions are included, for, compared to Social-democrats and Communist Party members, they only sharpen and radicalise that apparent resolution into subjective relations between wills. In his polemic against Grossman, Pannekoek rages:

> Capitalism is for him a mechanical system in which men participate as economic persons, capitalists, buyers, sellers, wage-workers, etc., but otherwise must submit in a purely passive way to what this mechanism imposes on them in view of its internal structure. [...]
> [T]he mechanism determines economic quantities while struggling and acting men stand outside this relation.[11]

It is an old tune that must sound familiar, but nonetheless is played periodically in radical left debates to this day. Pannekoek abstracts completely from *the social form of consciousness and of the will itself*. He would like to attribute a transcending potency of the will to "struggling and acting men" that is *independently* of whether or not this form (the value-form) and its substance (labour) are addressed as topics. This means acting with false immediacy to impute to subjects as they are in everyday life, constituted by capital, something that they could attain only through a radical critique of this form. All this "struggling and acting" remains under the spell of false objectivity as long as it has not gone through a critique of the form and substance of abstract labour. And if that does not happen, then people will just suffer *through their own "struggling and acting"* exactly "what this mechanism imposes on them" – simply *because* they do not "stand outside this relation."

This connection is for Pannekoek (and not only him) utterly incomprehensible, and he too ends up exactly opposite of where he intended, in the same place as Bukharin with the objectivity of the subject and the determinateness of the will itself:

> The collapse of capitalism in Marx does depend on the act of will of the working class; but this will is not a free

11. Pannekoek, www.marxists.org/archive/pannekoe/1934/collapse.htm

choice, but is itself determined by economic development. The contradictions of the capitalist economy, which repeatedly emerge in unemployment, crises, wars, class struggles, repeatedly determine the will to revolution of the proletariat. Socialism comes not because capitalism collapses economically and men, workers and others, are forced by necessity to create a new organisation, but because capitalism, as it lives and grows, becomes more and more unbearable for the workers and repeatedly pushes them to struggle until the will and strength to overthrow the domination of capitalism and establish a new organisation grows in them, and then capitalism collapses.[12]

Pannekoek does not even notice that it is six of one and half-dozen of the other, whether the will of the working-class 'determined by economic development' then brings capitalism subjectively to breakdown, or whether capitalism breaks down by itself, thus objectively forcing the working-class to "establish a new organisation." He unwillingly makes clear the exchangeability of subject and object in the fetishistic structure of reproduction, something that in the end is even raised to a metaphysics of history:

For Marx all social necessity is accomplished by men; this means that a man's thinking, wanting and acting - although appearing as a free choice in his consciousness - are completely determined by the action of the environment; it is only through the totality of these human acts, determined mainly by social forces, that conformity to laws is achieved in social development [...] The accumulation of capital, crises, pauperisation, the proletarian revolution, the seizure of power by the working class form together, acting like a natural law, an indivisible unity, the collapse of capitalism.[13]

12. Ibid.
13. Ibid.

This is really grotesque: the subjective determination appears directly as objective, without the context of mediation being reflected; like this, the emancipatory will itself appears as a component of exactly that pseudo-lawlike 'nature' that actually represents the scandal of false objectification. What shines forth here is a conceptualisation of the capital relation itself that falls far too short, for it is missing the decisive moments of the critique of the fetish form and of the substance of labour. The structuralism of an Althusser, for whom even the revolution will be a "process without a subject", already sends its love – even though Pannekoek is seemingly settled in at the other end of the Marxian and radical left subject-object scale. The price for keeping the working-class as the subject of history, and not letting the butter be taken from its bread by the 'economic determinism' of an objective breakdown, is paid by 'the class' itself only being able to act as enforcer of supposed social 'laws of nature'. This is an unmistakable indication that in reality this construct is imprisoned under the spell of capitalist categories and that the notion of 'proletarian revolution' is nothing more than the developmental ideology of abstract labour and an extension of the valorisation system.

It was, naturally, not hidden from Grossman that there was an ideological metacritique of his work based of the problem of the subject and beyond the immanent determinations of crisis theory. While still in exile in the USA, more than a decade after the debate had been broken off, he attempted to defend himself indirectly against the allegation of 'economic determinism' by protesting similarly to Rosa Luxemburg that the objective tendency to breakdown in no way made emancipatory activity redundant. An essential moment "in Marx's general theory" consists in the doctrine that:

> ...no economic system, no matter how weakened, collapses by itself in automatic fashion. It must be 'overthrown.' The theoretical analysis of the objective trends leading to a paralysis of the system serves to discover the 'weak links' and to fix them in time as a sort of barometer indicating when the system becomes ripe for change. Even when that point is reached, change will come about only through

active operation of the subjective factors. [...]
By this activity the objective tendencies can be realized.[14]

Now Grossman has arrived at the same place as Pannekoek; the (negative, false) objectivity is subjectified, the subjective action therefore contrariwise objectified ('execution of the objective tendencies'), the subject itself is only a 'factor' and confusion is complete. Grossman had obviously never occupied himself with this metalevel and he now belatedly even slips up on it, long after it has become clear that his analytical attempt at the level of the categories and the of crisis theory that draws on them fell flat everywhere.

It only requires one little step still to resolve this dilemma completely into the pure subjectivity of relations between wills, and to declare Marx's categories of the critique of political economy to be practically entirely irrelevant. The capital relation as an external relation between wills is then nothing more than 'will against will' (but in turn given objectified expression as 'class against class', since the category of class is as everyone knows itself systemically constituted and consequently initially belongs to objectivity). Put more exactly: the unconceptualised objectification of the category of class is transformed down to being a pure question of the will, so that the capitalist fetish objectivity seems to be resolved into a simple 'relation of forces' exercised between mutually opposed wills.

It was Karl Korsch who helped prepare this turn in the dispute about the metalevel complex of problems around the subject-object relation in the debate on crises and breakdown. For him every breakdown theory represented an 'objectivist deformation':

> *Such a theory of all objectively given economic tendency of development whose ultimate goal can be grasped* in advance employs pictorial notions rather than unequivocally determined scientific concepts. Furthermore, it is founded inevitably on insufficient induction and appears to me as not suitable for bringing forward that full earnestness of self-disciplined activity of the proletarian class struggling

14. Henryk Grossman, *The Evolutionist Revolt against Classical Economics, pt. I and II* in *The Journal of Political Economy, vol. 51 no.5 and 6* (Chicago 1943). See: www.marxists.org/archive/grossman/1943/evolutionist.htm

> for its own goals, which is as much necessary for the class
> war of the workers as it is for every other ordinary war.[15]

According to his commentator, Giacomo Marramao, Korsch goes so far as "to regard the dialectical method of presentation in the mature Marx as mere *allegory* that should arouse the will to struggle and revolutionary spirit of the proletariat."[16]

Giacomo Marramao, who concerned himself with the problem in the context of the Marxism of the New Left in the 1970s, correctly characterised Korsch's thinking as "a pragmatic reduction of the dialectical-morphological moment of the critique of political economy".[17] Taken to its logical conclusion this thinking must dissolve the categories of abstract labour, value, commodity, price, surplus-value, organic composition, tendency of the rate of profit to fall, etc., that is to say the theoretical determinations both of capitalist reproduction and of its crisis, into mere 'allegories' of the determinations of the wills of 'classes', thought of as presuppositionless subjects expressing their wills. The level of the fetish constitution and the 'automatic subject', that had in any case never been understood, was conclusively eliminated without any replacement, and the real objectifications transform themselves into the mere guises taken by purely subjective relations between wills.

It is true that Korsch turned against any mere subjectivism of unmediated direct action, but this only relates to the levels of mediation within the assumed pure relations between subjects, not to the negative objectivity of the fetish relation and crisis as objective limit:

> This position explains the question of the objective necessity
> or avoidability of capitalist crises as *a senseless question in
> this general form...* The materialist stance rather believes

15. Karl Korsch, *Some Fundamental Pressuppositions for a Materialist Discussion of Crisis Theory* (first published in *Proletarier #1* 1933) trans. Karl-Heinz Otto and Andrew Giles-Peters in *Class against Class*. See: www.marxists.org/archive/korsch/1933/crisis-theory.htm (emphasis in the original)

16. Giacomo Marramao, *Krisentheorie und >Konstitutionsproblematik<* in *Gesellschaft, Beiträge zur Marxschen Theorie 10* (Frankfurt/Main 1977) p21 (emphasis in the original)

17. Ibid. p42

> that certain, if only always limited, prognostic statements
> sufficient for practical action can be made on the basis of
> always, more exact and thorough empirical investigation
> of the present capitalist mode of production and its
> recognizable immanent tendencies of development.[18]

This shows the consequence of that 'pragmatic reductionism' of the categories of capitalist form and substance: the historical movement no longer appears as that of the categories themselves that would have to be first comprehended by a corresponding theory, but it appears only in its reduction to relations between wills, this is reduced to the 'empirical level' and its 'investigation', whereby this empirical level is grasped directly as that of 'the balance of forces' between opposed determinations of the will. Thus was the notorious class analysis born: no more investigation into and debate on the movement of the categories and their inner connection, no more debate on theories of crisis and breakdown, tendency of the rate of profit to fall, realisation problems and the like – everything written off as "a senseless question in this general form." Instead, what we have is only an empirical analysis in the sense of class structures and their changes, therefore also of the changes in relations between wills. It was that then, that Autonomism at once placed on its agenda with its theory of the 'recomposition of the working-class' as a permanent, reductionist research programme.

There is, naturally, no escaping the subject-object relation of the modern fetish constitution. It just advances that dilemma that already shines forth in Pannekoek and more generally in the reductive understanding rooted in labour movement Marxism: the more subjective, the more objective; the more the fetish relation is thought of as sheer relation between the wills of presuppositionless subjects expressing their wills ('classes'), whose real presuppositions remain dark, the more the negative, false objectivity creeps in by the backdoor. Theoreticians of the direct approach, who no longer reflect upon their own presuppositions, must also completely reify the structure of consciousness of their famous 'proletarian volitional subject' and 'investigate' it as if it were a natural object, and in so doing

18. Korsch, *Some Fundamental Pressuppositions for a Materialist Discussion of Crisis Theory* See: www.marxists.org/archive/korsch/1933/crisis-theory.htm (emphasis in the original)

they naturally deny meticulously their emphasis on the "self-disciplined activity of the proletarian class struggling for its own goals."

As the secret history of the crisis and breakdown debate in traditional Marxism beyond the reductive level of political economy consisted in awkwardly addressing the topic of that unexplained subject-object structure of modern socialisation in the value form, so, too, did the secret programme for its resolution consist in the reduction of the objectified categories of capital to pure relations between wills that can then be regarded and investigated under various aspects. The history of the postwar New Left was shaped by this paradigm. This unresolved, generally unreflected result of the breakdown debate was quite simply adopted; and just for this reason not only did the concept of breakdown become, a taboo word, a mere ghost, but the way to any further development towards a critique of labour-ontology was blocked and the concepts of reification and alienation, which were thoroughly addressed, were not formulated beyond a shallow social philosophy.

The level at which society is constituted, the problem of the fetish relation and 'automatic subject', had to remain without further treatment, indeed it was even expressly repudiated. This is also not contradicted by the outer appearance of the line of debate around Althusserian structuralism. Althusser left the 'proletarian subject' quite unreflected, on his emphasis, however, it was stripped down and reduced to being the 'executor' of structural processes. Pannekoek, however, as has been indicated, had already arrived at this point, and it was also, implicitly or explicitly, actually the presupposition of the whole of traditional 'historical materialism'. The opposite pole of Autonomism just formed the reverse side of the same coin. It is no coincidence that both Louis Althusser and Toni Negri likewise expressly repudiate the concept of the fetish and all of Marx's line of argument that is built on it. In this way, the problem of the objective inner limit to valorisation, together with the social form of the subject and its (labour) substance are suppressed once and for all as possible objects for reflection and radical critique.

15

Crisis and critique, political illusion and the relation of gender-dissociation

The reductionist subjectification of the categories was grounded in political economy with the development of capitalism itself to an 'organised' system (Hilferding). In reality, the valorisation problems resulting from a secular process of desubstantialisation of value itself, which since the late 19th Century had exponentially increased state interventions (further driven by the war economies of the era of the world wars and later the Fordist regulation of the second half of the 20th Century), appeared to be a virtual "overthrow of the law of value" by the seemingly direct command of policy and company management over capitalist reproduction. This notion haunted the entire realm of interpretation that in the meantime had pigeonholed itself as 'Western Marxism' and claimed to have gone beyond the 'economism' of traditional Marxism – while in reality only representing the subject-ideological reverse of the same coin.

This is how the *political illusion*, as the old labour movement Marxism already characterised it from the outset, was continued and raised exponentially. The 'struggle for recognition' on the ground of abstract labour and therefore of socialisation in the value form could only be carried on in a political form precisely because of its limitedness, since politics is nothing other than the secondary 'processing sphere' for the area of social problems that permanently grows out of the capital relation. This sphere, by its nature, positively presupposes valorisation, it is an immanent component of value as a social form. Every counterposition of economy and politics that stands by this distinction and sets the two spheres as external to one another, without being able to grasp their overarching connection in the value relation and substance of labour, remains crucially reductive and boils down to some variant of the political illusion. Politics, by its very nature, is related to the state, but the state represents both as a category and as a concrete apparatus the *political processing mechanism* of capitalism that *per se* cannot go beyond the end in itself of valorisation, but is nothing but a function of this compulsion (friction in the course of the political processing procedure can unwittingly set free potential for critique, but this changes nothing in the structural circumstances).

The insight into the system-linked character of the state and politics does, however, presuppose insight into the false objectification of the capitalist categories in general, and into the character of the 'automatic subject' as an end in itself. A quite different critique of the state results from this than that of traditional Marxism. The way of speaking of the state as "a committee for managing the common affairs of the whole bourgeoisie", used even by Marx from time to time, and cemented finally in the concept of the 'class state', is not nearly adequate and is an expression of sociological subjectification. The classes, whose presuppositions have not been determined, are in reality categories derived from the fetish relation and taken for presuppositionless subjects, then seem to subsume all the reproductive categories of capital under this sociological subjectification as their underlying reason. However, it is precisely in this way that the categories of labour, value, state, politics, etc. are ontologised, since they only seem to be attributively determined as objects of critique, as 'labour (transhistorically) exploited by capital', as 'value (surplus-value) appropriated by the rulers', as a 'state of the bourgeoisie', etc., so that we could imagine a 'liberated labour', a 'proletarian state' and, note well, an 'emancipatory politics'.

In this respect false subjectification already lay in the hypostasis of the sociologically reductive concept of class as supposed starting-point for all reflection (while Marx begins with the capitalist cell-form of the commodity, with the fetishistic form determination of reproduction, not with sociological class). In traditional Marxism, however, the categories developed by Marx of the critique of political economy, that express nothing other than the negative objectification of the fetish constitution, of the 'automatic subject', led for some time still a ghostly life of their own and brought forth those debates about capitalist development, crises and breakdown tendencies, which with the supposedly 'actual' complex problem of 'classes' and their 'politics' remained systemically unmediated. This, therefore, led to the unresolved question of the abstract subject-object structure and to failure in finding its answer.

As the labour movement was successful in its 'struggle for recognition' of workers as subjects, legal persons and citizens, a struggle that necessarily took the political form, so it became itself a bourgeois subject in the 'iron cage' (Max Weber) of socialisation in the value form. This success was at the same time a self-imprisonment within and self-imposed duty to the fetish form, and politics remained the vehicle for this restriction. The rise of the labour movement, whose success in the 'struggle for recognition' (a blood-soaked victory, since it found its fulfillment in World War I – full political recognition took the hand of those sacrificed in the war at the altar of the democratic nation), and the rise of state intervention went hand in hand. What could be more reasonable than now consummating the subjectification of the categories, conclusively misunderstanding politics as the form of emancipation and grounding this in the development of capital itself?

The theory of 'organised capitalism', of the alleged 'overcoming of the law of value' and of the 'political command' over the real categories of abstract labour and value had two consequences. Firstly, it only continued the classical tendency of Social-democracy to go for an unbroken 'growing into' the 'socialism' of a self-determined self-immolation in an organised factory society, or 'total social factory'. Secondly, it consummated subjectification and could therefore also be linked to radical left interpretations that, nonetheless, remained rooted in the same logic. This is true for Horkheimer and Adorno's theory of the 'authoritarian state' that supposedly operates beyond the law of value and it likewise holds for the later positions of Autonomism. Whether the supposed political command over abstract labour/value-form appears as something positive (Social-democracy), whether (not least because of the impression left by National Socialism) it is understood as 'doom' (Horkheimer/Adorno), or whether it figured as the sheer 'determination of the will' of the class enemy provoking and mobilising ever anew the 'counter will' of the proletariat (Negri/Autonomism) – an objective inner limit is no longer thinkable against a background like this where everything has dissolved itself into politics. This, however, was the way in which the apparent 'overcoming' of breakdown theory became identical with the consummated political illusion, with the bending back of emancipatory thought to the sphere of political functions in capitalist Modernity.

Giacomo Marramao correctly indicated in the 1970s that it was:

> ...precisely the theoreticians of Austromarxism who in European Marxism opened that 'season of subjectivity' consisting in a renewed, activist reading of Marx's

works through the filter of certain themes from Neo-
Kantianism[1]

It is no coincidence that the radical left activists of Autonomism and
related currents in the 1970s (and to some extent up to today) relied upon
Hilferding's theory of 'organised capitalism' of all things. This overall
orientation had as a consequence, however, as Marramao confirms,

> ...both with the Neo-Kantian Austromarxists as well as with
> the majority of left communists a *gnoseological curtailing*
> of that area which in Marx is determined by the social
> relations of production. The postulate of the (universal-
> ethical) subjective moment stands over against the empirical
> sociological analysis of the 'manifold of the real'. Instead of
> making the laws determining the tendencies of the mode
> of production recognisable, the economic analysis dissolves
> into an exercise in microsociology.[2]

However, this critical insight remained undeveloped, a mere trace
element, and it could not hinder the mainstream of the New Left from
moving to variants of Negri-style false subjectification. That was also
down to Marramao's arguments themselves, as they did not push forward
to the problem of the constitution of the fetish and the dissolution of
the subject-object dilemma, but itself already started *a priori* from the
conceptless reduction to the political. The aim of his essay, as he explains
right at the beginning, lay "in the perspective of *complex new definition*
of a politics appropriate to the situation in late capitalist countries".[3]
That brings back fatal memories of Christoph Deutschmann, whose
approach towards the problem of the desubstantialisation as objective
limit straightaway reverted to the political paradigm. What appears to
Deutschmann at the level of the categories of capital as 'economic policy',
is to Marramao on the metalevel of the subject-object problem the empty
abstraction of 'politics' in general.

1. Marramao, *Krisentheorie und >Konstitutionsproblematik<* p26
2. Ibid. p26 (emphasis in the original)
3. Ibid. p26 (emphasis in the original)

This is how things have remained up to today. Negri's post-Autonomism, making a furore for some time, as well as the postmodern left more generally, but also the more traditional Marxist 'class struggle' positions cling to a concept of 'politics' that is just as diffuse as it is inflationary, and which has become debased into a hollow phrase. They have no idea at all of the history of which they themselves are the result. Politics is somehow equated with intervention in general, bypassing the categories that have been degraded more than ever to mere background noises. What Pannekoek still foresaw indistinctly has reached its consummation in the categorial stupefaction of the Left. Subjects, or 'the subject' *per se*, are invoked, form is nothing and the will is everything. Unconcerned about abstract labour, substance of value and value-form, development and crisis, whatever humans have that is not 'absorbed' by valorisation is to be mobilised in false immediacy, as if that were possible without mediation by the critique of the subject form and its social substance. 'Capacity to intervene' is everything, and just for that reason it always turns into nothing. In the left milieu, saturated with this inflationary, emptied out and bloated concept of politics, the thought of an objective inner limit can only still bring forth some kind of grunting noises, every few months giving the 'breakdown theorists' their final farewell. In fact the more hissing and spitting it does, the more embarrassingly 'political intervention' regularly makes a complete fool of itself.

There is little sense in wanting this scene or milieu, itself nothing other than the glacial end of Marxist history, to come up with a reformulation of categorial reflection as long as they cannot win access to it by their own efforts by first confronting their own political-interventionist lemming like behaviour. Nevertheless, categorial reflection can and must be developed independently of the capacity of those in the final stages of political illusion over social policy to receive it. The dispute may be taken up at that point where the historical debate of the subjectification of the categories was broken off. In what sense is the problem newly posed if the Marxist labour-ontology is criticised and overcome, but in such a way that the categorial fabric of abstract labour is also newly determined?

Traditional Marxism could live with the objectification of the categories, despite its sociology of class and political reduction by making them positive and turning them into ontological objects of a merely attributive political management, whose result in the end was complete categorial subjectification. The driving force of this subjectification was the controversy over breakdown theory, leading through an unsolvable subject-object aporia to paralysis. The return to the categories after the passage through the radical critique of labour-ontology can no longer grasp the categorial connection of abstract labour positively, but only negatively (as was made explicit in Part I). However, this also poses the subject-object problem in another way within the context of the crisis and breakdown question. Subject and object can no longer be short-circuited as a positive unity, but have to be perceived in their *inner conflict*.

The question of crisis and breakdown is then logically placed purely at the level of the false, negative objectification and of a categorial movement of the capitalist dynamic that has made itself independent. The question of crisis and breakdown has therefore to be strictly separated from the question of emancipation. Initially, both questions diverge conceptually and in reality, as the modern fetish society constitutes itself in the first place by opposing polarities that have become independent. Emancipation can only be conscious activity, whereas crisis and breakdown, according to their concept, can only occur in the unconscious activity of objectified developments, and have nothing *directly* to do with conscious activity. This means that capitalism can break down without human self-emancipation. The result of that would be the self-destruction of humanity, or the "regression into barbarity", as Marx metaphorically characterised this alternative. The concept is problematic and of Euro-centric provenance, but it still describes best the ultimate possibility for negative objectification. This is why we can, indeed, watch 'social natural disasters' on television until they overtake us, but not our own emancipation from the context that creates such catastrophes. Conversely, human beings can emancipate themselves in principle, *without capitalism breaking down*. This breakdown is not an indispensable social precondition for emancipation, but can become in its blind objectivity the social environmental condition of emancipatory thought and activity, if the emancipatory transformation takes too long to arrive and capitalism is given the opportunity to fully develop its inner contradictions. Critique and crisis are therefore two pairs of boots, and whoever pulls on one boot from each pair, wanting to run in this false unity, must trip over their own feet.

Looked at in this way statements like the one from Paul Mattick are simply impossible in short-circuiting the two poles and abstracting from their inner conflict in favour of an unmediated monism of subject and object: "The *theoretical awareness* that the capitalist system can only end in breakdown because of its driving contradictions, *does not in the least bind us* to the view that the real breakdown is an automatic process, independent of human beings."[4] The helpless formula of the 'real' breakdown, as if there were both a real and an unreal one, only indicates that the problem has not been penetrated. Both the secular breakdown tendency as desubstantialisation or devaluation of value, as well as a real breakdown process at the close of the capitalist capacity to develop, are in fact as the lawlike nature of the system an 'automatic process', as long as humans act within the form determination of capital, but another, emancipated society can never emerge 'automatically' from this form.

Up to this point the problem was already dealt with elsewhere.[5] This did not, however, exhaust the question, even if the subject-object problem in the context of themes of crisis and breakdown is at least rectified in this way. It could, nevertheless, be countered that the emphasis on the strict objectivity of tendencies of crisis and breakdown, in contrast to critique and emancipation, would even further reify the problem, since here it is not a matter of the objectivity of processes of real 'first nature', but of the objectivity of a social pseudo-nature, that must in the end be mediated by human actions. Since it cannot be otherwise, the next question to be posed is obviously the one about 'subjective' mediation of social objectivity, instead this objectivity is either subjectified in an unmediated way (as in the larger part of class sociological Marxism, and particularly in Left Communism/Autonomism), or misunderstood as objectivity in the sense of natural science (as in economics). At root it is the same problem that in bourgeois social science from the beginning has been traded on as the opposition between structure and agency.

If all social appearances, categories and processes are not, in the last instance, brought forth and controlled by some kind of 'thing out there', but are traced back to human actions and decisions, then there cannot actually be any determinism at all, or in any case no absolute determinism. All that has happened and happens, including the objectifications of 'second nature', is determined by actions and decisions. The pure objectivity of an historical process and a positive philosophy of history built of it is always an *ex post* interpretation that glorifies a merely real order of events to be 'necessary' (built up into a system by Hegel and merely 'turned on its

4.   Mattick cited in Marramao, op. cit., p25 (emphasis in the original)
5.   See Robert Kurz, *Die antideutsche Ideologie* (Münster 2003) p226

head' by historical materialism). In reality all social processes are always to a certain extent open and undetermined as long as decisions are not taken and actions not carried out. Analogous to popular explanations of quantum mechanics, history may be visualised as a *probability cloud* of undetermined possibilities that only solidify in the moment of action.

First of all, however, there are actions and decisions of different scope; secondly, actions and decisions form concatenations, since once implemented they can no longer be reversed. This is the way that all actions always relate to the results of earlier actions by which they are also partly conditioned. For as long as human society has not attained the self-consciousness of an 'association of free individuals' that reflects the conditions and consequences of its social actions, which are determined in free, conscious decisions over the realisation of its possibilities, then these concatenations coalesce again and again to blind patterns of behaviour, to the matrix of a 'second nature' that makes itself independent and stands over against the individuals, appearing just like a 'thing out there'.

This may generally be termed the fetish constitution, and all history up to now has been the history of fetish relation. One such matrix is called by Marx an historical *mode of production*, which could be expanded to the concept of a *mode of production and life*. *Cultures* are often spoken of in bourgeois historiography, *social formations* in Marxism from time to time. Pushing the comparison with physics even further, an historical field could also be spoken of. At issue here is precisely what was criticised at the beginning of this study as a systematic deficit in postmodern thinking's perception, seeing as it does contingency at work in a virtually undifferentiated way, without developing a concept of these historical fields and the differences between their respective matrices. It is in exactly this sense of a merely diffuse relation of contingency that postmodern thinking is ahistorical.

However, once such a field has formed itself, then it limits contingency and reduces it to possibilities still within its matrix. We are thus dealing with two probability clouds in social-historical contingency. Once with the superordinate probability cloud of history, out of which such historical fields or formations condense, and once with a secondary probability cloud, out of which the internal history of such a field develops according to the pattern of its specific matrix.

Naturally, it has to be said straight away that this conceptualisation, even if it represents a generalisation, owes itself totally to the critically processed experience of the social constitution of modern capitalism. For the investigation of earlier conditions and of history up to now as a whole as an 'history of fetish relations' is only to add a cautious heuristic claim and not a new ideological 'philosophy of history'. So the errors of the philosophy of the Enlightenment and of historical materialism are to be avoided, both of them – one affirmative, one with critical intent – transhistorically ontologised the categories of capitalist Modernity. In doing this, historical materialism imposed upon history a dynamic logic of development as the 'dialectic of forces and relations of production', which in reality only characterises capitalism, modern socialisation in the value form.

From all historical fields it is only capitalist Modernity whose matrix brings forth the inner dynamic of a blind contradictory process in executing its pattern of activity, and with it an objectivity of second nature that can trigger an objective breakdown process. This is different from all premodern ways of constituting society, for instance the historical fields of agrarian society, in which the fetishistic objectivity did not configure itself into any such inner dynamic. That is why it is solely the capitalist society that in virtue of this destructive dynamic advanced to the boundary of a 'history of fetish relations' and made at all possible awareness of the fetish character, not however, positively as the crowning achievement of a 'necessary' history of progress, but purely negatively as the problem of an inner dynamic of breakdown belonging specifically to this field.

In this context we now have to inquire (again only in a limited way as a historical generalisation) into how characteristics of the probability cloud for the possibilities for action differ from those of the probability cloud for decision. According to whether we are located at the level at which the historical field is constituted as such, or at the level of its internal history, contingency expresses itself differently. There is no transhistorical process of necessity from which capitalism as an historical formation 'had' to emerge, but a kind of climate change for the probability cloud of possibilities for action when contingency reaches a state where a particular historical field of agrarian society begins to disintegrate. The plague played a role in this decomposition, but an even greater one was played by the military revolution of firearms in the so-called early modern age; the more exact explication of this development is a theme in its own right and does not belong here. However, what is important is the finding that like this there emerged in the probability cloud of history the possibility of a qualitative leap in the condensation of actions and decisions, the transition to the process of constituting a new historical field whose nature initially still remains undetermined.

This means that in this transformative phase a quite different new field could have been constituted other than capitalism. Or the condensation of the probability cloud to the capitalist field could have been broken off at a certain stage of development and transformed itself into another configuration. There are three turning-points in history where this is particularly clear. The peasant wars of the 15th and 16th Centuries expressed a rebellion against the early process of constituting the capitalist matrix, when it was only in its embryonic formation. Had those wars been successful (there was absolutely nothing 'necessary' about their defeat), then another matrix would have constituted itself out of the probability cloud, so presumably without any overcoming of the history of fetish relations, but just another new historical field with patterns of activity not capitalist, but different. The social movements and revolts of the 18th and early 19th Centuries were indeed already more shaped by the capitalist matrix, but they did contain the negation of abstract labour, and had they been victorious (and even their defeat was not absolutely 'necessary'), then the process of capitalist constitution would have been broken off at this point and the probability cloud would have taken on another quality in its condensation. The classical modern labour movement of the late 19th Century had indeed already practically internalised to a large extent the patterns of discipline of abstract labour, but at the same time this movement also went through the reception of Marxist theory that for the first time radically and critically addressed not only the concepts of abstract labour and the value-form, but also of the fetish relation generally, pregnant with the possibility of a conscious break. There is a definite flash of this in the early Marxist programmes and intentions, it was, however, given up just as quickly – but even this was not absolutely 'necessary'. At this point as well, the process of capitalist constitution could have been broken off and a transformation instituted. This would indeed have been accompanied by severe friction, but would not have been 'impossible' (it would have surmounted the problem of abstract labour, i.e. the movement of transformation would have to have emancipated itself from this matrix, including its own internalisation moments, through the development of critique).

Only because the probability cloud at these breakpoints condensed into static factual decisions that were not in any way *a priori*, and each time turned out in favour of a further solidification and evolvement of the capitalist field, could the contradictory capitalist dynamic further develop, by means of the fully-formed matrix, its logic of an objectified movement of categories that have made themselves independent. The contingency of a second-order probability cloud that remained over each time, of an inner history of the capitalist field, was in turn only determined with respect to the general logic of development. However, within this determinism of the total field the individual decisions and actions carried out are open and undetermined. For instance, it was not inevitable that the Germany in the 19th Century would catch up in building a state, for the individual components of the later German Empire could have been distributed among other state structures and humanity would have been spared considerably (similarly this nation building could have taken place the other way round with the inclusion of Austria). The victory of National Socialism and the following catastrophe were also not inevitable or 'historically necessary', for even with the further development of the capitalist field humanity would not necessarily have to have experienced this extreme culmination of the inner-capitalist potential for barbarity.

The question here is not one of capitalism's inner historical contingency, but of its breakdown logic which distinctly relates to the capitalist field as such. If capitalism's contradictory dynamic conceals a breakdown tendency, then it is the result of that objectification of the field with these qualities. Even the way this objectivity of the categories is constituted as well as their blind breakdown dynamic as a logically determined process is, it is true, determined by human actions and is carried out by human actions, but not *directly* by the actions and their intentions, but because these actions themselves in an uncontrolled process have initially brought forth a matrix, a pattern of activity. This pattern has then objectified itself in social categories and set free an independent contradictory dynamic, and to the extent that further activity is carried out *in these categories* and *according to this matrix*, human beings are even driving the categorial motor of self-contradiction and the breakdown programme, without being aware of this and without having any control over it, until they are overtaken by its results. The 'automatic subject' is nothing other than the self-movement of the capitalist real categories that are unconsciously created by human beings and move independently precisely through the individuals living out their lives within these categories not wanting to imagine anything differently and seeking their happiness by hook or by crook , and through their satisfying the demands brought forth by this matrix.

The breakdown tendency is consequently determined objectively precisely by human beings subjectively aligning their actions according to the predefined capitalist matrix, thus executing the system of abstract labour and its value-form, and executing it ever more, until they have, so to say, hanged themselves by it. The more subjects act and struggle and move, without questioning either the matrix of this action, struggling, etc., the system of abstract labour, or even perceiving it as a problem at all, then the more they themselves wind up the clockwork of the 'automatic subject'. They do not want to do so, and do not know they are doing it, but they do it anyway, because the social machine of the 'automatic subject' that has been created in long historical chains of activity and further and further developed in its contradictory dynamic simply cannot be stopped. The more subjective, the more objective - this puzzle of the modern subject-object structure can be thoroughly resolved then by means of the conceptualisation of the fetish constitution and of the historical field or its matrix.

Insight into the automatic breakdown tendency therefore has the exact opposite of fatalism as a consequence, namely *a completely new quality of radical critique itself.* The false subjectification of the categories, the insistence on the supposedly free, generally contingent capacity to act of subjects while bypassing the categories, leads even more surely to the objective automatism of breakdown, because the matrix of activity itself is ignored and remains uncriticised. Conversely, insight into the character of that automatism of breakdown leads to the critique of the categories themselves and the underlying matrix, and so to the deeper radicalism that is needed to blow up the historical field.

It is not only the form and substance of abstract labour that belong to the matrix, but also the actors of this entire blind system that sets the 'automatic subject' in motion through its own prestructured patterns of activity – *the subject.* This subject is no more determined in a transhistorical and ontological manner than labour itself. The subject represents much more the modern actor of abstract labour and its derived functions - it

6.   For detail see: Robert Kurz, *Blutige Vernunft* (Bad Honnef 2004)

is nothing other than the social form of individuals' own activity: form of perception, of thought, of relation, of activity.[6] *The question, therefore, is not how the new quality of critique is seen by the subject, but how this new quality implies the critique of the subject itself.* This critique is that of the 'subject form', which is nothing other than the modern capitalist form of activity. This may, at first, be difficult to imagine, since we are used to thinking actions and decisions exclusively within the category of the subject. Exactly that constitutes the fixation upon the capitalist matrix. Critique of the subject does not mean abandoning the struggle and wallowing in fatalism, but on the contrary a new quality of struggle itself that consciously makes breaking with the capitalist matrix its aim.

What is also decisive for a radical critique of the 'subject form' is the insight into the structure of this subject. It simply is not the 'human being' as such, but the *white Western male subject of Modernity*. Here we must return to Part I of this study where, in connection with Roswitha Scholz's dissociation theory the, in itself, *broken* conceptualisation of the real abstraction of labour was taken up. Real abstraction always goes hand in hand, not accidentally or empirically, but according to its logical essential determination, with the gender-determined dissociation of material, socio-physical and cultural-symbolic moments of social reproduction that are not absorbed by abstract labour/value-form. This dissociation is not to be understood as a separate 'sphere' (the merely 'private', for instance), or as a subordinate area (and therefore misunderstood), but as the overarching essential moment right through all spheres, because it is located at the level of the basic logic, or matrix, itself. The capitalist totality is therefore fundamentally not a monist totality that is absorbed in itself, as it still appears, for instance, in Moishe Postone, but a broken totality that is not absorbed in itself (implying a fundamental critique of Hegel's concept of totality) as a dissociation structure that also has to be considered.

Dissociation as an essential structural moment of abstract labour has to find itself again, therefore, in the subjects of this form and substance. Women in Modernity are always 'doubly socialised' (Regina Becker-Schmidt), in that they are to a certain extent only half in the subject form, because at the same time they must represent and attend to the dissociated in whatever broken and differentiated way they can. Dissociation stretches as an essential moment not only through all spheres of reproduction that are constituted by the capitalist matrix, but also through all eras of its inner history in each case with a different specificity right up to the postmodern.[7] Similarly, this is also true for non-white, non-Western human beings who, below the elites of modernisation, have never wholly entered into the modern subject-form, and so are always the first to be threatened by the failure of the capitalist matrix held up to them as a job specification, the necessary conditions for which they can never reach.

The new quality of radical critique, the way it accompanies the dissolution of the modern subject-object dilemma (not only) in crisis and breakdown theory, therefore demands not only the critique of labour-ontology, but also a critique of the subject as actor of this ontology; and not only a critique of the subject, but also of the essential logic of the structure of dissociation connected with it. Every reductionist 'critique of labour' that only leads halfway to a critique of the subject (i.e. to a gender-neutral concept of the subject), and ignores the logic of dissociation or degrades it to something merely historical and empirical, remains under the spell of the *white Western male* subject and is doomed to failure. Only an integrated radical critique of abstract labour, subject-form and gender-determined dissociation to the same degree can gain enough penetrating power for an overcoming of labour-ontology and thereby also of the matrix of the capitalist field. Once again for those taking notes: the content of the critique cannot be the eternal invocation of the subject either within the categories, or bypassing them, but must be the critique and in the end practical destruction of the categorial matrix, and thereby the subject, the *white Western male* subject itself.

For the Left, also particularly the radical Left, this insight is so heavy and almost unbearable, because they, as heirs of the false subjectification of the categories that was invested in labour movement Marxism, and particularly in the concept of class, have so to say become icebound. The 'working class' is, nevertheless, nothing other than simply - a subject, a subject of abstract labour and thereby a *white Western male* subject, something proven more than sufficiently by the history of gender relations and its shallow or completely ignored reflection in the context of class struggle history. The class struggle is androcentric-universalist, since it is arrested in the ontology of labour, declaring it to be the lever of emancipation, which is nothing other than the form and substance of the capitalist matrix. In the end the working class remains a character mask of

7. For detail see: Roswitha Scholz, *Das Geschlecht des Kapitalismus* (Bad Honnef 2000)

variable capital, and class struggle, according to its concept, a movement for modernisation in the inner space of the capitalist field. Today the class struggle label is decomposing empirically, because at the new node in the history of capitalist crisis the substance of labour is itself becoming obsolete, and the empirical categories of society, those exposed to crisis management, no longer allow themselves to be subsumed under 'value-creating labour' as their overarching category. Nonetheless, this empirical matter *does not correspond to a new concept of critique*. The concept of critique is missing, precisely because the concept of crisis is missing, and that in turn is because the subjectification of the categories has not been overcome.

For all that, the central problem does shimmer through, even with the last class war politicians who have for a long time now been condemned to a merely virtual existence. For example, in a text from the late-Autonomist journal *Wildcat* that goes quite in the opposite direction to the usual categorial subjectification of Marx's fetish concept:

> He speaks ironically in connection with capitalism of the 'natural laws' of production, which both structuralist Marxists and critics of determinism take at its word, without seeing the critique contained within.[8]

This approach partially addresses the problem of the matrix (overarching over the structure of classes and society) or false objectification as an object of critique. It also goes in the right direction when it continues:

> As a key accusation against every materialist analysis the accusation of determinism throws the baby out with the bathwater and confronts the ahistorical, structuralist determinism with a mirror image of an equally ahistorical and philosophical concept of 'freedom' or historical arbitrariness, or 'contingency'.[9]

8. *Wildcat-Zirkular Nr. 56/57, Mai 2000: Vom schwierigen Versuch, die kapitalistische Krise theoretisch zu bemeistern* See: http://www.wildcat-www.de/zirkular/56/z56kris2.htm

9. Ibid.

What also becomes clear is that categorial critique still stands in its infancy, because it is incomplete:

> Breakdown and determinist theories have to be criticised in any case if they deny people the possibility of becoming self-determined subjects of their own history over the course of time.[10]

The subject-form appears here still in the condition of supposedly emancipatory innocence, even though this form makes exactly self-determination impossible since it is the categorial form of thought and action in the fetishistic matrix. This might be because the class subject should be saved without fail, even though it is 'in itself' a component of negative socialisation, that is to say, it is constituted quite without ontological counterinsurance from the matrix of the capitalist field itself, and is the form of being of the *white Western male* subject.

On the other hand, without having a shadow of doubt about the ontology of labour and fetishistic objectification, there is Freerk Huisken, an ideologue of the Marxist journal *Gegenstandpunkt*, when he sticks an exclamation mark in brackets on to the very idea of a categorial break with labour and commodity production in the literature of value-critique, as if he had discovered an especially obvious lunacy. In his cramped way he attempts to ironise the "matter of the 'categorial break'...",[11] in order, finally, to consign it to esoteric irrationality and 'revisionism':

> The reader ...needs no grounds for his philosophical anticapitalism, but only the *belief* in the message of the *dawning end-times*, the *vision of a better world* and the '*categorial break*' with *Marx's critique of capitalism*, that is to say the total *rejection of class struggle*.[12]

10. Ibid.
11. Freerk Huisken, *Zum "Manifest gegen die Arbeit"(Gruppe KRISIS): "Wir sitzen alle in einem Boot – in dem der kollabierenden Arbeitsgesellschaft!"* (1999) See: http://www.fhuisken.de/krisis.htm
12. Ibid. (emphasis in the original)

This is just a collection of buzzwords in italics gathered as a reflex around the concept of the categories, that now only seem to consist of meaningless sounds. Well, categorial critique is in fact a break with his, Huisken's, understanding of "Marx's critique of capitalism". The only thing is that he, as well as the whole circle around *Gegenstandpunkt*, is not in the least aware that this understanding of his is a matter of the residuum of a fallen historical theory.

A lot of water still has to flow under the bridge before the rump Marxist scene with its belief in 'doing politics', 'subject' and 'class struggle' has died out. This scene will only ever interpret the concepts of categorial crisis (of absolute inner limit) and categorial critique as some kind of quietism and capitulation, simply because they can only think critique and emancipation within the categories of the capitalist matrix. Drawing once again on an analogy from the latest physics: it is perhaps something like that parable so beloved of cosmologists and quantum physicists which is supposed to illustrate to everyday consciousness the difficulties in understanding the 'impossible' world of quanta, strings, etc.

> A peasant asks an engineer to explain how a steam engine works. The engineer gives a detailed explanation, drawing diagrams, explaining fundamental concepts, showing where the fuel goes in and the steam goes out, how heat is transformed into motion and so forth. When the engineer is finished, the peasant says: Now I understand perfectly. But where is the horse?[13]

This, says a physicist, reflects "...how he felt about Einstein's general relativity. 'I understand it perfectly. But I don't know where the horse is.'"[14] A leftover Marxist like Huisken, if he really wanted to concern himself with the concepts of the socially constituted subject-object relation, historical field, capitalist matrix, objectification of the categories, etc., would somehow understand everything. But at the end he would again and again ask where the horse was.

13. K.C. Cole, *A Hole in the Universe: How Scientists Peered over the Edge of Emptiness and Found Everything* (Orlando 2001) p171

14. Ibid. p171

16

The quantitative concept of abstract labour and the accusation of 'naturalism'

In the meantime, it has been particularly postmodern inspired neo-Marxism that has erected another barrier against breakdown theory and categorial critique, one that expresses itself in a somewhat more sophisticated style. In doing this, the substance concept, still used unproblematically by Marx, is totally rejected – without noticing that this is only an imitation of the history of bourgeois theory from (positive) substantialism to mere functionalism and relationalism. The *negative, critical concept of substance in Marx* is thereby fundamentally missed. In Part 1 of this study this ideologeme of anti-substantialism was already briefly presented and criticised by means of the concept of abstract labour as real abstraction, it shall now undergo a more detailed critique, since it essentially belongs to an anti-crisis ideology that can be either bourgeois or neo-Marxist, and serves categorially to ward off the thought of an absolute inner limit of the movement of valorisation, in order to 'save' the subjectified categories of the capitalist field and, in particular, elements of the *white Western male* subject.

It was, in turn, the Russian theoretician Isaak Illich Rubin who had not only been the first to ontologise abstract labour with a hairsplitting conceptual dissociation into a specifically capitalist abstraction of labour on the one hand, and a transhistorical "socially equated labour" on the other (see the discussion in Part 1), but who can also claim to have opened the season of left-Marxist anti-substantialism. Like Michael Heinrich who bases his whole line of argument on him, Rubin wants to impute to Marx at all costs the view "that in a commodity economy only exchange transforms concrete labour into abstract labour."[1]

Just as later with Heinrich, Marx's concept of value is in this way reduced to exchange-value, in cross opposition to Marx, making explicit the simplification of the whole of traditional Marxism, that is its reduction of social relations to circulation and to an external juridical relation of

---

1. Rubin, *Essays on Marx's Theory of Value* p148

domination. Abstract labour no longer appears as a relation of production, but only of circulation, real abstraction only as 'exchange abstraction.'

Inevitably accompanying this superficial reductionism is an anti-substantialism, because a mere exchange abstraction would have to remain by nature without substance - a consequence already drawn in the 19th Century from the subjective value theory of bourgeois economics. Rubin wanders onto their tracks without blushing when he attacks Marx's concept of substance from the standpoint of circulatory simplification, because the concept no longer suits him.

In Marx's well-known words:

> On the one hand, all labour is an expenditure of human labour-power, in the physiological sense, and it is in this quality of being equal, or abstract, human labour that it forms the value of commodities. On the other hand, all labour is an expenditure of human labour-power in a particular form and with a definite aim, and it is in this quality of being concrete useful labour that it produces use-values.[2]

The issue is real abstraction as a "a productive expenditure of human brains, muscles, nerves, hands etc.",[3] and the products in this sense are already products of labour (not only as objects of exchange on the market) "merely congealed quantities of homogeneous human labour, i.e. of human labour-power expended without regard to the form of its expenditure."[4]

This is the sense in which the expenditure or combustion of abstracted human energy is already labour in action, or "value-forming substance"[5] and the result is a "mass of labour crystallised"[6] and the "common substance"[7] of commodities; "Labour is the substance, and the immanent

2. Marx, *Capital I* p137
3. Ibid. p134
4. Ibid. p128
5. Ibid. p129
6. Ibid. p131
7. Ibid. p151

measure of value."[8] It is only in the capital relation that value becomes the substantial, universal abstraction of labour at all in this "physiological sense", therefore only here that the real abstraction "...suddenly presents itself as a self-moving substance which passes through a process of its own, and for which commodities and money are both mere forms"[9] as substance of "wealth in the abstract".[10]

These determinations are not compatible with a mere 'exchange abstraction'. So Rubin, at least posing the problem openly, attempts a hasty disposal of Marx's concept of substance, upon which the edifice of the whole critique of political economy is based, as merely "the preliminary definitions which Marx gave on the first pages of his work" when he was apparently not yet quite in his right senses.[11]

So as not to incriminate himself in heresy, Rubin explains this 'preliminary definition' consistently on the one hand as the mere misunderstanding of a 'false' reception of Marx, and on the other as just an insinuation by bourgeois opponents, whereby the concept of substance is fortunately externalised over and against Marx's line of argument, even though the concept underlies the argument. Rubin merely remarks, rather weakly, that proponents of this supposedly false viewpoint can "find support in the cited passages and understand abstract labor in a physiological sense."[12] Rubin now attempts to denounce this 'understanding', in reality an unambiguous determination in Marx, as a supposed 'naturalism' or as a 'naturalistic standpoint': "Only a few analysts understand that the characteristics of abstract labor do not in any way coincide with a physiological equality of different labor expenditures."[13]

Rubin systematically attempts to strip Marx's concept of substance of every physical determination, and to counterpose it to the 'societal' as such as a purely relational exchange abstraction independent of every physical 'expenditure of nerves, muscles, brains, etc.'

8.   Ibid. p677
9.   Ibid. p256
10. Ibid. p254
11. Rubin, *Essays on Marx's Theory of Value* p135
12. Ibid. p135
13. Ibid. p133

> Abstract labor is the expenditure of human energy as such, independently of the given forms. Defined in this way, the concept of abstract labor is a physiological concept, devoid of all social and historical elements. The concept of abstract labor exists in all historical epochs independently of this or that social form of production.[14]

Rubin imputes to Marx (for it is actually Marx's basic theory that he is attacking here) exactly what he himself does, that is an ontologising of abstract labour just as Rubin had done by introducing his concept of a supposed transhistorical 'socially equated labour', as was shown in Part I. In speaking of abstraction 'in a physiological sense', Marx should now, according to Rubin, for his part have used an 'eternal' determination 'applicable to all historical epochs'. Rubin does not criticise Marx, therefore, in the way he, Rubin himself, must be criticised, that is by criticising his ontologisation of a specific capitalist determination (socially equated labour), but conversely because he maintains that there is in fact a transhistorical character of physiological expenditure of human energy that Marx falsely identified with the abstract labour specific to capitalism.

Rubin confuses here the simple fact that human beings are also creatures of nature in the physiological sense, with the specifically capitalist real abstraction that isolates the physiological combustion process, the 'expenditure of nerves, muscles, brains' from the concrete form of this expenditure and 'represents' it for itself alone. That human beings anyway permanently and always burn energy comes into consideration as a fact 'for itself' in no other historical field than the capitalist one; outside of this field such a statement is especially and flatly senseless. 'Abstraction' does not mean that something not yet present beforehand is only made, but that something already present is isolated, taken out of its context and made into an object for itself. Capitalism does this, and in practice, with the moment of the physiological expenditure of energy always present in human expressions of life. It does this by detaching this moment from its context, not generally, but from one definite process, commodity production, and treating it as a real abstraction. This practical paradox only exists in capitalism, and it is not just a process in the realm of circulation,

14. Ibid. p132

but of production, that operates in a way that *practically abstracts* what it, in however more concrete a form, manufactures.

Rubin understands real abstraction so little that taking Marx's statement concerning the body of the commodity, that this body "does not contain a single atom of physical matter"[15] that could be found by physicists or chemists, he seeks to make an argument against physical human expenditure of energy being determined as an object of capitalist abstraction. He confuses here the material objectivity of the commodity with the fetishistic *form of representation* of expended human energy in a specific social and historical field of relationships. Naturally, the body of the commodity does not 'contain' the expended human energy in a physically detectable way, because it firstly only appears in practice as real, but essentially as the combustion process it cannot really be held fast (otherwise even frozen fire would exist), and secondly, because it is just an abstraction that cannot really be physically detached from the concrete form of its expenditure.

However, what happens socially through the fetish form as a matter of fact, that is, in the money-form (Marx said in the first edition of *Capital* that it were as if next to the various concrete animals such as lions, elephants, etc., 'the animal' as such would also run around, the abstraction as concrete), constitutes the specifically social, capitalist paradox in which the physical moment of past human energy expenditure interlocks with the social fetish form.

Rubin, however, externally counterposes the (abstracted) physical energy expenditure on one side to the social character of value as the relational form on the other:

> One of two things is possible: if abstract labor is an expenditure of human energy in physiological form, then value also has a reified-material character. Or value is a social phenomenon, and then abstract labor must also be understood as a social phenomenon connected with a determined social form of production. It is not possible to reconcile a physiological concept of abstract labor with the historical character of the value which it creates.[16]

15. Marx, *Capital I* p128
16. Rubin, *Essays on Marx's Theory of Value* p135

Here he is behaving as if physical human existence had nothing at all to do with their sociality and history, as if it were not *this physical, bodily existence itself that is located in a social and historical form*. Rubin's line of argument would have long fallen into oblivion as a mere curiosity, if it did not accommodate certain ideological constructs in which it can be thankfully taken up. What Rubin achieved is the complete division of form (social value-form) from its substance (social expenditure of human energy). However, the essence of this form consists precisely in not only having to incarnate itself repeatedly in the commodity body, but also in having a physical substance as such, admittedly not matter, but energy. This energetic substance could only 'redeem' itself by burning the whole world in an *ultimative labour* (the immanent death drive of capital). For domestic ideological purposes Rubin's argument comes down to transmuting the form through desubstantialisation into a *contentless relationalism* that can only be placed in the sphere of circulation. The ideology of circulation in turn represents the basis of the bourgeois ideology of the Enlightenment generally, one that defines humans as 'having a propensity to truck, barter and exchange', so that Rubin's theoretical parody of Marx's concept of substance is superbly suited to explicitly asserting this exchange ideology of the commodity subject within Marxism.

This context also explains the at first glance astounding fact of how it is that a forgotten theoretician like Rubin had already experienced a boom in the 1990s with many leftist adepts of postmodernism. Going beyond the basal bourgeois ideology of circulation, his sleight of hand with the physiological substance of value accommodated to a nicety the virtualism and antinaturalism of postmodernism. With postmodernism the universal idealism of form comes to a head and is consummated. The natural basis of humanity is completely ignored and the relationalism already further developed in the 19th Century completely emptied out. It is not for nothing that postmodernism generally has its theoretical roots in the subjective value-theory of economics and in the purely relational linguistic theory of Saussure (who for his part drew positively from the marginalist school of economics). This connection within the context of the credit system and 'fictitious capital' is to be addressed in detail in Part IV of this study. In any case there must be something that 'has' or accounts for relationships. An empty relationship for itself would be a paradox like the grin of the cat without a cat in Lewis Carroll. In the meantime, however, postmodernism has been flattened out so far that every Tom, Dick and Harry, Little Moritz and the average person already believes they have pronounced wise judgement when they mindlessly and with smug stupid laughter give voice to: "But that is substantialism!" or "But that is naturalism!"

Michael Heinrich also has Rubin to thank for the core of his line of argument (without disclosing this, for Rubin is only incidentally handled in Heinrich's *The Science of Value*). Just in the same way that Heinrich has fallen into the traditional Marxist aversion to the thought of an absolute and objective inner limit to valorisation (and this is coated in the usual neo-Marxist manner by his projecting onto, of all things, this traditional Marxism, Leninism, etc. an insinuation of 'breakdown theory'), so does he also share the secret limitation to the sphere of circulation of the reductive critique of capitalism in labour movement Marxism, which even appears quite openly in his work. Already in his work *The Science of Value* he claims something that he then later repeats in his elementary text *An Introduction to the Three Volumes of Karl Marx's Capital*: "Money and exchange" are "the specific mode of socialisation"[17] in capitalism. The mode of production is thus reduced to the mode of circulation, while production appears as usual as 'only concrete' and labour, therefore, as ontological. Heinrich even makes this explicit when he maintains: "Looked at by itself in isolation, outside exchange, the body of the commodity is not a commodity, but merely a product".[18] With this Heinrich confirms perfectly his reductive 'naturalism of production' as well as the most vulgar Marxism of labour standing in glaring contrast to all findings of the last decades of the destructive character of abstract labour in practice. Capitalism is an essentially destructive mode of production in the form of economic rationality, and circulation is a secondary moment of this specific negative socialisation, not the 'actual' specifically capitalist form determination.

Heinrich has to polemicise all the more against the 'naturalism of the value substance', because he himself represents an ahistorical *naturalism of production,* to which the "specific mode of socialisation" as purely circulatory

17. Michael Heinrich, *Die Wissenschaft vom Wert. Die Marxsche Kritik der politischen Ökonomie zwischen wissenschaftlicher Revolution und klassischer Tradition* (3rd revised and expanded edition, Münster 2003) p217

18. Ibid. p216

is supposed to be external. To legitimate this construct that was already applied by Rubin and is charged in the meantime with postmodern anti-substantialism and virtualism, Heinrich shifts the concept of the 'social' (in contrast to 'natural', 'physiological', or 'substantial', that are simply equated) exclusively to the level of circulation. So even he conforms optimally to the basal bourgeois ideology since Adam Smith of humans as 'having a propensity to truck, barter and exchange'. The 'specific mode' of the social formation or of the historical field could accordingly only be determined by the specific mode of the respective 'exchange'. In Marxist terminology we would no longer be dealing with different modes of production, but only with different modes of circulation, while the differences in the 'eternal' purely natural production would be by nature only technical. It could hardly get more reductive than that.

Heinrich, just like Rubin, can only confront the 'social' with the 'substance', because he has already reduced the concept of sociality implicitly and *a priori* to the level of circulation. This construct is then supported by a line of argument that can only be described as a kind of peasant cunning. Heinrich takes the problem of the quantity of value as an opportunity to make the determination of the 'valid' quantity of value in each case an argument against any substantial character of value at all. What counts for the commodity producer is:

> Whether his individually expended private labour is in fact recognised as a component part of total social labour, only emerges in retrospect. If one could attribute 'value' to the products already before exchange, then this problem would already be assumed solved.[19]

The concept of the substance of value is here being illegitimately equated or muddled with the concept of the magnitude of value (based on Heinrich's false equating of value and exchange-value, already criticised in Part I). In circulation, 'in retrospect', it is indeed determined as a matter of fact, what quantum of the substance of value in each individual commodity as value-objectivity is socially 'valid.' Only in this purely quantitative sense is the sphere of circulation determined as 'relation of social validation' of value. But quantity can just simply only ever be

19. Ibid. p216

the *quantity of something*, that must be there as such so that it may be 'measured', or have its quantitative 'validity' determined. That is, however, something quite different from what Heinrich claims and that is that the value-objectivity itself as a social quality is only 'brought about' as circulation, while the individual commodity would be merely a 'product' without this social quality. He reduces the social quality of the substance of value to a pure determination of quantity, a logical impossibility. Ascertaining a quantitative validity from something that is supposed to be subsumed into this determination, without already being an existing substance, would be measuring without an object of measurement, that is in some way the grin of the cat without a cat.

Against all this, it must be fundamentally asserted once more that abstract labour, commodity-producing system or capitalism (the same social and historical field and its matrix, only looked at under different aspects) essentially represents a *relation of production* or a *mode of production*. The process of real abstraction is the production process itself, here abstraction takes place in practice from the material as well as social content, and with disastrous consequences for producers, society and natural resources, here is where value as such, with its 'ghostlike' value-objectivity, is manufactured. Circulation as an integral component part of this relation of production (and not the other way round!) measures the socially valid quantity of this already present value-objectivity; the process of circulation establishes how large the value-objectivity is, but does not manufacture it. The unity of production and circulation therefore consists in production being essentially the production of value, and of value-objectivity in a real process of abstraction (abstract labour appears as economic rationality to the producers and to their objects), while circulation determines the socially valid quantity of this value-objectivity by 'realising' it (the commodity is converted into money).

Heinrich, on the contrary, plays off the social character of value as a supposedly pure 'relation of social validation' in circulation against the value-objectivity of the individual commodity, that is the measurement of quantitative validity in the realisation process against the negative qualitative character of the real abstraction as a relation of production. His trick consists of seeking to make an argument out of the impossibility of determining the socially valid quantity of value in the measure of direct labour-time for an individual commodity against the real value-objectivity of the product before the exchange process (precisely because he cannot differentiate value from exchange-value). He wants to shuffle the 'fantastic objectivity', the 'abstract objectivity', the paradoxically real 'thing made of thought' as 'spectral or ghostlike objectivity', etc. purely onto the circulation process. He claims to have proven this by indicating the problem of determining quantity - if the product itself were already value, according to Heinrich, then the labour-time expended on this product every time would already have to be the socially valid measure of value, the problem of quantity would already be solved in advance and would not have to emerge only afterwards through circulation. He makes the merely quantitative relation of social validation in circulation into the qualitative social relation of value abstraction in general and thereby misses the historical field as a relation of production.

This line of argument essentially serves to 'naturalise' the real abstract production process itself, abstract labour in practice as a purely technical process, as mere concrete labour, etc., while the social relation is supposed to be purely circulatory. For Heinrich the problem of the quantitative measure is a mere vehicle for this ideological simplification:

> If, therefore, 'value-forming substance', abstract labour, is measured by socially necessary labour-time, then in the end abstract labour is measured by concrete labour. Such a view is indeed compatible with the idea of abstract labour as a physiological quality of labour, insofar as in doing this abstract labour is identified with simple unqualified labour. If, however, abstract labour is conceived of as a definite social relation of private labours to one another, then it is impossible to declare the length of time labour-power is expended without further circumstance to be the measure of the amount of abstract labour. Abstract labour as a social relation cannot be 'expended' at all. By readily measuring abstract labour by the length of time of concrete labour, Marx falls onto the ground of classical political economy. This did not differentiate abstract labour from concrete, its measure of value, labour-time, was always related to concrete labour.[20]

20. Ibid. p216

Heinrich's confusion is so overwhelming that at first one does not know where to begin with the critique. Initially, the relation of concrete and abstract labour may perhaps be taken as a starting point. Heinrich makes out as if it were an issue of two quite different things (corresponding to his classification of 'concrete labour' as a purely natural-technical process in production and 'abstract labour' as mere exchange abstraction in the circulation process). Precisely what is central to Marx, though, is that abstract and concrete labour are a matter of one and the same process, admittedly in a quite different relationship. This is why he also speaks about the "The double character of the labour embodied in commodities";[21] this is why he even says that "all labour" ('in capitalist commodity production' should be added) on the one hand is "an expenditure of human labour-power in the physiological sense" and insofar as it is that, it is abstract labour, and on the other hand it is "an expenditure of human labour-power in a particular form and with a definite aim", and insofar, it is concrete labour.[22]

This means that the social abstraction is undertaken on concrete labour itself; that is to say that the capitalist reversal of abstract and concrete as social *a priori* (not merely as something specific to circulation, but as an overarching moment) already appears in capitalist production itself. So-called concrete labour is only the *form of appearance* of abstract labour. And this is no process merely happening in thought or imagination, but a practical one that already asserts itself in the content and purpose of production (destructive or senseless content of production, while production necessary for life can even be shut down, etc.), because the content (the concrete labour and its product) are already determined by abstraction.

Concrete labour is no innocent, but by being only the concrete form of appearance of real abstraction for the end in itself of capital valorisation, it takes upon itself as "a definite aim" the indifference towards human needs and towards the sensuous material world in general, not only in its direct content (from landmines to private transport, from the denaturing of foodstuffs to the functionalist uglification and de-aestheticising of architecture, etc.), but also in the configuration of the instruments of

21. Marx, *Capital I* p5 as emended by Ehrbar pi
22. Ibid. p137

production, the degradation of the producers, in the indifference towards natural resources, etc., as has already been shown in Part I.

Marx's decisive step beyond classical bourgeois political economy was precisely his introduction of the conceptual difference between abstract and concrete labour in relation to the unified process of production. And it was precisely the circulation-ideological fixation of political economy on human beings as 'having a propensity to truck, barter and exchange' which led it to tear apart the relation between abstract and concrete without having any concept of doing so, and on the one hand relating the value abstraction only to circulation, while the quantum of value was, nevertheless, to be determined by a labour that, however, only appears as concrete. It is Heinrich himself who cannot free himself from this dilemma of the classical political-economists, because, just like them, he cannot recognise the real abstraction and 'double character of labour' in production itself. However, because concrete labour is only the form of appearance of abstract labour as a real abstraction, the product is not only qualitatively an object with a 'purpose', but at the same time in its negative social quality, a value-objectivity. Consequently, the quantity expended, appearing as magnitude of value, relates to abstract labour as the overarching moment in the production process itself.

Here is where Heinrich now continues his confusion, for after tearing apart concrete and abstract labour and dividing them between two different spheres, he now claims that abstract labour as 'a social relation' cannot be 'expended' at all. Since abstract labour is nothing other than the real abstraction from concrete labour itself, the abstraction from its concrete objective determination, the expenditure of labour-power on this concrete purpose, itself already determined by abstraction, is *socially* nothing other than the 'expenditure of nerves, muscles, brains' leaving aside any definite material and social content, in other words, abstract labour.

It is one and the same expenditure, however according to its social quality it is separated from the material content of this expenditure, as Marx makes clear:

> While, therefore, with reference to use-value, the labour contained in a commodity counts only qualitatively, with reference to value it counts only quantitatively, once it has been reduced to human labour pure and simple. In the

> former case, it was a matter of the 'how' and the 'what'
> of labour, in the latter of the 'how much', of the temporal
> duration of labour.[23]

However, it is as the social *a priori*, so also the *a priori* of production itself that labour "has been reduced to human labour pure and simple." As such it is expended in a forced, but nevertheless concrete-content, determination, but from which already in the process of expenditure, or production, it is *socially* separate. Naturally, insofar as it is a 'social relation', abstract labour is expended simply as a relation of production. The 'how much', the duration, refers right from the beginning not to the duration in respect of some concrete objective determination (even practically in economic calculation), that is what is manufactured with which material qualities, but solely to the expenditure of 'nerves, muscles, brains', to abstract labour – and its optimisation. This reduction of quantity to a quantity of abstract labour, in contrast to Heinrich's claim, has absolutely nothing to do with the idea of "simple unqualified labour", for it counts for every qualification, just because it disregards content.

What is expended is, as a social relation of production, precisely abstract labour, and what is counted as quantity is precisely the duration of labour solely in its character as abstract labour. Heinrich stumbles through his complete conceptual error in such a way that he externally confronts the mode of mediation where this quantum of actually expended abstract labour is determined as valid or invalid through circulation, with the thing itself conceptually, that is the actual 'expenditure'. He believes himself justified in his argument by the indication that "it is impossible to declare the length of time labour-power is expended without further circumstance to be the measure of the amount of abstract labour." But the phrase 'without further circumstance' does not save him here. On the contrary, it just indicates that in fact the duration of the expenditure of abstract labour forms the measure of the amount of abstract labour, exactly as Marx had established, - only just not 'without further circumstance.' But Heinrich has already confronted the mediating 'circumstance' with the thing itself; for him abstract labour can not be expended at all and the duration of expenditure of labour-power in no way represents the measure of the amount of abstract labour.

23. Ibid. p136

We now turn to examine this 'circumstance', this time after posing the matter correctly. It is, in fact, the problem of mediation to be more precise. *Socially*, concrete labour is nothing other than the form of appearance of abstract labour, *socially*, the expenditure of labour-power nothing other than a quantum of abstract labour. However, this social character of labour as really abstract *cannot directly* assume a form, because the relation of production is not a directly social relation, but manifests itself as in separate production units ('firms', 'companies'). That does not mean, though, that the "specific mode of socialisation" in capitalism is merely a circulatory one, nothing but "money and exchange" as Heinrich maintains; it is much more the case that circulation merely *mediates the specific social character of production*. Capitalist production is not at all coincidental or arbitrary; just as it already represents materially a system of functional division, so does it already represent formally and substantially a system for the expenditure of abstract labour, mediated, however, only in circulation. "Money and exchange" are not the social relation and they do not constitute it, but they merely mediate it and insofar as they do they are moments of this relation, which is something quite different. Directly, the sociality of abstract labour only appears negatively in its destructive manipulation of humans and nature, and not positively in the shape of 'abstract wealth' (Marx). It is circulation as an integral element of the relation of production that mediates and at the same time 'realises' the sociality of abstract labour – but does not manufacture it or constitute it alone. For *what* it mediates and realises is just the real expenditure of abstract labour in the production process itself.

How does the quantity problem of expended abstract labour present itself now in this 'circumstance' of mediation by circulation? From the social point of view every single production process is nothing other than a *fraction* of the expenditure of a *total social mass* of abstract labour. Consequently, the 'validity' of the expenditure can only be a total social one, but cannot present itself directly as such. This is why this presentation does not directly appear as *labour-time*, but only in transmuted shape *as money*, as the price realised (value and price are in no way directly identical, but the total social identity is brought about in turn only through mediation; but this treatment does not belong here). Through the individual commodity as value-objectivity, as a 'ghostlike' social quality, entering into circulation, the *quantity* of this abstract labour can only appear and be observed in the already transmuted, reified objectivity of money. The fetishism of abstract labour as an end in itself *appears* in the fetishism of money as an end in itself. While the metamorphosis of the commodity into the money-form takes place, value in the form of exchange-value 'realises' itself and separates the money-form from the body of the commodity, at the same time what quantum of really expended abstract labour this commodity represents as a fraction of the total social mass of expended labour is 'measured', and only in this reified shape. The process of realisation in circulation therefore only establishes how much of the abstract labour individually expended as a fraction of the total social abstract labour is, in fact, 'valid.' *Therefore, it is already presupposed that abstract labour is actually expended and that the individual act of production in an element of the total social mass of expended abstract labour.*

The 'validity' refers not only to the average degree of productivity, from which the individual act of production can deviate above or below. Rather, it is also dependent upon whether each commodity sufficiently (i.e. corresponding to the yardstick of social profitability) represents *surplus-value*, whereby as is well-known surplus-value is nothing other than the value shape of *surplus-labour* performed in excess of the reproduction costs of the commodity labour-power. The use-value of the commodity labour-power has absolutely nothing to do with the use-value of the goods produced, nor has the expenditure of this labour-power anything to do with the concrete objective determination of production, which is incidental and external for capital. Heinrich already misses the problem here. The use-value of labour-power and its expenditure consists solely in its potential to create abstract value above its reproduction costs.

Abstract labour and value as a social relation are only possible at all as surplus-labour and surplus-value. This must at once be asserted against a reductive 'value-critical' way of speaking that declares the concept of surplus-value to be utterly irrelevant so as to fall back ultimately, in a similar manner to Heinrich, unintentionally and ashamed into a reductive and circulatory understanding of socialisation in the form of value. However, the decisive determination is that the commodity represents the socially valid quantum of the amount of abstract *surplus-labour* expended, not of abstract labour pure and simple. A commodity can by all means be produced at the socially average degree of productivity, yet still be completely or partially 'invalid' as an amount of expended abstract labour, because it does not represent sufficient surplus-value. This problem will be reflected in the actual crisis-theoretical determination of the value substance, or the desubstantialisation or devaluation of value in Part III of this study.

What has to be grasped initially here is that Heinrich with his reduction of value, and therefore abstract labour, to the sphere of circulation also misses the specifically capitalist character of circulation itself. For insofar as he says that socially necessary labour-time (which he relates to concrete labour, just like the bourgeois classical political-economists) "does not depend on technology alone",[24] the only thing he understands by the specific social relation upon which socially necessary labour-time also depends, in connection with Marx, is the 'use-value for others' in a sense that is in turn natural-material or 'concrete.' The issue then, according to Heinrich, is not only the 'average skill' of the producers 'under average conditions', but also in respect of its 'validity' how far the labour "was required for the satisfaction of social need",[25] whereby it only concerns the concrete level (needs/use-values).

However, this is only the way it appears from the standpoint of 'simple circulation'. The 'social need' in capitalism is, in truth, the need for valorisation, and the use-value for the satisfaction of this specific need is itself already located at the level of abstract labour, that is the use-value of the commodity labour-power of expending additional abstract labour over and above its reproduction costs, of forming the substance of value over and above its own equivalent. Heinrich is saying more than he knows at this decisive point, when he indicates in connection with Reichelt and Pollock that socially necessary labour-time is "not only determined by technology, but also by social demand that is only effective in the exchange process through the relationship of commodities to money".[26] An exceptional own goal; for the *demand* that appears in circulation and its *restriction* (lack of the ability to pay), which can even make commodities manufactured at the technologically average degree of productivity substantially 'invalid', is really nothing other than the appearance of the substantial mass of socially expended abstract labour as surplus-labour. And where there is not enough abstract surplus-labour 'in it', even the social validity of the still present substance of labour in the form of past combustion of human

24. Ibid. p218
25. Ibid. p244
26. Heinrich, *Die Wissenschaft vom Wert* p241

energy declines. Lack of demand is not simply a problem of circulation (where it only 'appears'), but an assertion of the lack of surplus-value production, i.e. additional expenditure of surplus-labour.

Heinrich has ensnared himself like this, because he is unable to recognise in his circulatory reductionism that abstract labour only counts as a formal 'validation relation', but not, however, as a *substantial relation of subjugation*. Abstract labour as a social relation is, however, essentially the subordination of individuals under the end in itself of valorisation precisely as a relation of production; they are subjugated to the compulsion to expend in a very real way abstract labour above and beyond their reproduction costs. Traditional Marxism is not to be criticised for addressing the topic of this relation of subjugation generally, but because it addressed it in a completely reductive way, that is reducing it to an external juridical property relation and in this way finally to a circulatory 'question of justice' about the supposed lack of equivalence in the sale of the commodity labour-power (misunderstood as 'unpaid labour'), whereas Marx proved precisely that there may very well be fair play in the sphere of circulation and the problem lies in the relation of abstract labour production, exactly what traditional Marxism has ontologised in a whole spectrum of variations with much hairsplitting and evasive manoeuvres. However, Heinrich does not go beyond traditional Marxism by adequately determining anew the relation of abstract labour production as a relation of subjugation under the end in itself of the 'automatic subject', but he falls behind traditional Marxism by presenting abstract labour generally only as a formal relation of validation in circulation.

This line of argument entangles itself in the bourgeois dichotomy of the 'two worlds' of production (of 'concrete' physical expenditure of labour-power) and circulation (exchange abstraction). Heinrich can only seemingly and implicitly regard himself above bourgeois economics by holding against it its "problems with value-objectivity":

> The classical political-economists attempted to reduce it to nature (as expression of the expenditure of an amount of physical labour), the subjective value theory attempts to grasp it by means of psychical processes (utility estimations, preferences). But value-objectivity eludes both attempts: contrary to an only subjective attribution it proves itself as material-objective, but without any physical magnitude

entering this objectivity. Value-objectivity is a matter of a
specific social objectivity: not only is it socially conditioned,
it also exists only in the social relationship of exchange.[27]

Heinrich does not in any way raise himself above the dilemma of
these 'two attempts.' By categorically denying the physical character of
abstract labour as combustion of human energy and roundly rejecting the
corresponding Marxian determination in order to add it to the bourgeois
classics, what escapes him is the decisive Marxian break with the classics
(for whose 'true' understanding he always gives credit): the Marxian
break consists precisely in explaining the specific historical character of
capitalism as a *mode of production* by determining the *double character of
labour itself* (labour in action), that is its logical and practical divergence
into abstract and concrete labour within the same expenditure of labour-
power, – and only thereby overcoming the direct dichotomy of production
and circulation.

Abstract labour and value are the overarching categories of production
and circulation, appearing in the latter only as exchange-value and money.
Contrary to the bourgeois classics Marx refers to the physical character
of value-objectivity and not simply to apparently innocent and 'eternal'
concrete labour, but he shows the specific reduction of this physical
character to abstract human energy expenditure, separated from every
concrete intended purpose. What appears as reified in circulation by
way of exchange-value and money, is already present in production: the
'living fire', the expenditure of human energy, perceived and mobilised as
socially separated from its content. This critical proof of the reductionist
abstraction process of human energy in production itself differentiates
itself fundamentally from the uncritical determination of physical labour
as the substance of value-objectivity by classical bourgeois political
economy that misses exactly this process of abstraction and thereby the
double character of labour, as well as not tackling how value is mediated
to circulatory objectivity. This Marxian break with the bourgeois classics
already establishes the break with the ontology of labour, even if Marx
himself did not consistently take this final step. Heinrich, on the other
hand, has completely blocked access to this understanding by banishing
value-objectivity wholly to circulation, and so he himself can no longer

27. Ibid. p217

establish any mediation to production (which is then only perceived as 'naturalised').

Heinrich himself, like his predecessor Rubin, has moved close to a subjective value theory, even if he does not want to admit it. The marginalist school and the whole of modern economics which has emerged from it solves the dilemma of classical bourgeois political economy just as one-sidedly as Heinrich. For all variants and further developments of subjective value theory, value-objectivity (always conceptually reduced to mere prices) is located solely in circulation, while production appears as only 'technical' (as has been shown this paradigm also surfaced briefly in the Marxist debate on breakdown theory).

If Heinrich now asserts himself against subjective value theory, value-objectivity proves itself nonetheless "as material-objective, but without any physical magnitude entering this objectivity", then his claim for this objective character remains completely unaccounted for. His whole line of argument leaves in darkness just what the objective character is to consist in. This is already shown in the second chapter of his *Science of Value* under the title *Marginalism and The Neoclassical School* where he goes into subjective value theory, but only superficially in every respect, both in scope and content, without being able to put forward a single stringent argument.[28] On the basis of his circulatory premise he can only ever smuggle in the 'objectivity' of value-objectivity as a vague, undetermined postulate. For in circulation alone and taken for itself there is absolutely no objectivity be be pinned down, because here in actuality there are only 'reckoning' commodity owners as legal subjects following their market calculations. Every act of purchase is at the same time an act of sale, it is always a matter of dual reciprocity and it is not at all evident from where some sort of objectivity is supposed to come as regards value-objectivity, that is only ever an exchange-value that is either paid for, or not. If, therefore, value-objectivity according to Heinrich has its place only in circulation, then there can be no further essential argument to assert against subjective value theory and the claim to an objective character must remain empty.

The objectivity of value-objectivity can only have its ground in the expenditure of labour-power, but Heinrich lacks any mediation to production in his purely circulatory value-objectivity. If abstract labour

28. Ibid. p62-78

'cannot be expended', as he maintains, then it cannot be measured either, that is determined in its magnitude, either directly or indirectly. But if labour does, nonetheless, underlie value-objectivity, where does the objectivity come from? For instance, does it lie solely in abstract time (not of the individual, but mediated by the whole society) of labour? Norbert Trenkle seeks refuge in this argument as representative of a reductive value-critique that is 'open' to all tendencies. Trenkle declares:

> When Marx [...] shows that abstract labour constitutes
> the substance of value and therefore also its magnitude is
> determined by the average labour-time expended, then he
> by no means falls under the spell of the physiologistic or
> naturalistic perspective of classical political economy.[29]

Against Heinrich this line of argument is spinelessly defensive and 'open' to postmodern anti-substantialism. "In fact", Trenkle continues, commodity producers confront their products "as expressions of reified abstract labour-time".[30] Absolutely nothing is gained by this argument. For this labour-time is the time 'of something' and not just time quanta for themselves. Time does not become abstract *per se*, but through being the time of a process made abstract. Abstract time is not value-objectivity itself, but the measure of this value-objectivity. A measure without the measured would once again be like the grin of the cat without the cat. Abstract time is the measure, but the object of this measure is the expenditure of human energy made abstract. The substance is not the measure, but the measured, the expended abstract-physical energy in time units. Without this physical basis for abstract labour there is no longer any objectivity at all to value-objectivity and also no time quantum for this social/phantasmal 'congealed time'. Whoever denies this physical (energetic) substance, such as Heinrich, or in a softer and more defensive way like Trenkle, must consequentially accept the central arguments of the subjective value-theory. The corresponding process of abstraction takes place in the expenditure of labour-power itself, as a reduction to

29. Norbert Trenkle, *Was ist der Wert, was soll die Krise* Presentation at the University of Vienna, June 1998 See: http://www.giga.or.at/others/krisis/n-trenkle_was-ist-der-wert-html (Trenkle 1998 p4)

30. Ibid. p4

the combustion of human energy in general, and only in this sense is the naturalism of bourgeois classical political economy to be criticised as it does not see through the double character of labour itself. Everything else is just hairsplitting oriented to the sphere of circulation, leaving nothing more to confront subjective value theory.

In a certain respect this is also true of Moishe Postone's line of argument that suffers an irruption here. Just like Heinrich, and basing himself likewise on Rubin, Postone claims of Marx that "the definitions he provides of abstract human labor in *Capital*, Chapter One, are very problematic",[31] because they are somehow 'naturalised': "They seem to indicate that it is a biological residue, that it is to be interpreted as the expenditure of human physiological energy."[32] Postone also believes that in this way value-objectivity is incomprehensibly defined no longer in the sense of "purely social objects",[33] only then to repeat almost exactly Rubin's argument, that Heinrich also picks up later: "If, however, the category of abstract human labor is a social determination, it cannot be a physiological category".[34]

It does not even cross Postone's mind that the social categories always, firstly, include the natural basis of human life, the 'metabolism with nature' (Marx) that is in no way external to social forms. That is why it also remains hidden to him that, secondly, the reduction to 'mere expenditure of physiological energy' already represents a social (in no way natural) abstraction, precisely the real abstraction that capitalism undertakes on the expenditure of human energy by separating it from the concrete content of expenditure. Postone completely misses the problem when he calls "to move beyond the physiological definition of abstract human labor provided by Marx and analyze its underlying social and historical meaning".[35] This analysis can only consist in singling out precisely the social and historical character of the reduction to 'mere expenditure of physiological energy' itself, but not in separating the social and historical character of abstract labour from the real expenditure of human energy. Counterposing the real expenditure of physical energy as

31. Postone, *Time, Labor, and Social Domination* p144
32. Ibid. p144
33. Ibid. p145
34. Ibid. p145
35. Ibid. p145

supposedly "transhistorical, natural, and thus historically empty"[36] to the 'purely social' character of abstract labour only leaves one way open, and that is just the purely circulatory definition of real abstraction found in Rubin, Sohn-Rethel, Heinrich, etc.

Postone foils his own central concern in this way, that is breaking open precisely that circulatory limitation and reduction in the traditional critique of capitalism and determining the character of abstract labour as a real relation of production. For Heinrich, on the contrary, the same argument is fully in line with his ideological Marx interpretation with its explicit reductionism, rooted as it is at decisive points in traditional Marxism. This allows us to specify quite precisely why Heinrich currently enjoys such favour in old and new Marxist discourse in the German speaking world, and why he appears so suited as a point of reference for both a defence of, as well as a dilution and reduction of, radical value-critique in the context of postmodern interpretations, so that every kind of superficial reasoning driven by unreflected identity claims refers to Heinrich, believing itself capable of sunbathing in the light of his very special 'reflexiveness'.

Firstly, the anti-substantialism of Heinrich, following Rubin, promises to overturn the value-critical crisis theory of an absolute inner limit to valorisation as desubstantialisation or devaluation of value in the cheapest way imaginable, by already vitiating the presupposition of this line of argument, the concept of the substance of abstract labour itself; and what is more with the obliging, 'sleek' comparison, at first glance so appealing to Marxist reflexes, as well as those of social theory more generally, of a 'purely social' character of value abstraction on the one hand, and a supposedly crude 'naturalistic' understanding on the other. This is where the applause may already surge up, even before the matter has even been thought out to the end.

Secondly, with this Heinrich naturally gives the postmodern monkeys ample cubes of sugar, but still postmodern theorems deny the natural basis of society or at least its relevance. At the same time Heinrich picks up on a central buzzword of postmodernism with his economic theory of anti-substantialism. Virtualism and arbitrary thinking are interlaced with resistance to crisis theory to form an ideology of a possible arbitrary prolongation of the value-form even if without substance. 'Practically',

36. Ibid. p145

this postmodern arbitrariness appeared in the ideology of the consumer, particularly virulent in the 1990s with the leftist postulate of the 'consumer as dissident'. How this ideology is mediated theoretically with the basal assumption of subjective value theory is explained by Heinrich himself: "It is no longer the producer, but the consumer who stands at the heart of economic observation."[37] However, this approach also gives nourishment to Heinrich, for consumers' subjective utility estimations and preferences are indeed located in the sphere of circulation, and Heinrich has likewise reduced value-objectivity to this framework. Even the latest precarious sequel to consumer ideology under the crisis conditions of its impossible fulfillment that peddles the consumerist and reductive concept of 'appropriation', can still relate positively to Heinrich in abstract economic theory.

Thirdly, Heinrich's interpretation makes explicit not only the hidden circulatory limitedness of traditional Marxism, but he also supports the subjectification of the categories in 'Western Marxism' discussed in this study that resulted from the history of Marxist theory (not least in the debate on breakdown theory). The proximity to economic subjectification in the subjective value theory corresponds to the proximity to political subjectification in a partly traditionally reformist, partly postmodern movement Marxism (for instance in the manner of Hardt/Negri) that is driving at merely political regulation or a vague urge for emancipation within the not yet overcome and uncritically presupposed formal context of value-socialisation. Exactly because the deeper dimension of the theoretical history of the weaknesses in Heinrich's line of argument remains unreflected, it is well suited as a point of reference for every possible version of a neo-Marxist continuation within the form of bourgeois volition, where one may feel superior to traditional Marxism and exquisitely 'reflected'.

Fourthly, in the end Heinrich's *Science of Value* in its interlacing of anti-substantialism, reduction of value-objectivity to the sphere of circulation and proximity to the subjectification of the categories is also compatible with the central ideology of circulation in bourgeois Enlightenment thinking in general. This basic ideology of Modernity as crisis ideology has become today the vanishing point of official bourgeois thought as well as of the disintegration of Marxism into its bourgeois Enlightenment

37. Heinrich, *Die Wissenschaft vom Wert* p75

components, whereas nothing more remains of the connected transcending moments which cannot be separated either from the concept of the fetish or from the negative substance concept of abstract labour.

In grim denial of any objective inner limit to valorisation, already appearing in the classical debate around breakdown theory, the bourgeois subject of circulation finally asserts itself today in both old and new Marxism, neither of which want to acknowledge the existence and decline of their own presuppositions. This subject is essentially the *white Western male* of Modernity that wants to hide its character in the apparent universality and egalitarianism of the sphere of circulation and so still affirm their identity at the historical limits of valorisation. The ideological prolongation of the value-form despite desubstantialisation accompanies the ideological prolongation of the gender-determined dissociation relation, crumbling even though its presuppositions are.

Precisely in the crisis can the *ideology of the subject as ideology of circulation* be arbitrarily mobilised: negatively as condemnation of 'injustice' and denunciation of 'the other' right up to structural or open anti-Semitism, positively as invocation of the democratic ideals of freedom and equality right up to late petty bourgeois utopias of 'circulation without competition' (copyleft, gift economy, consumerist 'appropriation', etc.) Even the deconceptualised leftist politicism as an empty appeal to the sheer unreflected subject of volition has its roots in the ideology of circulation. For the political subject, or legal person, is indeed essentially a subject of circulation (commodity owners in a general sense). The prefix 'anti' changes nothing in this context, even antipolitics remains politics as long as the *white Western male* subject still wants to gain some sort of transcending moments, dragging along elements of the circulatory ideology of the Enlightenment. Heinrich has supplied a political-economic justification for the retreat of neo-Marxism to the last line of defence of democratic and Enlightenment ideals, that does indeed stand on feet of clay as far as its arguments are concerned, but just for that reason finds all the more resonance since it seems to offer a bolthole for the leftwing *white Western male* subject in its despair.

Bibliography
(including English editions used for translation purposes)

Autorenkollektiv. *Politische Ökonomie des Sozialismus und ihre Anwendung in der DDR,* Berlin 1969

Bauer, Otto. *Die Akkumulation des Kapitals,* in: *Die Neue Zeit,* 1912
In: Paul Mattick, *Economic Crisis and Crisis Theory,* 1974
See: www.marxists.org/archive/mattick-paul/1974/crisis/

Bernstein, Eduard. *Die Zusammenbruchstheorie und die Kolonialpolitik,* in *Die Neue Zeit,* 19 Jan 1898. In: Friedemann 1978 (see below)

Braunthal, Alfred. *Der Zusammenbruch der Zusammenbruchstheorie,* in: *Die Gesellschaft. Internationale Revue für Sozialismus und Politik,* Berlin, Oktober 1929

Bucharin, Nikolai. *Der Imperialismus und die Akkumulation des Kapitals,* in: *Unter dem Banner des Marxismus,* Jahrgang 1, 1925. Reprint:Erlangen 1970
Imperialism and the Accumulation of Capital trans. Rudolf Wichman. In: Luxemburg/Bukharin 1972 (see below)

Cole, K.C. *A Hole in the Universe: How Scientists Peered over the Edge of Emptiness and Found Everything,* Orlando 2001

Deutschmann, Christoph. *Die Weltwirtschaftskrise als Problem der marxistischen Krisentheorie,* in: *Krisen und Krisentheorien,* Frankfurt/Main 1974

Eckstein, Gustav. *Rosa Luxemburg, Die Akkumulation des Kapitals, eine Besprechung,* in: *Vorwärts* 1913. In: Luxemburg 1970 (see below)
Also in: Luxemburg/Bukharin 1972 (see below)

Friedemann, Peter (Ed.) *Materialien zum politischen Richtungsstreit in der deutschen Sozialdemokratie 1890-1917, Bd. 1,* Frankfurt/Main, Berlin, Wien 1978

Gallas, Alexander. *Marx als Monist? Versuch einer Kritik der Wertkritik,* Berlin 2003

Grossmann, Henryk. *Das Akkumulations – und Zusammenbruchsgesetz des kapitalistischen Systems (Zugleich eine Krisentheorie).* First pub. Leipzig 1929; reprint: Frankfurt/Main 1967.
The Law of Accumulation and Breakdown of the Capitalist System (Being also a theory of crises) translated and abridged by Jairus Banaji (1979) See: www.marxists.org/archive/grossman/1929/breakdown/

Grossmann, Henryk. *Die evolutionistische Revolte gegen die klassische Ökonomie*, in: *Aufsätze zur Krisentheorie*. First pub. Chicago 1943; Frankfurt/Main 1971 *The Evolutionist Revolt against Classical Economics, pt. I and II*, in: *The Journal of Political Economy, vol. 51: no.5 and 6*, Chicago 1943. See: www.marxists. org/archive/grossman/1943/evolutionist.htm

Heinrich, Michael. *Kritik der politischen Ökonomie, Eine Einführung.* Stuttgart 2004
An Introduction to the Three Volumes of Karl Marx's Capital trans. Alexander Locascio, New York 2012

Heinrich, Michael. *Die Wissenschaft vom Wert. Die Marxsche Kritik der politischen Ökonomie zwischen wissenschaftlicher Revolution und klassischer Tradition,* (Third revised and expanded edition), Münster 2003

Huisken, Freerk. *Zum "Manifest gegen die Arbeit"(Gruppe KRISIS): "Wir sitzen alle in einem Boot – in dem der kollabierenden Arbeitsgesellschaft!"* 1999. See: http://www.fhuisken.de/krisis.htm

Initiative Sozialistisches Forum. *Der Theoretiker ist der Wert,* Freiburg 2000

Kautsky, Karl. *Bernstein und das Sozialdemokratische Programm. Eine Antikritik,* Berlin 1899, Bonn 1979

Kantorowics, Ernst H. *Die zwei Körper des Königs: Eine Studie zur politischen Theologie des Mittelalters,* München 1990
The King's Two Bodies: A Study in Medieval Political Theology, Princeton 1957, 1997

Kolakowski, Leszek. *Die Hauptströmungen des Marxismus in 3 Bänden. Band 1: Entstehung, Band 2: Entwicklung, Band 3: Zerfall,* München 1989 (First pub. 1978)
Main Currents of Marxism, Vol. 2: The Golden Age trans. PS Falla, London 1981

Korsch, Karl. *Über einige grundsätzliche Voraussetzungen für eine materialistische Diskussion der Krisentheorie,* in: *Proletarier #1* 1933 in: *Politische Texte,* (eds. Erich Gerlach and Jürgen Seifert) Frankfurt 1974
Some Fundamental Presuppositions for a Materialist Discussion of Crisis Theory, trans. Karl-Heinz Otto and Andrew Giles-Peters (Source: *Class against Class*) See: www.marxists.org/archive/korsch/1933/crisis-theory.htm

Kurz, Robert. *Abstrakte Arbeit und Sozialismus,* in: *Marxistische Kritik 4,* Erlangen 1987

Kurz, Robert. *Die antideutsche Ideologie,* Münster 2003

Kurz, Robert. *Blutige Vernunft: Essays zur emanzipatorischen Kritik der kapitalistischen Moderne und ihrer "westlichen Werte",* Bad Honnef 2004

Luxemburg, Rosa. *Die Akkumulation des Kapitals.* First pub. 1912, reprint: Frankfurt/Main 1970 (based on edition of 1923).
The Accumulation of Capital trans. Agnes Schwarzschild, London 1951, New York 2003

Luxemburg, Rosa. *Die Akkumulation des Kapitals oder Was die Epigonen aus der Marxschen Kritik gemacht haben. Eine Antikritik.* First pub. 1914. In: Luxemburg 1970 (see above)
The Accumulation of Capital - An Anti-critique: The Accumulation of Capital, or What the Epigones Have Made of Marx's Theory In: *The Accumulation of Capital - An Anti-critique and Imperialism and the Accumulation of Capital* by Rosa Luxemburg and Nikolai Bukharin respectively, trans. Rudolf Wichman, London/New York 1972

Lukács, Georg. *Zur Ontologie des gesellschaftlichen Seins, Teilband, Die Arbeit,* Neuwied und Darmstadt 1973
Zur Ontologie des gesellschaftlichen Seins, Teilband, Die ontologischen Grundprinzipien von Marx, Neuwied und Darmstadt 1972
Published in English in three volumes as: *Ontology of Social Being 1: Hegel; 2: Marx; 3: Labour* trans. David Fernbach, London 1978, 1978, 1980

Malin, Shimon. *Dr. Bertlmanns Socken. Wie die Quantenphysik unser Weltbild verändert,* Leipzig 2003

Marx, Karl. *Das Kapital, Bd. I-III,* Marx-Engels Werke 23-25, Berlin 1965 (Vol. I based on 4th edition of 1890)
Capital vol. I trans. Ben Fowkes, London 1976
Emendments to above translation: Ehrbar, Hans G. *Annotations to Marx's Capital,* 2002 see: http://content.csbs.utah.edu/~ehrbar/akmc.htm
Capital vol. II trans. David Fernbach, London 1978
Capital vol. III trans. David Fernbach, London 1981

Marx, Karl. *Grundrisse der Kritik der politischen Ökonomie (Rohentwurf),* Berlin 1974
Grundrisse: Foundations of the Critique of Political Economy (Rough Draft) trans. Martin Nicolaus, London 1973
Emendments to above translation: Ehrbar, Hans G. *Annotations to Karl Marx's Intoduction to Grundrisse,* 2010 see: http://content.csbs.utah.edu/~ehrbar/akmc.htm

Marx, Karl. *Economic and Philosophic Manuscripts (1844)* in *Early Writings* trans. Rodney Livingstone and Gregor Benton, London 1975

Marramao, Giacomo. *Krisentheorie und >Konstitutionsproblematik<,* in: *Gesellschaft, Beiträge zur Marxschen Theorie 10* Frankfurt/Main 1977

Mattick, Paul (with contributions by Christoph Deutschmann and Volkhard Brandes). *Krisen und Krisentheorien*, Frankfurt/Main 1974
Economic Crisis and Crisis Theory (Source: *Class against Class*) 1974
See: www.marxists.org/archive/mattick-paul/1974/crisis/

Mattick, Paul. *Marx und Keynes. Die Grenzen des >gemischten Wirtschaftssystems<*, Frankfurt/Main 1974
Marx and Keynes: The Limits of the Mixed Economy, Boston 1969
See: www.marxists.org/archive/mattick-paul/1969/marx-keynes/

Moszkowska, Natalie. *Zur Kritik moderner Krisentheorien*, Prag 1935

Neusüß, Christel. *Imperialismus und Weltmarktbewegung des Kapitals*, Erlangen 1972

Pannekoek, Anton. *Die Zusammenbruchstheorie des Kapitalismus*, in: *Rätekommunist Nr.1* Juni 1934 See: www.marxists.org/deutsch/archiv/pannekoek/1934/06/z-bruch.htm
The Theory of the Collapse of Capitalism, trans. Adam Buick in *Capital and Class*, Spring 1977 See: www.marxists.org/archive/pannekoe/1934/collapse.htm

Postone, Moishe. *Zeit, Arbeit und gesellschaftliche Herrschaft. Eine neue Interpretation der kritischen Theorie von Marx*, Freiburg 2003
Time, Labor, and Social Domination: A reinterpretation of Marx's critical theory, Cambridge 1993

Rosdolsky, Roman. *Zur Entstehungsgeschichte des Marxschen >Kapital<*, Frankfurt/Main 1973 (First pub. 1968)

Rubin, Isaak Iljitsch, *Studien zur Marxschen Werttheorie*, Frankfurt/Main 1973 (First pub. 1924)
Essays on Marx's Theory of Value, trans. Miloš Samardžija and Fredy Perlman, Detroit 1972

Scholz, Roswitha. *Das Geschlecht des Kapitalismus*, Bad Honnef 2000

Sohn-Rethel, Alfred. *Warenform und Denkform*, Frankfurt/Main 1978

Sternberg, Fritz. *Eine Umwälzung der Wissenschaft?* Berlin 1930

Trenkle, Norbert. *Was ist der Wert, was soll die Krise*, Referat an der Uni Wien im Juni 1998. See: http://www.giga.or.at/others/krisis/n-trenkle_was-ist-der-wert-html

Trottmann, Martin. *Zur Interpretation und Kritik der Zusammenbruchs-theorie von Henryk Grossmann*, Zürich 1956

Varga, Eugen. *Akkumulation und Zusammenbruch des Kapitalismus*, in: *Unter dem Banner des Marxismus, 4. Jhg.*, Wien 1930; Reprint, Erlangen 1970

Walther, Rudolf. *"...aber nach der Sündflut kommen wir und nur wir". "Zusammenbruchstheorie", Marxismus und politisches Defizit in der SPD 1890-1914,* Frankfurt/Main, Berlin, Wien 1981

Wildcat-Zirkular Nr. 56/57, Mai 2000. Vom schwierigen Versuch, die kapitalistische Krise theoretisch zu bemeistern, See: http://www.wildcat-www.de/zirkular/56/z56kris2.htm

Wolf, Dieter. *Der dialektische Widerspruch im Kapital. Ein Beitrag zur Marxschen Werttheorie,* Hamburg 2002

Index

15th and 16th Century, 182

18th Century, 46, 108, 182

19th Century, 8, 10, 37, 147, 173, 182, 182-183, 191, 195

20th Century, 8, 122, 126, 137, 153, 173; 1920s, 33; 1930s, 148-149; 1950s, 60, 148; 1960s, 120, 155; 1970s, 60, 147, 155-157, 170, 175-176; 1980s, 50, 60, 71, 155; 1990s, 60, 195, 212

Abstract human energy, 32, 98, 102-103, 207

Abstract labour, 5-6, 8, 21-24, 27, 29-31, 33-42, 44, 48, 50, 52-54, 57-58, 60, 64, 67, 70-74, 82-85, 87-94, 96-98, 101-105, 107-108, 111-113, 117-118, 120, 125, 140, 143, 156, 164, 166, 168, 173, 175, 177-178, 182, 184-186, 190-194, 194, 194, 196, 199-211, 213; and concrete, 27, 42-43, 73, 199-201, 207; as commodity, 10, 34, 204; as economic rationality, 198; as exchange, 70, 96; as human labour, 54, 57-59, 70, 87-88, 191, 210; as labour expended, 87; as logic of production, 92; as social, 72, 83, 86; as substance of value, 177; as surplus-labour, 205; as value, 5, 47, 70, 74-75, 93, 107, 175, 204, 207; commodity-producing system, 198; concept of, 53, 64-65; disembedded, 89; fetishism, 58; Gallas, 85; Heinrich, 202; Marx, 5, 21, 23, 29, 43, 193; Marxist, 5, 33; measure, 199; mediation, 58, 203; Postone, 63; production of, 206; Rubin, 34; subject-form, 186; subject-object, 165; to circulation, 70; under state communism, 92; value commodity, 38, 170; value-creating, 43; value-form, 185; value-forming, 42; value-objectivity, 73, 83. *See also* Labour, Labour abstraction, Work

Accountancy, periods of absolute, 55

Accounting, social, 36, 54

Activist, Autonomism, 176; reading of Marx, 175

Adorno, Theodor, 92, 175

Aesthetic, 107-108

Agamben, Giorgio, 90

Agrarian, mode of production, 99, 181; society, 55, 181

Ahistorical, concrete-useful labour, 54; disembedded economic continuum, 112; freedom or contingency, 187; Heinrich's 'naturalism of production', 196; Platonic model, 146; postmodern, 180; space-time of economics, 112; structuralist determinism, 187; time of value-socialisation, 113

Alienation, active, 52; as shallow social philosophy, 172; human, 53, 62; not ontological, 57; temporal, 100; versus having 'enough time', 55

Althusser, Louis, 168, 172. *See also*
    Structuralism
Americana, Pax, 153
Anderson, Perry, 49
Animals, concrete, 194; farm, 107;
    treatment, 109
Anti-semitism, 213
Anti-substantialism, 30, 190, 211;
    Heinrich, 190, 211; Trenkle, 209. *See
    also* Substantialism
Aporia, Adorno, 92; Marx, 25, 27, 33-34,
    37, 67, 84; subject-object, 25, 178. *See
    also* Labour-ontology
Arendt, Hannah, 60
Aristotle, 14, 44
Army, 93; reserve (of labour), 141-143
Astronomical, dimension, 98; flow of time,
    97-98, 100
Austromarxist, 131, 175-176
Automatic subject, 19, 22, 30, 98, 101-
    102, 116, 170, 172, 174, 183-184, 206;
    Marx, 18, 100, 139; valorisation, 107.
    See also Self-moving end in itself
Autonomism, 61, 86, 171-172, 175-176,
    179; post-, 177
Backhaus, Hans-Georg, 81
Barbarity, 147-148, 183; and Socialism,
    153, 165
Bauer, Otto, Austromarxist, 131;
    Bukharin, 133-134; Grossman,
    138-139, 142, 145-146, 149, 152;
    Luxemburg, 137, 159, 164; Platonist
    model, 144, 151; prosperity and crisis,
    132; working class rebellion, 159
Becker-Schmidt, Regina, 185
Bentham, Jeremy, 95
Bernstein, Eduard, 122-124, 126, 216-217
Biosphere, 20-21, 109; and human
    society-110
Boom (economic), 144; 1990s, 195
Bourgeois, circulation of ideas, 148;
    cleansing function, 148; debate
    on 'crisis in working society', 60;
    economics, 77, 147, 153, 191, 206;
    enlightenment, 212; exchange relations,
    92; historical approach, 117, 180;
    ideology, 10, 108, 195, 197; petty,
    159, 213; political economy, 137, 201,
    205, 207-208, 210; subject, 12, 174,
    213; theory, 190; thought, 14, 21, 212;
    two worlds of production, 206; work
    ethic, 37
Braunthal, Alfred, 140, 151, 164-165, 216
Breakdown theory, 120-126, 158,
    160; absolute inner limit, 136,
    158; apparent overcoming, 175;
    Bukharin, 133; Deutschmann, 156;
    economic determinism, 161, 165;
    Great Depression, 147; Grossman,
    137, 145, 148-149, 151, 154, 157;
    Heinrich, 196, 208, 212-213; Korsch,
    169; Luxemburg, 130, 154, 160;
    neo-Marxism, 190, 196; Pannekoek,
    135; subject-object, 178, 186. *See also*
    Catastrophe theory (Luxemburg),
    Collapse of capitalism , Crisis theory
Bukharin, Nikolai, 130, 133-134, 149,
    158, 161-163, 166, 216, 218; Bauer,
    133, 137, 145; imperialism, 133,
    162; Luxemburg, 133, 159, 162, 164;
    subject-object, 164
Bureaucracy, 101, 103
Bureaucratic, 13, 90, 94
Business, census, 149; cycle, 154;
    disembedded space, 90, 93-94, 96-97;
    functional space, 94; management,

65, 71

Cabinet making, 87-88. *See also* Carpentry and weaving

Capitalist matrix, 182, 184-186, 189

Capital-relation, 13, 21

Carpentry and weaving, 23, 87

Carroll, Lewis, 195

Catastrophe theory (Luxemburg), 130, 161. *See also* Breakdown theory, Collapse of capitalism, Crisis theory

Chemical and physical reduction, 108, 110

Circulation, and value-objectivity, 198; ideology of, 195, 201, 212-213; level of, 197; mode of, 126, 196-197; process, 92, 135, 198-200; sociality of abstract labour, 203; theory of, 73, 85, 135-136, 157, 195; velocity of, 134

Citizens, 38, 174

Civilisation, standard of, 140-141

Class, against class, 169; analysis, 171; -based appropriation, 42; concious, 123; enemy, 175; proletarian, 169, 172; sociological, 174, 179; structures, 171; subject, 159, 163, 188; value-creating, 72

Class struggle, 140, 163, 167, 169, 172, 177, 186-189

Class war, 170, 187

Classes, 12, 115, 170-171, 174, 187. *See also* Proletariat, Working-class

Cleansing (function of economic crises), 132, 134, 147-148. *See also* Crisis theory

Climate change, 110, 181

Coercion, social, 92

Cole, K.C., 189

Collapse of capitalism, Bauer, 159; Bukharin, 162; Grossman, 168; Heinrich, 121; Luxemburg, 130; Pannekoek, 135, 166-167; rate of growth, 152; Varga, 163-164. *See also* Breakdown theory, Catastrophe theory (Luxemburg), Crisis theory

Communist, council, 130, 135, 151, 166; state, 164-165

Community, [non-]capitalist, 57; academic, 62; socialist, 34-36

Concrete labour, 27-28, 42-43, 64, 66, 70, 72-73, 85, 87-89, 98, 103-105, 108, 190, 199-201, 203, 205, 207. *See also* Labour

Consumer, 47, 102, 107, 132, 161, 212, 212

Consumerist, 212-213

Consumption, and production, 107; Bukharin, 133; capitalist, breakdown in, 143, 146, 151; commodity, 78, 105; Eckstein, 131; individual capitalist/ luxury, 138-139, 141-142; Luxemburg, 127-128, 130; Pannekoek, 135

Co-operation, 103-104

Copernicus, 161

Cosmologists, 189

Countries, capitalist, 108, 128, 147, 163; industrialised, 38; non-capitalist, 129; workers of, 122. *See also* Periphery, the

Credit system, 195

Crisis, 5, 29-30, 60, 94, 97, 112, 119-122, 133-134, 137-138, 141-149, 153, 156, 158, 162, 173, 177, 189, 212-213; and breakdown, 154-155, 157, 164, 172, 178-179, 186; anti-, 190; Commercial, 124; Economic, 123, 132, 154; global, 101, 110

Crisis theory, 6, 12, 82, 125-127, 132,

135-136, 149-150, 154, 157-158, 163, 168-171, 187, 211; Marx, 118, 156; Marxist, 155, 159. *See also* Breakdown theory, Catastrophe theory (Luxemburg), Collapse of capitalism

Culture, human, 20, 110; or social formations, 10, 180. *See also* Society

Cunow, Heinrich, 124, 126

Darwinism, social, 108

Democracy, 68; social, 122, 161. *See also* Social-democracy

Democrat, social, 164

Democritus, 14

Deportation policies, 11

Depression, Great, 126, 147-148, 153, 158, 165; Long 1873-1879, 121; underaccumulation, 132

Determinism, absolute, 179; economic, 161-162, 164-165, 168; structuralist, 187

Deus ex machina, 159, 163

Deutschmann, Christoph, 155-156, 176

Devaluation of value, 118, 140, 142, 179, 205, 211. *See also* Valorisation

Dialectic, capitalist development, 112; matter and form, 143; production, 181; time, 112-113

Dissociation, feminine, 91, 96; gendered, 90-91, 93, 96-97, 106, 115-116, 173, 185-186, 213; Rubin, 190; social use-value, 115; structure, 185-186; theory (Scholtz), 185; value, 97. *See also* Feminine, Gender

Divine, absolute, 16, 19. *See also* God

Double-character of labour, 63

Dualist, non-, 86; understanding, 85-86

Eckstein, Gustav, 131, 161

Ecological, debates of the 1980s, 71; socio-

-72, 110

Ecologism, 110

Ecology (social movement), 93

Economic, rationalisation , 94, 107, 109; rationality, 196, 198

Economics, bourgeois, 77, 191, 206, 208; marginalist school, 195, 208; modern, 26, 208; postmodernism, 195; since Adam Smith, 108; space-time of, 112 *See also* Political economy, Keynesian

Economists, bourgeois, 147, 153; vulgar Marxist, 75, 82. *See also* Political-economists

Egypt, ancient, 27, 30, 55

Einstein, general relativity, 189

Emancipated society, 58, 179

Engels, Friedrich, 45, 124

Enlightenment, 15, 18, 34, 92, 181, 195, 212-213

Equalisation (of labour - Rubin), 34-38, 55

Equality, 91-93, 95, 192, 213

Erfurt Programme, 124. *See also* Social-democracy

Europe, Western, 38, 99

Everyday, the, 16, 112

Everyday life, 93, 100, 107, 166

Exchange, 33, 38, 40-41, 47, 56, 73, 75, 81, 86, 95, 150, 190, 195-197, 201; abstraction, 41, 52, 70, 72, 83, 91-92, 96, 191-192, 200, 206; Heinrich, 74, 207; ideology, 195; process, 71, 198, 205; relation, 76-78, 92

Exchange-value, 28, 73-78, 82-83, 105, 190, 197, 199, 204, 207-208

Factory, 42-43, 74, 89, 108; hospital-109; social, 175

Family, Traditional, 97, 115

Fatalism, 184-185

Feminine, 91, 96-97. *See also* Dissociation, Gender

Fetishism, 8, 42; abstract labour and money, 204; commodity, 161; Grossman schema, 58; value-form, 31

Feudal, 90, 139. *See also* Pre-capitalist, Pre-modern

Fordist, 173

Foucault, Michel, 90

Freud, Sigmund, 161

Gallas, Alexander, 82-86

Gegenstandpunkt, 188-189. *See also* Huisken, Freerk

Gender, 91-93, 185-186. *See also* Dissociation, Feminine

German, Democratic Republic, 42; Empire, 158, 183; Idealism, 19; Marxist theory, 148; Social-democracy, 124; value-critique, 60, 211. *See also* State

God, 14-15, 19. *See also* Divine

Goods, 132, 204; and services, 36; destructive, 108; material, 42-43; produced, 31; useful, 74, 97

Grossman, Henryk, 5-6, 126, 137, 139-154, 156-157, 163-164, 166, 168-169

Grundrisse, 25

Hardt, Michael, 212

Hegel, G.W.F., 22, 44, 50, 179, 185

Hegelian, 19, 48, 67

Heinrich, Michael, 73-75, 77-80, 82, 85, 120-122, 124, 126, 132, 135-136, 145, 147, 190, 196-213

Hilferding, Rudolf, 161, 173, 176

Historical materialism, 172, 180-181

Horkheimer, Max, 175

Huisken, Freerk, 188

Idealism, 19-22, 92, 95, 195

Ideology, 8-9, 11, 18, 38, 48, 70, 107, 112, 159, 168, 190, 195, 211-213; bourgeois, 10, 108, 195, 197

Illusion, political, 6, 173, 175, 177

Imperialist, 129, 160-162

Individualisation, abstract, 115

Industry, 123, 128, 131, 165; agricultural, 90, 109; armaments, 107, 131; car, 108

Inner limit, 12, 118, 141-142, 153, 175, 177, 189; capital, 29, 120, 139, 143; production, 124, 126, 132; Protestant, 24; valorisation, 136, 157-158, 162, 172, 190, 196, 211, 213

International, The, London congress 1896, 122; Third, 149

Kant, Emmanuel, 46, 65

Kantian, 19; Neo-, 176

Kantorowicz, Ernst, 17

Kautsky, Karl, 124

Keynesian, 156-157. *See also* Economics

Kolakowski, Leszek, 130-131

Korsch, Karl, 169-171

Kurz, Robert, 2, 82, 153, 179, 184

Labour, agricultural, 25; concrete-useful, 53-54; embodied, 200; expended, 43, 73, 87, 204; forced, 55; market, 81, 103; obsolescence of, 137, 141-142, 144; ontologist, 41, 49, 84; socialist equalised, 35-36; socially equalised, 34-35; wage, 61, 95-96, 106, 138-139. *See also* Abstract-labour, Concrete-labour, Work

Labour abstraction, 30, 34, 52, 58, 62, 64, 72, 120 *See also* Abstract-labour

Labour movement, 24, 67, 121-122, 140, 174-175, 182; Heinrich (as "worker's movement"), 121; Marxism, 10, 23, 33, 41, 47, 51, 68, 70, 72, 85, 116, 120,

126, 130, 137, 145, 155, 158, 171, 173, 186, 196; Marxist, 13, 49, 58, 84, 121-122, 125; Western, 38

Labour ontology, 50, 52, 84, 125, 156-157, 172, 178, 186; bourgeois, 60; Lukács, 56; Marxist, 5, 33, 50, 54, 158, 177; modern, 33

Labour substance, 29, 45-46, 172

Labour Theory of Value (Lukács), 47

Labour-power, 24, 47, 56, 71, 76, 80, 88, 93, 95-96, 101, 105-106, 128, 133, 137, 140, 142, 191, 199-204, 206-209; commodity, 81, 94, 103, 105-106, 113, 204-206; expended, 31, 76, 191; redundancy, 141

Labour-time, 55, 65, 98, 199, 203, 209; direct, 63, 198; expended-199, 209; necessary, 47, 100, 199, 205

Law of, accumulation, 131, 138; breakdown, 137, 142, 163; tendency of rate of profit to fall, 153, 155; value, 47, 173, 175. *See also* Overaccumulation, Profit, Surplus-value, Underaccumulation

Left, Communism/Autonomism, 179; Marxist, 190; milieu, 177; New, 120, 155-156, 170, 172, 176; old, 2; postmodern, 124, 130, 177; radical, 166, 168, 175-176, 186; the, 59, 117, 124, 166, 186; ultra, 124; Western, 50. *See also* Socialism

Leibnitz, Gottfried, 15

Lenin, V.I., 146, 151

Leninist, 85, 120, 124, 130, 135, 144, 149

Life-world, 20, 90, 93-94, 100, 104, 116

Locke, John, 46

Lukács, Georg, 44-50, 54, 56, 58, 61, 65

Luxemburg, Rosa, 5, 126-131, 133-137, 147, 149, 151, 154, 156-159, 161-162, 164, 168

Malin, Shimon, 15

Marramao, Giacomo, 170, 175-176, 179

Mars (planet), 110

Marx, Karl, abstract labour, 21, 23, 26, 29-30, 33-34, 38, 43-44, 64, 73, 75, 82, 84-85, 90, 96, 190, 193, 199-203, 207, 209-211; accumulation, 129, 138-139, 143, 160; and Engels, 124; aporia, 25, 27, 33-34, 63, 84; automatic subject, 18, 100, 139; breakdown, 118, 121-122, 124, 143, 154, 156, 158, 163, 166-168, 178; circulation, 39-40, 95, 135, 206; class, 174; concrete labour, 87-88; disembedded space, 90, 94; fetish, 18, 31, 161, 172, 187, 194; labour critique, 60-61; labour ontology, 24, 33, 37, 50, 54, 56, 67, 84-86; necessary labour, 66, 205; organic composition, 137, 144, 150; political economy, 23, 51, 121, 169, 199, 201; premodern, 16; production, 80, 103, 106, 109, 128, 130-131, 176, 180; socialist stage, 37-38; substance, 45, 190-192, 195; substance of capital, 125; time economy, 55, 65; value, 20, 28, 47, 64, 74-75, 77-79, 81-83, 140, 207

Marxism, Buddhist, 117; class sociological, 179; commonplace variants, 120; European, 175; labour, 50; labour movement, 10, 23, 33, 41, 47, 51, 68, 70, 72, 85, 116, 120, 126, 130, 137, 145, 155, 158, 171, 173, 186, 212; labour-ontological, 144; leftover 1970s, 157; mainstream, 137; neo-, 190; old and new, 213; old orthodox, 120; Ricardian, 49; traditional, 12-13,

21, 29-30, 40, 60, 68, 70-72, 74, 77-78, 92, 96, 101, 112, 116-118, 120, 123, 125, 127, 135-136, 139, 145, 151, 154, 172-174, 177, 190, 196, 206, 211-212; traditional academic, 51; traditional half, 73; vulgar, 196; Western, 38, 49, 85, 173, 212

Marxists, 72, 90, 132; academic, 85; labour movement, 58; neo-, 83; structuralist, 187; traditional, 29, 58, 84, 130; Western, 58. *See also* Neo-Marxist

Masses, the, 127, 151, 159. *See also* Producers, Proletariat, Workers, Working-class

Materials, Building, 107; Natural, 31-32, 53, 108, 113; Raw, 162

Mattick, Paul, 132, 135, 153-154, 178-179

Metabolic process(es), 53, 92

Metaphysics, real, 8, 14, 16-17, 19-22

Military, 90, 131; machine, 89, 91; revolution, 89, 101, 181

Mill, John Stuart, 137

Money, 10, 17-18, 21, 50, 74, 78, 80-82, 90, 100, 104, 106, 128-129, 133-134, 153, 192, 196, 198, 203-204, 207

Money-form, 38, 72, 81, 128, 194

Money-owner, 95, 105

Moszkowska, Natalie, 153

National liberation movements, 38, 50. *See also* Periphery, the, Recuperative modernisation

National Socialism, 175, 183

National Socialist, 153, 164-165

Naturalism, 192, 196, 210

Negri, Antonio, 86, 172, 175-177, 212

Neo-Marxist, 82, 190, 196, 212. *See also* Marxists

Nerves, muscles and brains, 87, 191-193, 201-202

Newton, Issac, time, 65, 99; universe, 15, 20

Newtonian, time, 114; universe, 15, 20, 97, 108

Non-capitalist, 55, 57, 63, 128-129, 131, 161. *See also* Pre-capitalist, Socialist mode of production

Non-white, non-Western, 186. *See also* White Western male subject

Overaccumulation, 132, 142, 150, 164

Pannekoek, Anton, 135, 151-152, 166-169, 171-172, 177

Periphery, the, 38, 141, 164-165. *See also* Countries, Recuperative modernisation

Physicists, 189, 194

Physics, 8, 20, 180, 189

Plato, 19

Platonic, Idealism, 19-20; Model, 146, 149-151

Pol Pot, 58-59

Political-economists, classical, 201-206. *See also* Economists

Political economy, 164, 172-173, 201; bourgeois, 137, 201, 207-208; classical, 199, 209-210. *See also* Economics

Pollock, Friedrich, 205

Polyanyi, Karl, 89

Postcapitalist, democracy, 68; economy, 65; society, 38, 58, 65, 67, 98

Postmodernism, 2, 83, 195, 211

Postone, Moishe, 13, 29, 39, 41, 49, 60-68, 70-71, 98-100, 112-114, 185, 210-211

Postwar, crisis, 148; Marxist thinking, 153; New Left, 172; prosperity, 153-154,

158. *See also* World War II

Pre-capitalist, 129. *See also* Feudal

Pre-modern, 14, 16, 27

Price, 18, 127, 170, 203, 208

Primitive accumulation, 90, 164

Probability cloud, 180-183

Producers, 71-73, 79, 100, 102-105,
    197-198, 201, 205, 209, 212; socialist,
    42-43. See also Masses, the, Proletariat,
    Workers, Working Class

Profit, extra, 152; greed for, 105; rate of,
    150, 152; tendency of rate to fall, 126,
    137, 141, 153-155, 170-171. *See also*
    Law of

Proletariat, 42, 49, 72, 124, 158, 160,
    162, 167, 175. *See also* Masses, the,
    Producers, Workers, Working-class

Property, 95; juridical concept, 72-74, 90,
    92, 101, 206; legal, 40, 71; private, 61,
    101-103

Protestant, 46; ethic, 37, 112. *See also*
    Work ethic

Protestantism, 56

Proudhon, Pierre-Joseph, 37

Quantum (theory), 8, 109, 180, 189

Recuperative modernisation, 38, 50,
    56, 59, 90, 94, 164-165. *See also*
    Communist, Countries. Periphery, the

Reductionism, 110, 171, 191, 206, 211;
    physical, 15, 108-109

Reichelt, Helmut, 205

Relativisim, 8, 10-13

Relativity, general theory of, 189

Revolution, 101, 155, 162, 165, 168;
    counter, 133; military, 89, 101, 181;
    October, 37, 162; proletarian, 165,
    167-168, 170; social, 124

Ricardo, David, 137

Rosdolsky, Roman, 136

Rubin, Isaak Illich, 33-37, 42, 46, 52, 55,
    65, 190-197, 208, 210-211

Russia, 37, 163-164

Salin, Edgar, 148

Saussure, Ferdinand, 8, 195

Schema, Bauer-Grossman, 149, 151; Marx
    Capital II, 128; Pannekoek, 152

Scholz, Roswitha, 91, 96, 185-186

Schumpeter, Joseph, 147

Science, 75, 137; and knowledge, 8-9;
    and productivity, 113; bourgeois social,
    179; fiction, 110; modern, 115; natural,
    8, 15, 22, 108-109, 179; of value
    (Heinrich), 196, 196, 208, 212; to
    industry, 128

Self-expanding value, 30, 36. *See also*
    Valorisation

Self-expansion of, capital, 29, 120;
    value, 17, 20, 22, 27, 96, 141. *See also*
    Valorisation

Self-moving end in itself, 81, 106, 145. *See
    also* Automatic subject

Smith, Adam, 25, 44, 46, 108, 137, 154,
    197

Social historians: Thompson, Gurjevich &
    Needham, 98

Social-democracy, 121, 123-124, 131,
    159, 175. *See also* Erfurt Programme

Socialism, Grossman, 143; historical
    necessity, 130; labour under, 35, 42-
    43; Lukács, 47-48; organised factory
    society, 175; Pannekoek, 167; political
    economy, 23; post October revolution,
    37-38; real existing, 23, 42, 49-50,
    52, 58, 70-71, 94; state, 38; through
    parliamentary channels, 161; two stage /
    communism, 37; Wolf, 51. *See also* Left

Socialist mode of production, 42-43. *See also* Non-capitalist

Society, 8, 27, 54, 63-64; agrarian, 55, 181; basic categories, 10; Bauer, 132; Bernstein, 123; bourgeois, 26, 159; Braunthal, 165; breakdown, 123; capitalist, 2, 20, 61, 78, 81, 99, 112, 149, 181; criticism, 71; emancipated, 58, 179; form, 25, 28, 37; Gallas, 85; Heinrich, 211; human, 15, 180; labour, 56-57, 62; Marx, 28, 84, 95; modern, 12, 26-27, 60, 178; non-capitalist, 63; organised factory, 175; postcapitalist, 38, 65, 67, 98; Postone, 49, 60-61, 63, 66, 70; pre-capitalist, 129; premodern, 54-55, 181; productive and consuming power, 127; real metaphysics, 8; Rubin, 36; socialist, 43, 123; underdeveloped, 165; value based form, 19; Wolf, 55-56

Sohn-Rethel, Alfred, 41, 61, 70, 72, 211, 220

Space-time, 15, 100-101; abstract-103, 112-113; alien (abstract labour), 102; and abstract labour, 101, 103, 111; disembedded, 110, 112, 117; economic, 101-104, 108-110, 112, 115-118; social reproduction, 101; specific, 101, 103

Stalin, Joseph, 58

Stalinism, 37

State, and politics, 27, 40, 115-116, 173-174; authoritarian (Horkheimer/ Adorno)-175; communist, 164-165; critique (of class state), 174; for the individual, 183; intervention, 72, 173, 175; Kolakowski (contra Luxemburg), 131; planning, 40, 44, 56; Postone, 13, 115; proletarian, 174; regulation, 42; Social-democracy, 161; socialist, 38, 44,

56, 103; welfare, 97; Wolf, 57

Structuralism, 161; Althusser, 168, 172

Subject-object, aporia, 178; dilemma, 176, 186; problem, 159, 163, 169, 176, 178-179; relation, 171, 189; scale (Marxian/radical left), 168; structure (issues around), 164-165, 172, 184. *See also* Aporia

Substantialism, against, 30; anti-, 190-191, 197, 209, 211-212; false, 29; positive, 190; postmodernism, 196; real, 12

Surplus-labour, 204-206

Surplus-value, accumulation, 133, 135, 138; and value, 102, 106, 113, 127, 136; and working class, 42, 131; appropriation, 174; Bauer, 131-132; Bukharin-134; Deutschmann, 155-156; end in itself, 106; Grossman, 137-139, 141-142; Heinrich, 136; inexhaustible, 127; irrelevant, 204; Luxemburg, 126, 159; Mattick, 135; Moszkowska, 153; production, 107, 113, 126-128, 130-131, 135-137, 141, 150, 155-156, 206; realisation, 78, 81, 92, 113, 126, 128-129; relative, 152-153; represents, 126, 204; substantial, 144; surplus-labour, 204; withheld, 125

Technical process, 39, 103, 152, 199-200

Third industrial revolution, 60, 97, 101, 141, 148, 155, 158, 164

Trenkle, Norbert, 209

Trottmann, Martin, 148

Truck, barter and exchange, 195, 197, 201

Underaccumulation, 132

Unemployed, 150, 158

Unemployment, 60, 167

USA (United States of America), 141, 168

Use-value, 23, 28, 41-43, 66, 72-73, 77,

88, 105-106, 113-114, 201, 204-205;
abstract, 28, 43, 107; and value, 77-78,
80; dimension, 113-114; of commodity,
23, 106, 113, 204-205; of products, 23,
106; to produce, 88, 106, 191

Valorisation, and crisis, 132, 145,
162; and dissociation, 91; and
overaccumulation, 142; and political
form, 173; and production, 103-105,
109; and proletarian subject, 168, 177;
and space-time, 102-103, 108, 116;
and time, 98, 100; as labour process,
109; as subject, 88; automatic subject,
100, 102, 107; capitalist, 39, 96,
205; Grossman, 138, 143-146, 157;
indifference to human needs, 107-108,
113, 200, 206; inner limit, 8, 120,
136, 211, 213; inner limit (rejection
of), 153, 158, 172, 190, 196; logic, 37;
Marx, 139; money-form, 81; of abstract
labour, 90; of value, 87, 90, 102, 141;
process, 18-19, 58, 71, 80-81, 97, 101;
reductionism, 110; social space, 89;
social use-value, 106; value-socialisation,
113; Varga (on Grossman), 150. *See also*
Devaluation of value, Self-expanding
value, Self-expansion of

Value-critique, 51, 58-60, 84-85, 188, 209

Value-form, 19-21, 28, 31, 42-43, 56, 58,
74, 79, 81-82, 92, 143, 150, 156, 164,
166, 177, 182, 184-185, 195, 211, 213

Value-objectivity, 73-83, 87, 89, 108-109,
113, 197-198, 201, 203, 206-210, 212

Value-socialisation, Luxemburg, 127;
Pannekoek, 166; postmodern Marxism
(Hardt/Negri), 212; Postone, 66, 98,
112-113; traditional Marxism, 117-
118; undisputed categories, 93

Value-theory, 195, 209

Varga, Eugene, 149-151, 163-164

Walther, Rudolf, 121-122

War, economies, 173; of annihilation, 110;
peasant 15th/16th Cent., 182. *See also*
World wars (era of)

Wealth, abstract, 106-107, 125, 127, 192,
203; and labour, 25; -creating activity-
26; form of, 78, 81; Postone, 49, 60, 65

Weber, Max, 174

White Western male subject, 15, 185-186,
189-190, 213

Wildcat journal, 187

Wolf, Dieter, 50-59, 64-65, 70

Women, 91, 93, 185

Work, 61, 71, 102, 115. *See also* Abstract-
labour

Work ethic, 37

Workers, 36, 84, 94, 96, 104, 122-123,
131, 133-134, 140-143, 150, 167,
170, 174; wage, 137,159, 166. *See also*
Masses, the, Producers

Working-class, 130, 145, 158, 165, 167-
168, 171. *See also* Proletariat

World War I, after, 133; Bukharin, 162;
labour movement, 175; Luxemburg,
159, 161; Neusüß, 147

World War II, after, 135-136, 147-148;
after - prosperity, 156; consequences,
153; Neusüß, 147

World wars (era of), 126, 137, 158, 173.
See also War

KETO SLOW COOKER

Vegetarian Recipes

Best Healthy LOW-Carb Recipe Cookbook to Succeed o Your Keto Diet Without Compromising on Taste!

By Dana Ray

TABLE OF CONTENTS

Broccoli quiche 8

Parmesan Potatoes 10

Zucchini Noodles... 12

Green Peas Risotto 13

Mushroom Stew 15

Curry Cauliflower 17

Veggie Bean stew 19

Fennel Bites 21

Carrot Soup 22

Peppers Chili.. 24

Okra Stew... 26

Vegan Curry 27

Tomato and Bell Pepper Gratin............................ 29

Beans and Rice.. 31

Mediterranean Veggie Mix.................................... 33

Indian Dhal... 35

Spinach Soup 37

Cheesy Corn 38

Artichoke Linguini.. 39

Butter Asparagus 41

Spicy Pumpkin Wedges.. 42

Tofu Greens... 43

Mashed Potatoes.. 45

Kale Quiche 47

Stew for Vegans.. 49

Vegetarian Lasagna..50

Potato Salad 52

Chickpea Curry 53

Lemony Lentils Soup..54

Mashed Cauliflower..56

Vegan Spicy Jambalaya...58

Green Beans and Mushrooms...59

Cheesy Tofu...60

Cabbage and Onion Mix...61

Lemon Artichokes 63

Minty Peas 64

Balsamic-glazed Beets 65

Spicy Quinoa..67

Sweet Potato Soup..68

Spelt Pilaf..70

Vegetable Lasagna...71

Cauliflower Rice Mix..73

Coconut Okra..74

Zucchini and Yellow Squash..75

Eggplant Parmesan...76

Thyme Tomatoes 77

Quinoa Dolma...78

Creamy Puree..79

Cauliflower Hash...80

Brussels Sprouts 81

Sautéed Garlic 82

Cheesy Corn 83

Shredded Cabbage Sauté 84

Ranch Broccoli 85

Sautéed Spinach 86

Cheddar Mushrooms 87

Fragrant Appetizer Peppers 89

Paprika Baby Carrot 90

Butter Asparagus 91

Jalapeno Corn 92

Garlic Cauliflower Steaks 93

Eggplant Gratin 94

Garlic Carrots Mix 96

Broccoli Mix 97

Minty Peas and Tomatoes 98

Lemon Artichokes 99

SLOW COOKER VEGETARIAN RECIPES

Broccoli quiche

Prep Time: 25 mins | Cooking Time: 4 hours | Servings: 7

INGREDIENTS:

- ✓ 7 oz. pie crust
- ✓ ¼ cup broccoli
- ✓ 1/3 cup sweet peas
- ✓ ¼ cup heavy cream
- ✓ 2 tbsps flour
- ✓ 3 eggs
- ✓ 4 oz. romano cheese, shredded
- ✓ 1 tsp cilantro
- ✓ 1 tsp salt
- ✓ ¼ cup spinach
- ✓ 1 tomato

DIRECTIONS:

1. cover the inside of the slow cooker bowl with

parchment.

2. put the pie crust inside and flatten it well with your fingertips.

3. chop the broccoli and combine it with sweet peas. combine the heavy cream, flour, cilantro, and salt together. stir the liquid until smooth.

4. then beat the eggs into the heavy cream liquid and mix it with a hand mixer. when you get a smooth mix, combine it with the broccoli.

5. chop the spinach and add it to the mix. chop the tomato and add it to the mix too. pour the prepared mixture into the pie crust slowly.

6. close the slow cooker lid and cook the quiche for 4 hours on HIGH.

7. after 4 hours, sprinkle the quiche surface with the shredded cheese and cook the dish for 25 minutes more. serve the prepared quiche

NUTRITION(per Serving): Calories 261, Fat 18g, Carbs 20g, Protein 9g

Parmesan Potatoes

Prep Time: 20 mins | Cooking Time: 4 hours | Servings: 5

INGREDIENTS:

- ✓ 1-pound small potato
- ✓ ½ cup fresh dill
- ✓ 7 oz. parmesan
- ✓ 1 tsp rosemary
- ✓ 1 tsp thyme
- ✓ 1 cup water
- ✓ ¼ tsp chili flakes
- ✓ 3 tbsp cream
- ✓ 1 tsp salt

DIRECTIONS:

1. peel the potatoes and put them in the slow cooker.
2. add water, salt, thyme, rosemary, and chili flakes.
3. close the slow cooker lid and cook the potato for 2 hours on HIGH.
4. meanwhile, shred parmesan cheese and chop the fresh dill. when the time is done, sprinkle the potato with the cream and fresh dill. stir it carefully.
5. add shredded parmesan cheese and close the slow cooker lid. cook the potato on HIGH for 2 hours

10

more.

6. then open the slow cooker lid and do not stir the potato anymore. gently transfer the dish to the serving plates.

NUTRITION(per Serving): Calories 239, Fat 6g, Carbs 25g, Protein 2g

Zucchini Noodles

Prep Time: 15 mins | Cooking Time: 1 hour | Servings: 4

INGREDIENTS:

- ✓ 2 zucchini
- ✓ 1 tsp dried oregano
- ✓ 1 tsp dried basil
- ✓ 2 tbsp butter
- ✓ ¼ tsp salt
- ✓ 5 tbsp water

DIRECTIONS:

1. peel the zucchini and spiralize it with a veggie spiralizer.
2. melt the butter and mix it together with the dried oregano, dried basil, salt, and water.
3. place the spiralized zucchini in the slow cooker and add the spice mixture.
4. close the lid and cook the meal for 1 hour on LOW.
5. let the cooked pasta cool slightly. Serve it!

NUTRITION(per Serving): Calories 68, Fat 6g, Carbs 2.5g, Protein 1.2g

Green Peas Risotto

Prep Time: 20 mins | Cooking Time: 3 hours | Servings: 6

INGREDIENTS:

- ✓ 7 oz. parmigiano-reggiano
- ✓ 2 cup vegetable broth
- ✓ 1 tsp olive oil
- ✓ 1 onion, chopped
- ✓ ½ cup green peas
- ✓ 1 garlic clove, peeled and sliced
- ✓ 2 cups long grain rice
- ✓ ¼ cup dry wine
- ✓ 1 tsp ground black pepper
- ✓ 1 carrot, chopped

DIRECTIONS:

1. spray a skillet with olive oil.
2. add the chopped onion and carrot and roast the vegetables for 3 minutes on the medium heat. then put the seared vegetables in the slow cooker. toss the long grain rice in the remaining oil and sauté for 1 minute on the HIGH heat.
3. add the roasted long grain rice and sliced garlic in the slow cooker.

4. add green peas, dry wine, salt, ground black pepper, and beef broth. after this, add the chicken broth and stir the mixture gently. close the slow cooker lid and cook the risotto for 3 hours.

5. then stir the risotto gently.

6. shred parmigiano-reggiano and sprinkle over the risotto. close the slow cooker lid and cook the dish for 30 minutes more. enjoy the prepared risotto immediately!

NUTRITION(per Serving): Calories 264, Fat 3g, Carbs 53g, Protein 7g

Mushroom Stew

Prep Time: 5 mins | Cooking Time: 6 hours | Servings: 8

INGREDIENTS:

- ✓ 10 oz white mushrooms, sliced
- ✓ 2 eggplants, chopped
- ✓ 1 onion, diced
- ✓ 1 garlic clove, diced
- ✓ 2 bell peppers, chopped
- ✓ 1 cup water
- ✓ 1 tbsp butter
- ✓ ½ tsp ground black pepper

DIRECTIONS:

1. place the sliced mushrooms, chopped eggplant, and diced onion into the slow cooker.
2. add garlic clove and bell peppers.
3. sprinkle the vegetables with salt and ground black pepper.
4. add butter and water and stir it gently with a wooden spatula.
5. close the lid and cook the stew for 6 hours on LOW.
6. ctir the cooked stew one more time and serve!

NUTRITION(per Serving): Calories 76, Fat 1.3g, Carbs 13g, Protein 4g

Curry Cauliflower

Prep Time: 5 mins | Cooking Time: 5 hours | Servings: 2

INGREDIENTS:

- ✓ 10 oz cauliflower
- ✓ 1 tsp curry paste
- ✓ 1 tsp curry powder
- ✓ ½ tsp dried cilantro
- ✓ 1 oz butter
- ✓ ¾ cup water
- ✓ ¼ cup vegetable stock

DIRECTIONS:

1. chop the cauliflower roughly and sprinkle it with the curry powder and dried cilantro.
2. place the chopped cauliflower in the slow cooker.
3. mix the curry paste with the water.
4. add chicken stock and transfer the liquid to the slow cooker.
5. add butter and close the lid.
6. cook the cauliflower for 5 hours on LOW
7. strain ½ of the liquid off and discard. Transfer the cauliflower to serving bowls.

NUTRITION(per Serving): Calories 164, Fat 13g, Carbs 8.5g, Protein 3.7g

Veggie Bean stew

Prep Time: 20 mins | Cooking Time: 7 hours | Servings: 8

INGREDIENTS:

- ✓ ½ cup barley
- ✓ 1 cup black beans
- ✓ ¼ cup red beans
- ✓ 2 carrots
- ✓ 1 cup onion, chopped
- ✓ 1 cup tomato juice
- ✓ 2 potatoes
- ✓ 1 tsp salt
- ✓ 1 tsp ground black pepper
- ✓ 4 cups water
- ✓ 4 oz. tofu
- ✓ 1 tsp garlic powder
- ✓ 1 cup fresh cilantro

DIRECTIONS:

1. place barley, black beans, and red beans in the slow cooker vessel.
2. add chopped onion, tomato juice, salt, ground black pepper, and garlic powder. after this, add water and close the slow cooker lid.

3. cook the dish for 4 hours on HIGH.

4. meanwhile, peel the carrots and cut them into the strips. peel the potatoes and chop.

5. add the carrot strips and chopped potatoes in the slow cooker after 4 hours of cooking.

6. chop the fresh cilantro and add it in the slow cooker too.

7. stir the mix and close the slow cooker lid. cook the stew for 3 hours more on LOW.

8. serve the prepared dish immediately or keep it in the fridge, not more than 3 days.

NUTRITION(per Serving): Calories 218, Fat 3g ,Carbs 37g, Protein 7g

Fennel Bites

Prep Time: 10 mins | Cooking Time: 2 hours | Servings: 6

INGREDIENTS:

✓ 1-pound fennel bulb

✓ 1 tsp cumin 1 teaspoon thyme

✓ 1 tsp salt

✓ 1 oz butter

✓ 1 tbsp olive oil

DIRECTIONS:

1. mix the cumin, thyme, salt, and olive oil.
2. slice the fennel bulb and sprinkle it with the spice mixture.
3. place the fennel in the slow cooker and add butter.
4. close the lid and cook for 2 hours on HIGH. Serve hot!

NUTRITION(per Serving): Calories 92, Fat 7.3g ,Carbs 6.7g, Protein 1.7g

Carrot Soup

Prep Time: 18 mins | Cooking Time: 12 hours | Servings: 9

INGREDIENTS:

- ✓ 1-pound carrot
- ✓ 1 tsp ground cardamom
- ✓ ¼ tsp nutmeg
- ✓ 1 tsp salt
- ✓ 3 tbsps fresh parsley
- ✓ 1 tsp honey
- ✓ 1 tsp marjoram
- ✓ 5 cups vegetable stock
- ✓ ½ cup yellow onion, chopped
- ✓ 1 tsp butter

DIRECTIONS:

1. toss the butter in a pan and add chopped onion.
2. chop the carrot and add it to the pan too.
3. roast the vegetables for 5 minutes on the LOW heat. after this, place the roasted vegetables in the sLOW cooker. add ground cardamom, nutmeg, salt, marjoram, and chicken stock.
4. close the sLOW cooker lid and cook the soup for 12 hours on LOW.

5. chop the fresh parsley.

6. when the time is over, blend the soup with a hand blender until you get a smooth texture. then ladle the soup into the serving bowls.

7. sprinkle the prepared soup with the chopped fresh parsley and honey. enjoy the soup immediately!

NUTRITION(per Serving): Calories 80, Fat 2g, Carbs 11g, Protein 4g

Peppers Chili

Prep Time: 10 mins | Cooking Time: 8 hours | Servings: 6

INGREDIENTS:

- ✓ 1 cup pumpkin, pureed
- ✓ 45 oz canned black beans, drained
- ✓ 30 oz canned tomatoes, chopped
- ✓ 1 yellow bell pepper, chopped
- ✓ 1 yellow onion, chopped
- ✓ ¼ tsp nutmeg, ground
- ✓ 1 tsp cinnamon powder
- ✓ 1 tbsp chili powder
- ✓ 1 tsp cumin, ground
- ✓ 1/8 tsp cloves, ground
- ✓ a pinch of sea salt
- ✓ black pepper to the taste

DIRECTIONS:

1. put pumpkin puree in your slow cooker.
2. add black beans, tomatoes, onion, bell pepper, cumin, nutmeg, cinnamon, chili powder, cloves, salt and pepper, stir, cover and cook on LOW for 8 hours.
3. stir your chili again, divide into bowls and serve.

NUTRITION(per Serving): Calories 240, Fat 22g, Carbs 5g, Protein 24g

Okra Stew

Prep Time: 5 mins | Cooking Time: 5 hours | Servings: 4

INGREDIENTS:

- ✓ 10 oz okra, chopped
- ✓ 1 onion, diced
- ✓ 5 oz cauliflower, chopped
- ✓ 1 cup water
- ✓ 1 tsp butter

DIRECTIONS:

1. Mix the chopped okra, diced onion, cauliflower, and spices.

2. stir the mixture and place it in the slow cooker.

3. add water and butter and close the lid.

4. cook the stew for 5 hours on LOW.

5. transfer the dish into serving bowls and serve!

NUTRITION(per Serving): Calories 59, Fat 1.2g, Carbs 10.4g, Protein 2.6g

Vegan Curry

Prep Time: 10 mins | Cooking Time: 4 hours | Servings: 6

INGREDIENTS:

- ✓ 3 cups sweet potatoes, cubed
- ✓ 2 cups broccoli florets
- ✓ 1 cup water
- ✓ 1 cup white onion, chopped
- ✓ 28 oz canned tomatoes, chopped
- ✓ 15 oz canned chickpeas, drained
- ✓ ¼ cup quinoa
- ✓ 29 oz canned coconut milk
- ✓ 1 tbsp garlic, minced
- ✓ 1 tbsp ginger root, grated
- ✓ 1 tabmexican souplespoon turmeric, ground
- ✓ 2 tsps vegan tamari sauce
- ✓ 1 tsp chili flakes

DIRECTIONS:

1. put the water in your slow cooker.

2. add potatoes, broccoli, onion, tomatoes, chickpeas, quinoa, garlic, ginger, turmeric, chili flakes, tamari sauce and coconut milk.

3. stir, cover and cook on HIGH for 4 hours.

4. stir your curry again, divide into bowls and serve.

NUTRITION(per Serving): Calories 302, Fat 22g, Carbs 4g, Protein 36g

Tomato and Bell Pepper Gratin

Prep Time: 15 mins | Cooking Time: 4 hours | Servings: 4

INGREDIENTS:

- ✓ 2 tomatoes, sliced
- ✓ 6 oz bell pepper, sliced
- ✓ 4 oz Parmesan, grated
- ✓ ¼ cup almond milk, unsweetened
- ✓ 1 tbsps dried parsley
- ✓ ¼ tsp ground coriander
- ✓ 1 tsp butter
- ✓ 1 garlic clove, diced

DIRECTIONS:

1. chop the butter and place it in the slow cooker.

2. make a layer of the sliced tomatoes in the bottom of the slow cooker on top of the butter.

3. next, make a layer of the bell peppers.

4. sprinkle the vegetables with the almond milk, dried parsley, ground coriander, and diced garlic clove.

5. place the grated cheese over the vegetables and close the lid.

6. cook the gratin for 4 hours on LOW. Serve!

NUTRITION(per Serving): Calories 204, Fat 1.2g, Carbs 15g, Protein 11.4g

Beans and Rice

Prep Time: 10 mins | Cooking Time: 8 hours | Servings: 4

INGREDIENTS:

✓ 3 cups water

✓ 8 ounces dry kidney beans

✓ 1 onion, chopped

✓ ½ green bell pepper, chopped

✓ ½ stalk celery, chopped, or to taste

✓ 2 cloves garlic, minced, or to taste

✓ 1 bay leaf

✓ salt and pepper to taste

✓ hot cooked rice, for serving

DIRECTIONS:

1. combine the water, kidney beans, onion, green bell pepper, celery, garlic, and bay leaf in the bowl of a slow cooker and stir to combine. Set the slow cooker to LOW, and cook for at least 8 hours. remove and discard the bay leaf.

2. meanwhile, cook the rice according to the package DIRECTIONS: . Serve with the red bean mixture.

3. season with salt and ground black pepper to taste.

NUTRITION(per Serving): Calories 286, Fat 9.2g, Carbs 42g, Protein 16g

Mediterranean Veggie Mix

Prep Time: 15 mins | Cooking Time: 7 hours | Servings: 8

INGREDIENTS:

- ✓ 1 zucchini
- ✓ 2 eggplants
- ✓ 2 red onion
- ✓ 4 potatoes
- ✓ 4 oz. asparagus
- ✓ 2 tbsp olive oil
- ✓ 1 tsp ground black pepper
- ✓ 1 tsp paprika
- ✓ 1 tsp salt
- ✓ 1 tbsp mediterranean seasoning
- ✓ 1 tsp minced garlic

DIRECTIONS:

1. combine the olive oil, mediterranean seasoning, salt, paprika, ground black pepper, and minced garlic together.

2. whisk the mixture well. wash all the vegetables carefully.

3. cut the zucchini, eggplants, and potatoes into the

medium cubes. cut the asparagus into 2 parts.

4. then peel the onions and cut them into 4 parts. toss all the vegetables in the slow cooker and sprinkle them with the spice mixture.

5. close the sLOW cooker lid and cook the vegetable mix for 7 hours on LOW.

6. serve the prepared vegetable mix hot.

NUTRITION(per Serving): Calories 226, Fat 4g, Carbs 44g, Protein 6g

Indian Dhal

Prep Time: 15 mins | Cooking Time: 5 hours | Servings: 11

INGREDIENTS:

- ✓ 1 tsp cumin
- ✓ 1 oz. mustard seeds
- ✓ 10 oz. lentils
- ✓ 1 tsp fennel seeds
- ✓ 7 cups water
- ✓ 6 oz. tomato, canned
- ✓ 4 oz. onion
- ✓ ½ tsp fresh ginger, grated
- ✓ 1 oz. bay leaf
- ✓ 1 tsp turmeric
- ✓ 1 tsp salt
- ✓ 2 cups rice

DIRECTIONS:

1. peel the onion. chop the onion and tomatoes and place them in a slow cooker.

2. combine the cumin, mustard seeds, and fennel seeds in a shallow bowl.

3. add the bay leaf and mix. sprinkle the vegetables in

the slow cooker with the spice mixture.

4. add salt, turmeric, and grated fresh ginger. add rice and mix.

5. add the lentils and water. stir gently.

6. then close the slow cooker lid and cook dal for 5 hours on LOW.

7. when the dish is done, stir and transfer to serving plates.

NUTRITION(per Serving): Calories 115, Fat 22g, Carbs 6g, Protein 32g

Spinach Soup

Prep Time: 15 mins | Cooking Time: 6-8 hours | Servings: 4

INGREDIENTS:

- ✓ 2 pounds spinach
- ✓ ¼ cup cream cheese
- ✓ 1 onion, diced
- ✓ 2 cups heavy cream
- ✓ 1 garlic clove, minced
- ✓ 2 cups water
- ✓ salt, pepper, to taste

DIRECTIONS:

1. pour water into the slow cooker. add spinach, salt, and pepper.

2. add cream cheese, onion, garlic, and heavy cream.

3. lose the lid and cook on LOW for 6-8 hours.

4. puree soup with blender and serve.

NUTRITION(per Serving): Calories 322 ,Fat 28g ,Carbs 17g, Protein 12g

Cheesy Corn

Prep Time: 12 mins | Cooking Time: 4 hours | Servings: 4

INGREDIENTS:

- ✓ 4 cups fresh or frozen corn
- ✓ ¾ cup cheddar cheese, shredded
- ✓ 8 ounces of cream cheese, cubed
- ✓ ¼ cup melted butter
- ✓ ½ cup heavy whipping cream
- ✓ ½ tsp salt
- ✓ ¼ tsp pepper

DIRECTIONS:

1. combine all the ingredients in the cooker.

2. stir well and cover.

3. cook for 3-4 hours on LOW or until the cheese is melted.

4. stir well just before serving.

NUTRITION(per Serving): Calories 219, Fat 10g, Carbs 28g, Protein 8g

Artichoke Linguini

Prep Time: 12 mins | Cooking Time: 6 hours | Servings: 6

INGREDIENTS:

- ✓ 12 ounces dry linguine or fettuccine
- ✓ 3 14-ounce tomatoes, diced with basil, garlic, and oregano
- ✓ 1 14-ounce cans artichoke hearts, drained
- ✓ 1 tbsp minced garlic
- ✓ ½ cup heavy cream

DIRECTIONS:

1. coat the inside of slow cooker with nonstick cooking spray.
2. drain 2 of the cans of diced tomatoes.
3. combine drained and undrained tomatoes, garlic, and artichoke hearts in the slow cooker.
4. cover and cook for 6-8 hours on LOW or 3-4 hours on HIGH.
5. stir the cream.
6. Cook pasta according to package DIRECTIONS: ; drain.
7. Serve artichoke sauce over hot cooked pasta.

NUTRITION(per Serving): Calories 439, Fat 1.2g, Carbs 68g, Protein 14g

Butter Asparagus

Prep Time: 15 mins | Cooking Time: 5 hours | Servings: 4

INGREDIENTS:

- ✓ 1-pound asparagus
- ✓ 2 tbsps vegan butter
- ✓ 1 tsp ground black pepper
- ✓ 1 cup vegetable stock

DIRECTIONS:

1. pour the vegetable stock in the slow cooker.

2. chop the asparagus roughly and add in the slow cooker.

3. close the lid and cook the asparagus for 5 hours on LOW.

4. then drain water and transfer the asparagus in the bowl.

5. sprinkle it with ground black pepper and butter.

NUTRITION(per Serving): Calories 77, Fat 6.2g, Carbs 4.8g, Protein 2.4g

Spicy Pumpkin Wedges

Prep Time: 10 mins | Cooking Time: 6 hours | Servings: 4

INGREDIENTS:

- ✓ 2-pound pumpkin, peeled
- ✓ 1 teaspoon ground cardamom 2 tbsps lemon juice
- ✓ 1 teaspoon lemon zest, grated
- ✓ 2 tbsps sugar
- ✓ 1 cup of water

DIRECTIONS:

1. cut the pumpkin into wedges and place them in the slow cooker.

2. add water.

3. then sprinkle the pumpkin with ground cardamom, lemon juice, lemon zest, and sugar.

4. close the lid and cook the pumpkin on LOW for 6 hours.

5. serve the pumpkin wedges with sweet liquid from the slow cooker.

NUTRITION(per Serving): Calories 103 ,Fat 0.8g ,Carbs 27g, Protein 6.2g

Tofu Greens

Prep Time: 10 mins | Cooking Time: 3 hours | Servings: 8

INGREDIENTS:

✓ 4 pounds mixed green leaves

✓ 1 red onion, finely diced

✓ 4 ounces tofu cut into 1" strips

✓ ½ cup tamari sauce

✓ ¼ cup olive oil

✓ Salt and pepper

DIRECTIONS:

1. marinate the tofu strips with the tamari sauce for 1 hour.

2. in the meantime, blanch the greens, drain, and roughly chop.

3. turn on the slow cooker and add onions and tofu with marinade.

4. toss in the greens and olive oil. season with salt and pepper.

5. cover and cook for 2 ½ hours on HIGH until the greens are soft.

6. taste and adjust the seasoning and serve hot.

43

NUTRITION(per Serving): Calories 173, Fat 14.8g, Carbs 10g, Protein 19g

Mashed Potatoes

Prep Time: 10 mins | Cooking Time: 5 hours | Servings: 8

INGREDIENTS:

✓ 5 lb russet potatoes, peeled and cut into 1-inch cubes

✓ 3 smashed garlic cloves

✓ 3 ½ cups milk, divided

✓ ½ cup unsalted butter

✓ ⅓ cup grated Parmesan cheese

DIRECTIONS:

1. grease the inside of the slow cooker with cooking spray.

2. place the prepared potatoes in the slow cooker. put the garlic cloves on top. season with salt and pepper.

3. separate 2 cups of the milk and set aside. pour the remaining 1 ½ cups of milk over potatoes. stir.

4. cover the slow cooker and cook 4 to 5 hours on HIGH, or until fork tender.

5. when the potatoes are soft enough to mash. Set the slow cooker at WARM.

6. in a saucepan, melt the butter over very low heat.

Add the 2 cups of milk to the butter to warm.

7. remove the garlic from the potatoes as well as any unwanted brown bits on the sides of the pot.

8. mash the potatoes while in the pot.

9. gradually add warmed milk with butter mixture and Parmesan to the potatoes while mashing.

10.   add more salt and pepper, if desired

NUTRITION(per Serving): Calories 103 ,Fat 0.8g ,Carbs 27g, Protein 6.2g

Kale Quiche

Prep Time: 15 mins | Cooking Time: 3-5 hours | Servings: 3

INGREDIENTS:

- ✓ 1 cup almond milk
- ✓ 4 eggs
- ✓ 1 cup carbquick baking mix
- ✓ 2 cups spinach, chopped
- ✓ ½ bell pepper, chopped
- ✓ cups fresh baby kale, chopped
- ✓ tsp garlic, chopped
- ✓ 1/3 cup fresh basil, chopped
- ✓ salt, pepper, to taste
- ✓ 1 tbsp olive oil

DIRECTIONS:

1. add oil to a slow cooker or use a cooking spray.

2. beat eggs into a slow cooker; add almond milk and baking mix, mix to combine.

3. add spinach, bell pepper, garlic, and basil, stir to combine.

4. close the lid and cook on LOW for 5 hours or on HIGH for 3 hours.

5. make sure the quiche is done, check the center with a toothpick, it should be dry.

NUTRITION(per Serving): Calories 273, Fat 24.8g, Carbs 5.6g, Protein 10.2g

Stew for Vegans

Prep Time: 10 mins | Cooking Time: 2 hours | Servings: 4

INGREDIENTS:

- ✓ ½ cup onions, finely diced
- ✓ 2 medium-sized sweet potatoes, diced
- ✓ Salt and pepper
- ✓ 2 cups frozen mixed vegetables
- ✓ 4-5 cups vegetable broth
- ✓ 1 large tomato, chopped

DIRECTIONS:

1. layer onions and potatoes in the slow cooker, and sprinkle with salt and pepper.

2. add frozen vegetables and broth and cover and cook for 2 hours on HIGH.

3. stir in tomatoes, and add salt or pepper to balance the taste.

4. serve hot!

NUTRITION(per Serving): Calories 87, Fat 1g, Carbs 15g, Protein 3g

Vegetarian Lasagna

Prep Time: 10 mins | Cooking Time: 4 hours | Servings: 6

INGREDIENTS:

- ✓ 32 oz ricotta cheese
- ✓ 6 cups baby spinach
- ✓ Salt and black pepper
- ✓ 10 oz frozen winter squash purée, thawed
- ✓ 12 ready-to-bake lasagna noodles
- ✓ 2 cups shredded mozzarella cheese

DIRECTIONS:

1. combine the ricotta, spinach, ½ teaspoon salt, and ½ tsp pepper.

2. in the bottom of the slow cooker, spread ½ cup of the squash purée. top with 3 pieces of lasagna noodles. top the lasagna with ⅓ of the ricotta mixture. repeat a layer of squash and noodles followed by ricotta mixture. repeat until all of the lasagna have been used. end with ricotta mixture on top. sprinkle with the mozzarella.

3. cover and cook for 3 to 4 hours on LOW, or until the lasagna are tender.

NUTRITION(per Serving): Calories 571, Fat 28g, Carbs 47g, Protein 32g

Potato Salad

Prep Time: 10 mins | Cooking Time: 3 hours | Servings: 2

INGREDIENTS:

- ✓ 1 cup potato, chopped
- ✓ 1 cup of water
- ✓ 1 tsp salt
- ✓ 2 oz. celery stalk, chopped
- ✓ 2 oz. fresh parsley, chopped
- ✓ ¼ onion, diced
- ✓ 1 tablespoon mayonnaise

DIRECTIONS:

1. put the potatoes in the slow cooker.

2. add water and salt.

3. cook the potatoes on high for 3 hours.

4. then drain water and transfer the potatoes in the salad bowl.

5. add all remaining ingredients and carefully mix the salad.

NUTRITION(per Serving): Calories 123 ,Fat 6.8g ,Carbs 12.7g, Protein 5.2g

Chickpea Curry

Prep Time: 10 mins | Cooking Time: 6 hours | Servings: 4

INGREDIENTS:

- ✓ 2 onions, diced
- ✓ 4 cloves garlic, minced
- ✓ 1 inch ginger, minced
- ✓ 2 (15-ounce) cans chickpeas
- ✓ 1 (15-ounce) can diced tomatoes
- ✓ 1 (15-ounce) can coconut milk
- ✓ 1–2 tablespoons curry powder
- ✓ ½ bunch cilantro
- ✓ basmati rice, for serving

DIRECTIONS:

1. mix everything except for the cilantro together in the slow cooker.

2. cook on LOW for 6–8 hours.

3. Just before serving, mix in the cilantro. Serve over rice.

NUTRITION(per Serving): Calories 219 ,Fat 7.8g ,Carbs 32g, Protein 7.2g

Lemony Lentils Soup

Prep Time: 10 mins | Cooking Time: 6 hours | Servings: 6

INGREDIENTS:

- ✓ 1 yellow bell pepper, chopped
- ✓ 1 yellow onion, chopped
- ✓ 6 carrots, chopped
- ✓ 4 garlic cloves, minced
- ✓ a pinch of cayenne pepper
- ✓ 4 cups veggie stock
- ✓ 3 cups red lentils, dried
- ✓ 3 cups water
- ✓ a pinch of sea salt
- ✓ 1 tbsp rosemary, chopped
- ✓ 1 lemon zest and juice from

DIRECTIONS:

1. put the stock and water in your slow cooker.

2. add bell pepper, onion, carrots, garlic, lentils, cayenne and salt.

3. stir, cover and cook on LOW for 6 hours.

4. add rosemary, lemon zest and juice, stir, ladle into bowls and serve.

NUTRITION(per Serving): Calories 335, Fat 22.8g, Carbs 6g, Protein 34g

Mashed Cauliflower

Prep Time: 15 mins | Cooking Time: 3-6 hours | Servings: 4

INGREDIENTS:

- ✓ 1 cauliflower head, cut into florets
- ✓ garlic cloves, peeled
- ✓ ½ tsp fresh rosemary, chopped
- ✓ ½ tsp fresh thyme, chopped
- ✓ ½ tsp fresh sage, chopped
- ✓ ½ tsp fresh parsley, chopped
- ✓ 1 cup vegetable broth
- ✓ 2 cups water
- ✓ 1 tbsps ghee
- ✓ salt, pepper, to taste

DIRECTIONS:

1. pour broth into the slow cooker, add cauliflower florets.

2. add water, it should cover the cauliflower.

3. close the lid and cook on LOW for 6 hours or on HIGH for 3 hours.

4. once cooked, drain water from the slow cooker.

5. add herbs, salt, and pepper, and ghee, puree with a

blender.

NUTRITION(per Serving): Calories 115, Fat 18.8g, Carbs 7.6g, Protein 6.2g

Vegan Spicy Jambalaya

Prep Time: 10 mins | Cooking Time: 4 hours | Servings: 6

INGREDIENTS:

- ✓ 1 green bell pepper, chopped
- ✓ 1 cup okra
- ✓ 1 small yellow onion, chopped
- ✓ 2 garlic cloves, minced
- ✓ 3 celery ribs, chopped
- ✓ 16 oz canned tomatoes, chopped
- ✓ 1 and ½ cups veggie stock
- ✓ ½ tsp paprika
- ✓ a pinch of salt and black pepper

DIRECTIONS:

1. in your slow cooker, mix bell pepper with okra, onion, garlic, celery, tomatoes, stock, paprika, salt and pepper, stir, cover and cook on LOW for 4 hours.

2. divide into bowls and serve.

NUTRITION(per Serving): Calories 375, Fat 18.8g, Carbs 29g, Protein 24g

Green Beans and Mushrooms

Prep Time: 15 mins | Cooking Time: 3 hours | Servings: 4

INGREDIENTS:

- ✓ 1 pound fresh green beans, trimmed
- ✓ 1 small yellow onion, chopped
- ✓ 1 garlic clove, minced
- ✓ 1 cup vegetable stock
- ✓ 8 oz mushrooms, sliced
- ✓ salt and black pepper to the taste
- ✓ A splash of balsamic vinegar

DIRECTIONS:

1. in your slow cooker, mix beans with onion, garlic, stock, mushrooms, salt, pepper and vinegar, stir, cover and cook on LOW for 3 hours.

2. divide between plates and serve as a side dish.

NUTRITION(per Serving): Calories 145, Fat 1.8g, Carbs 6g, Protein 4g

Cheesy Tofu

Prep Time: 12 mins | Cooking Time: 7 hours | Servings: 4

INGREDIENTS:

- ✓ 8 ounces marinated tofu
- ✓ 1 cup frozen peas, thawed
- ✓ ½ cup onion, minced
- ✓ Salt and pepper to taste
- ✓ 1 ½ cups mashed potatoes
- ✓ 2 tablespoons sharp cheddar cheese, shredded

DIRECTIONS:

1. in the slow cooker, combine the tofu, peas, onion, and salt and pepper.

2. add the mashed potatoes and stir them in.

3. close the lid and make sure that the valve is sealed properly.

4. cover, and cook on LOW for 7 ½ hours.

5. sprinkle the cheese on top, and cover. Cook 30 minutes more on LOW, until the cheese is melted.

NUTRITION(per Serving): Calories 465, Fat 6.8g, Carbs 56g, Protein 34g

Cabbage and Onion Mix

Prep Time: 15 mins | Cooking Time: 2 hours | Servings: 2

INGREDIENTS:

- ✓ 1 and ½ cups green cabbage, shredded
- ✓ 1 cup red cabbage, shredded
- ✓ 1 tbsp olive oil
- ✓ 1 red onion, sliced
- ✓ 2 spring onions, chopped
- ✓ ½ cup tomato paste
- ✓ ¼ cup veggie stock
- ✓ 2 tomatoes, chopped
- ✓ 2 jalapenos, chopped
- ✓ 1 tbsp chili powder
- ✓ 1 tbsp chives, chopped
- ✓ A pinch of salt and black pepper

DIRECTIONS:

1. grease your slow cooker with the oil and mix the cabbage with the onion, spring onions and the other **INGREDIENTS:** inside.

2. toss, put the lid on and cook on HIGH for 2 hours. divide between plates and serve as a side dish.

NUTRITION(per Serving): Calories 210, Fat 4g, Carbs 9g, Protein 8g

Lemon Artichokes

Prep Time: 15 mins | Cooking Time: 3 hours | Servings: 2

INGREDIENTS:

- ✓ 1 cup veggie stock
- ✓ 2 medium artichokes, trimmed
- ✓ 1 tbsp lemon juice
- ✓ 1 tbsp lemon zest, grated
- ✓ salt to the taste

DIRECTIONS:

1. in your slow cooker, mix the artichokes with the stock and the other **INGREDIENTS:** , and then toss it, put the lid on and cook on LOW for 3 hours.

2. divide artichokes between plates and serve as a side dish.

NUTRITION(per Serving): Calories 103. Carbs 10g. Protein 5g. Fat 14g

Minty Peas

Prep Time: 15 mins | Cooking Time: 3 hours | Servings: 2

INGREDIENTS:

- ✓ 1 pound okra, sliced
- ✓ ½ pound tomatoes, cut into wedges
- ✓ 1 tbsp olive oil
- ✓ ½ cup veggie stock
- ✓ ½ tsp chili powder
- ✓ salt and black pepper to the taste
- ✓ 1 tbsp mint, chopped
- ✓ 3 green onions, chopped
- ✓ 1 tbsp chives, chopped

DIRECTIONS:

1. grease your slow cooker with the oil, and mix the okra with the tomatoes and the other **INGREDIENTS:** inside.

2. put the lid on, cook on LOW for 3 hours, divide between plates and serve as a side dish.

NUTRITION(per Serving): Calories 69, Fat 4g, Carbs 9g, Protein 6g

Balsamic-glazed Beets

Prep Time: 15 mins | Cooking Time: 7 hours | Servings: 6

INGREDIENTS:

- ✓ 1 lb. beets, sliced
- ✓ 5 oz. orange juice
- ✓ 3 oz. balsamic vinegar
- ✓ 3 tbsp. almonds
- ✓ 6 oz. goat cheese
- ✓ 1 tsp. minced garlic
- ✓ 1 tsp. olive oil

DIRECTIONS:

1. toss the beets with balsamic vinegar, orange juice, and olive oil in the insert of slow cooker.

2. put the slow cooker's lid on and set the cooking time to 7 hours on LOW settings.

3. toss goat cheese with minced garlic and almonds in a bowl.

4. spread this cheese garlic mixture over the beets.

5. put the cooker's lid on and set the cooking time to 10 minutes on HIGH settings.

6. serve warm.

NUTRITION(per Serving): Calories 196, Fat 11.4g, Carbs 12g, Protein 10g

Spicy Quinoa

Prep Time: 15 mins | Cooking Time: 2 hours | Servings: 2

INGREDIENTS:

- ✓ 1 cup quinoa
- ✓ 2 tsps butter, melted
- ✓ salt and black pepper to the taste
- ✓ 1 tsp turmeric powder
- ✓ 2 cups vegetable stock
- ✓ 1 tsp cumin, ground

DIRECTIONS:

1. grease your slow cooker with the butter, add the quinoa and the other **INGREDIENTS:** - toss, put the lid on and then cook on HIGH for about 2 hours

2. divide between plates and serve as a side dish.

NUTRITION(per Serving): Calories 150, Fat 3g, Carbs 9g, Protein 4g

Sweet Potato Soup

Prep Time: 10 mins | Cooking Time: 8 hours | Servings: 5

INGREDIENTS:

- ✓ 5 cups veggie stock
- ✓ 2 celery stalks, chopped
- ✓ 3 sweet potatoes, chopped
- ✓ 1 cup yellow onion, chopped
- ✓ 2 garlic cloves, minced
- ✓ 1 cup rice milk
- ✓ 1 tsp tarragon, dried
- ✓ 2 cups baby spinach
- ✓ 8 tbsps almonds, sliced
- ✓ a pinch of salt

DIRECTIONS:

1. put the stock in your slow cooker.
2. add celery, potatoes, onion, garlic, salt, pepper and tarragon.
3. stir, cover and cook on LOW for 8 hours.
4. add rice milk and blend using an immersion blender.
5. add almonds and spinach, stir, cover and leave aside for 20 minutes.

6. ladle into bowls and serve.

NUTRITION(per Serving): Calories 306, Fat 21.4g, Carbs 6g, Protein 28g

Spelt Pilaf

Prep Time: 15 mins | Cooking Time: 4 hours | Servings: 2

INGREDIENTS:

- ✓ ½ tbsp balsamic vinegar
- ✓ ½ cup whole spelt
- ✓ a pinch of salt and black pepper
- ✓ 1 cup chicken stock
- ✓ ½ tbsp olive oil
- ✓ 1 tbsp green onions, chopped
- ✓ 1 tbsp mint, chopped

DIRECTIONS:

1. in your slow cooker, mix the farro with the vinegar and the other **INGREDIENTS:** , toss, put the lid on and cook on LOW for 4 hours.

2. divide between plates and serve

NUTRITION(per Serving): Calories 162, Fat 3g, Carbs 9g, Protein 3g

Vegetable Lasagna

Prep Time: 20 mins | Cooking Time: 6 hours | Servings: 4

INGREDIENTS:

- ✓ 1 eggplant, sliced
- ✓ 1 cup kale, chopped
- ✓ 3 eggs, beaten
- ✓ 2 tbsps Keto tomato sauce
- ✓ ½ tsp ground black pepper
- ✓ 1 cup Cheddar, grated
- ✓ ½ tsp chili flakes
- ✓ 1 tbsp tomato sauce
- ✓ 1 tsp coconut oil
- ✓ ½ tsp butter

DIRECTIONS:

1. place coconut oil in the skillet and melt it.

2. then add sliced eggplants and roast them for 1 minute from each side.

3. after this, transfer them in the bowl.

4. toss butter in the skillet.

5. place 1 beaten egg in the skillet and stir it to get the shape of a pancake.

6. roast the egg pancake for 1 minute from each side.

7. repeat the steps with remaining eggs.

8. separate the eggplants into 2 parts.

9. place 1 part of eggplants in the slow cooker. you should make the eggplant layer.

10. then add ½ cup chopped parsley and 1 egg pancake.

11. sprinkle the egg pancakes with 1/3 cup of parmesan.

12. then add remaining eggplants and second egg pancake.

13. sprinkle it with ½ part of remaining parmesan and top with the last egg pancake.

14. then spread it with tomato sauce, kale and sprinkle with chili flakes and ground black pepper.

15. add tomato sauce and top lasagna with remaining cheese.

16. close the lid and cook lasagna for 6 hours on LOW.

NUTRITION(per Serving): Calories 253, Fat 16g, Carbs 12g, Protein 23g

Cauliflower Rice Mix

Prep Time: 15 mins | Cooking Time: 2 hours | Servings: 2

INGREDIENTS:

- ✓ 1 cup cauliflower rice
- ✓ 1 tbsp coconut butter
- ✓ ¼ tsp salt
- ✓ ¾ tsp turmeric
- ✓ 1 tsp cayenne pepper
- ✓ 1 tsp curry powder
- ✓ 2 oz. Provolone cheese
- ✓ 1 ½ cups chicken stock

DIRECTIONS:

1. in the slow cooker, mix the cauliflower with the butter and the other **INGREDIENTS:** except the cheese, close the lid and cook on HIGH for 1 hour.

2. add the cheese, cook on HIGH for 1 more hour, divide between plates and serve.

NUTRITION(per Serving): Calories 134 Fat 5g Carbs 6.4g ,Protein 5g

Coconut Okra

Prep Time: 15 mins | Cooking Time: 3 hours | Servings: 6

INGREDIENTS:

- ✓ 1-pound okra, trimmed
- ✓ 1/3 cup coconut cream
- ✓ 1/3 cup butter
- ✓ ½ tsp salt
- ✓ ½ tsp turmeric powder
- ✓ ¾ tsp ground nutmeg

DIRECTIONS:

1. in the slow cooker, mix the okra with cream, butter and the other ingredients

2. cook okra for 3 hours on HIGH.

NUTRITION(per Serving): Calories 203, Fat 6.3g, Carbs 6.4g, Protein 3.2g

Zucchini and Yellow Squash

Prep Time: 15 mins | Cooking Time: 6 hours | Servings: 2

INGREDIENTS:

- ✓ 2/3 cup zucchini, sliced
- ✓ 2/3 cups yellow squash, sliced
- ✓ 1/3 tsp Italian seasoning
- ✓ 1/8 cup butter

DIRECTIONS:

1. place zucchini and squash on the bottom of the slow cooker.

2. sprinkle with the italian seasoning with salt, pepper, and garlic powder to taste. top with butter.

3. cover and cook within 6 hours on LOW

NUTRITION(per Serving): Calories 122, Fat 9.3g ,Carbs 3.7g, Protein 4g

Eggplant Parmesan

Prep Time: 40 mins | Cooking Time: 4 hours | Servings: 2

INGREDIENTS:

- ✓ 1 large eggplant, 1/2-inch slices
- ✓ 1 egg, whisked
- ✓ 1 tsp Italian seasoning
- ✓ 1 cup marinara
- ✓ 1/4 cup Parmesan cheese, grated

DIRECTIONS:

1. put salt on each side of the eggplant, then let stand for 30 minutes.

2. spread some of the marinara on the bottom of the slow cooker and season with salt and pepper, garlic powder, and italian seasoning.

3. spread the eggplants on a single the slow cooker and pour over some of the marinara sauce. repeat up to 3 layers. top with parmesan. cover and cook for 4 hours.

NUTRITION(per Serving): Calories 159, Fat 12g, Carbs 8g, Protein 15g

Thyme Tomatoes

Preparation time: 10 min | Cooking time: 5 h | Servings: 4

INGREDIENTS:

- ✓ 1-pound tomatoes, sliced
- ✓ 1 tablespoon dried thyme
- ✓ 1 teaspoon salt
- ✓ 1 tablespoons olive oil
- ✓ 1 tablespoon apple cider vinegar
- ✓ ½ cup of water

DIRECTIONS:

1- Put all ingredients in the slow cooker and close the lid.

2- Cook the tomatoes on Low for 5 hours.

NUTRITION(per Serving: Calories 83, Protein 1.1 g, Carbs 4.9 g, Fat 7.3 g, Fiber 1.6 g, Cholesterol 0 mg, Sodium 588 mg, Potassium 277 mg

Quinoa Dolma

Preparation time: 15 min |Cooking time: 3 h |

Servings: 6

INGREDIENTS:

- 2 sweet peppers, seeded
- 1 cup quinoa, cooked
- ½ cup corn kernels, cooked
- 1 teaspoon chili flakes
- 1 cup of water
- ½ cup tomato juice

DIRECTIONS:

1- Mix quinoa with corn kernels and chili flakes.
2- Fill the sweet peppers with quinoa mixture and put in the slow cooker.
3- Add water and tomato juice.
4- Close the lid and cook the peppers on High for 3 hours.

NUTRITION(per Serving: Calories 171, Protein 6.6 g, Carbs 33.7 g, Fat 2.3 g, Fiber 4.8 g, Cholesterol 0 mg, Sodium 29 mg, Potassium 641 mg

Creamy Puree

Preparation time: 10 min | Cooking time: 4 h |

Servings: 4

INGREDIENTS:

- ✓ 2 cups potatoes, chopped
- ✓ 2 cups of water
- ✓ 1 tablespoon vegan butter
- ✓ ¼ cup cream
- ✓ 1 teaspoon salt

DIRECTIONS:

1- Pour water into the slow cooker.

2- Add potatoes and salt.

3- Cook the vegetables on high for 4 hours.

4- Then drain water, add butter and cream.

5- Mash the potatoes until smooth.

NUTRITION(per Serving): Calories 87, Protein 1.4 g, Carbs 12.3 g, Fat 3.8 g, Fiber 1.8 g, Cholesterol 10 mg, Sodium 617 mg, Potassium 314 mg

Cauliflower Hash

Preparation time: 10 min | Cooking time: 2.5 h | Servings: 4

INGREDIENTS:

- ✓ 2 cups cauliflower, roughly chopped
- ✓ ½ cup potato, chopped
- ✓ oz. Provolone, grated
- ✓ 1 tablespoons chives, chopped
- ✓ 1 cup milk
- ✓ ½ cup of water
- ✓ 1 teaspoon chili powder

DIRECTIONS:

1- Pour water and milk into the slow cooker.
2- Add cauliflower, potato, chives, and chili powder.
3- Close the lid and cook the mixture on high for 2 hours.
4- Then sprinkle the hash with provolone cheese and cook the meal on High for 30 minutes.

NUTRITION(per Serving): Calories 134, Protein 9.3 g, Carbs 9.5 g, Fat 7.1 g, Fiber 2.4 g, Cholesterol 20 mg, Sodium 246 mg, Potassium 348 mg

Brussels Sprouts

Preparation time: 10 min | Cooking time: 2.5 h | Servings: 4

INGREDIENTS:

- ✓ 1-pound Brussels sprouts
- ✓ oz. tofu, chopped, cooked
- ✓ 1 teaspoon cayenne pepper
- ✓ 2 cups of water
- ✓ 1 tablespoon vegan butter

DIRECTIONS:

1- Pour water into the slow cooker.

2- Add Brussels sprouts and cayenne pepper.

3- Cook the vegetables on high for 2.5 hours.

4- Then drain water and mix Brussels sprouts with butter and tofu.

5- Shake the vegetables gently.

NUTRITION(per Serving): Calories 153, Protein 9.2g, Carbs 10.8g, Fat 9.3g, Fiber 4.4g, Cholesterol 23mg, Sodium 380mg, Potassium 532mg

Sautéed Garlic

Preparation time: 10 min | Cooking time: 6 h | Servings: 4

INGREDIENTS:

- ✓ oz. garlic cloves, peeled
- ✓ 2 tablespoons lemon juice
- ✓ 1 teaspoon ground black pepper
- ✓ 1 cup of water
- ✓ 1 tablespoon vegan butter
- ✓ 1 bay leaf

DIRECTIONS:

1- Put all ingredients in the slow cooker.

2- Close the lid and cook the garlic on Low for 6 hours.

NUTRITION(per Serving): Calories 135, Protein 4.7 g, Carbs 24.1 g, Fat 3.3 g, Fiber 1.7 g, Cholesterol 8 mg, Sodium 36 mg, Potassium 303 mg

Cheesy Corn

Preparation time: 5 min | Cooking time: 5 h | Servings: 5

INGREDIENTS:

- ✓ 2 cups corn kernels
- ✓ ½ cup Cheddar cheese, shredded
- ✓ 1 tablespoon vegan butter
- ✓ 1 teaspoon ground black pepper
- ✓ 1 teaspoon salt
- ✓ cups of water

DIRECTIONS:

1- Mix corn kernels with ground black pepper, butter, salt, and cheese.

2- Transfer the mixture to the slow cooker and add water.

3- Close the lid and cook the meal on Low for 5 hours.

NUTRITION(per Serving): Calories 173, Protein 6.9 g, Carbs 23.6 g, Fat 7.5 g, Fiber 3.5 g, Cholesterol 18 mg, Sodium 573 mg, Potassium 351 mg

Shredded Cabbage Sauté

Preparation time: 10 min | Cooking time: 6 h | Servings: 4

INGREDIENTS:

- ✓ 2 cups white cabbage, shredded
- ✓ 1 cup tomato juice
- ✓ 1 teaspoon salt
- ✓ 1 teaspoon sugar
- ✓ 1 teaspoon dried oregano
- ✓ 1 tablespoons olive oil
- ✓ 1 cup of water

DIRECTIONS:

1- Put all ingredients in the slow cooker.

2- Carefully mix all ingredients with the help of the spoon and close the lid.

3- Cook the cabbage sauté for 6 hours on Low.

NUTRITION(per Serving): Calories 118, Protein 1.2 g, Carbs 6.9 g, Fat 10.6 g, Fiber 1.7 g, Cholesterol 0 mg, Sodium 756 mg, Potassium 235 mg

Ranch Broccoli

Preparation time: 10 min | Cooking time: 1.5 h | Servings: 3

INGREDIENTS:

- ✓ 2 cups broccoli
- ✓ 1 teaspoon chili flakes
- ✓ 2 tablespoons ranch dressing
- ✓ 2 cups of water

DIRECTIONS:

1- Put the broccoli in the slow cooker.

2- Add water and close the lid.

3- Cook the broccoli on high for 1.5 hours.

4- Then drain water and transfer the broccoli in the bowl.

5- Sprinkle it with chili flakes and ranch dressing. Shake the meal gently.

NUTRITION(per Serving): Calories 34, Protein 2.7 g, Carbs 6.6 g, Fat 0.3 g, Fiber 2.4 g, Cholesterol 0 mg, Sodium 91 mg, Potassium 291 mg.

Sautéed Spinach

Preparation time: 10 min | Cooking time: 1 h | Servings: 3

INGREDIENTS:

- ✓ 2 cups spinach
- ✓ 1 tablespoon vegan butter, softened
- ✓ 2 cups of water
- ✓ oz Parmesan, grated
- ✓ 1 teaspoon pine nuts, crushed

DIRECTIONS:

1- Chop the spinach and put it in the slow cooker.

2- Add water and close the lid.

3- Cook the spinach on High for 1 hour.

4- Then drain water and put the cooked spinach in the bowl.

5- Add pine nuts, Parmesan, and butter.

6- Carefully mix the spinach.

NUTRITION(per Serving):: Calories 108, Protein 7.1 g, Carbs 1.9 g, Fat 8.7 g, Fiber 0.7 g, Cholesterol 24 mg, Sodium 231mg, Potassium 176 mg.

Cheddar Mushrooms

Preparation time: 10 min | Cooking time: 6 h |
Servings: 4

INGREDIENTS:

- ✓ 2 cups cremini mushrooms, sliced
- ✓ 1 teaspoon dried oregano
- ✓ 1 teaspoon ground black pepper
- ✓ ½ teaspoon salt
- ✓ 1 cup Cheddar cheese, shredded
- ✓ 1 cup heavy cream
- ✓ 1 cup of water

DIRECTIONS:

1- Pour water and heavy cream into the slow cooker.

2- Add salt, ground black pepper, and dried oregano.

3- Then add sliced mushrooms and Cheddar cheese.

4- Cook the meal on Low for 6 hours.

5- When the mushrooms are cooked, gently stir them and transfer to the serving plates.

NUTRITION(per Serving): Calories 239, Protein 9.6 g, Carbs 4.8 g, Fat 20.6 g,   Fiber 0.7 g, Cholesterol 71 mg, Sodium 484 mg, Potassium 38 6mg.

Fragrant Appetizer Peppers

Preparation time: 15 min | Cooking time: 1.5 h | Servings: 2

INGREDIENTS:

- ✓ 2 sweet peppers, seeded
- ✓ ¼ cup apple cider vinegar
- ✓ 1 red onion, sliced
- ✓ 1 teaspoon peppercorns
- ✓ ½ teaspoon sugar
- ✓ ¼ cup of water
- ✓ 1 tablespoon olive oil

DIRECTIONS:

1- Slice the sweet peppers roughly and put in the slow cooker.

2- Add all remaining ingredients and close the lid.

3- Cook the peppers on high for 1.5 hours.

4- Then cool the peppers well and store them in the fridge for up to 6 days.

NUTRITION(per Serving): Calories 171, Protein 3.1 g, Carbs 25.1 g, Fat 7.7 g, Fiber 4.7 g, Cholesterol 0 mg, Sodium 11 mg, Potassium 564 mg.

Paprika Baby Carrot

min | Cooking time: 2.5 h | Servings: 2

Preparation time: 10

INGREDIENTS:

- ✓ 1 tablespoon ground paprika
- ✓ 2 cups baby carrot
- ✓ 1 teaspoon cumin seeds
- ✓ 1 cup of water
- ✓ 1 teaspoon vegan butter

DIRECTIONS:

1- Pour water into the slow cooker.

2- Add baby carrot, cumin seeds, and ground paprika.

3- Close the lid and cook the carrot on High for 2.5 hours.

4- Then drain water, add butter, and shake the vegetables.

NUTRITION(per Serving): Calories 60, Protein 1.6 g, Carbs 8.6 g, Fat 2.7 g, Fiber 4.2 g, Cholesterol 5 mg, Sodium 64 mg, Potassium 220 mg.

Butter Asparagus

Preparation time: 15 min | Cooking time: 5 h | Servings: 4

INGREDIENTS:

- ✓ 1-pound asparagus
- ✓ 2 tablespoons vegan butter
- ✓ 1 teaspoon ground black pepper
- ✓ 1 cup vegetable stock

DIRECTIONS:

1- Pour the vegetable stock into the slow cooker.

2- Chop the asparagus roughly and add to the slow cooker.

3- Close the lid and cook the asparagus for 5 hours on Low.

4- Then drain water and transfer the asparagus in the bowl.

5- Sprinkle it with ground black pepper and butter.

NUTRITION(per Serving): Calories 77, Protein 2.8g , Carbs 4.9 g , Fat 6.1 g, Fiber 2.5 g, Cholesterol 15 mg, Sodium 234 mg, Potassium 241 mg.

Jalapeno Corn

Preparation time: 10 min | Cooking time: 5 h | Servings: 4

INGREDIENTS:

- ✓ 1 cup heavy cream
- ✓ ½ cup Monterey Jack cheese, shredded
- ✓ 1-pound corn kernels
- ✓ 1 jalapenos, minced
- ✓ 1 teaspoon vegan butter
- ✓ 1 tablespoon dried dill

DIRECTIONS:

1- Pour heavy cream into the slow cooker.

2- Add Monterey Jack cheese, corn kernels, minced jalapeno, butter, and dried dill.

3- Cook the corn on Low for 5 hours.

NUTRITION(per Serving): Calories 203, Protein 5.6 g, Carbs 9.3 g, Fat 16.9 g, Fiber 1.5 g, Cholesterol 56 mg, Sodium 101 mg, Potassium 187 mg.

Garlic Cauliflower Steaks

Preparation time: 15 min | Cooking time: 3 h | Servings: 4

INGREDIENTS:

- ✓ 14 oz cauliflower head
- ✓ One teaspoon minced garlic
- ✓ Four tablespoons butter
- ✓ Four tablespoons water
- ✓ One teaspoon paprika

DIRECTIONS:

1- Wash the cauliflower head carefully and slice it into the medium steaks.
2- Mix up together the butter, minced garlic, and paprika.
3- Rub the cauliflower steaks with the butter mixture.
4- Pour the water into the slow cooker.
5- Add the cauliflower steaks and close the lid.
6- Cook the vegetables for 3 hours on High.
7- Transfer the cooked cauliflower steaks to a platter and serve them immediately!

NUTRITION(per Serving): Calories 129, Fat 11.7 g, Fiber 2.7 g, Carbs 5.8 g, Protein 2.2 g

Eggplant Gratin

Preparation time: 15 min | Cooking time: 5 h | Servings: 7

INGREDIENTS:

- ✓ One tablespoon butter
- ✓ One teaspoon minced garlic
- ✓ Two eggplants, chopped
- ✓ One teaspoon salt
- ✓ One tablespoon dried parsley
- ✓ 4 oz Parmesan, grated
- ✓ Four tablespoons water
- ✓ One teaspoon chili flakes

DIRECTIONS:

1- Mix the dried parsley, chili flakes, and salt.
2- Sprinkle the chopped eggplants with the spice mixture and stir well.
3- Place the eggplants in the slow cooker.
4- Add the water and minced garlic.
5- Add the butter and sprinkle with the grated Parmesan.
6- Close the lid and cook the gratin for 5 hours on Low.
7- Open the lid and cool the gratin for 10 minutes.

8-   Serve it.

NUTRITION(per Serving): Calories 107, Fat 5.4 g, Fiber 5.6 g, Carbs 10 g, Protein 6.8 g

Garlic Carrots Mix

Preparation time: 15 min | Cooking time: 4 h | Servings: 2

INGREDIENTS:

- ✓ 1 pound carrots, sliced
- ✓ 2 garlic cloves, minced
- ✓ 1 red onion, chopped
- ✓ 1 tablespoon olive oil
- ✓ ½ cup tomato sauce
- ✓ A pinch of salt and black pepper
- ✓ ½ teaspoon oregano, dried
- ✓ 2 teaspoons lemon zest, grated
- ✓ 1 tablespoon lemon juice
- ✓ 1 tablespoon chives, chopped

DIRECTIONS:

1- In your slow cooker, mix the carrots with the garlic, onion and then add the other Ingredients, toss, put the lid on and cook on Low for 4 hours.

2- Divide the mix between plates and serve.

NUTRITION(per Serving): Calories 219, Fat 8 g, Fiber 4 g, Carbs 8 g, Protein 17 g

Broccoli Mix

Preparation time: 15 min | Cooking time: 2 h | Servings: 10

INGREDIENTS:

- ✓ 6 cups broccoli florets
- ✓ 1 and ½ cups cheddar cheese, shredded
- ✓ 10 ounces canned cream of celery soup
- ✓ ½ teaspoon Worcestershire sauce
- ✓ ¼ cup yellow onion, chopped
- ✓ Salt and black pepper to the taste
- ✓ 1 cup crackers, crushed
- ✓ 2 tablespoons soft butter

DIRECTIONS:

1- In a bowl, mix broccoli with cream of celery soup, cheese, salt, pepper, onion and Worcestershire sauce, toss and transfer to your slow cooker.
2- Add butter, toss again, sprinkle crackers, cover and cook on High for hours.
3- Serve as a side dish.

NUTRITION(per Serving): Calories 159, Fat 11 g, Fiber 1 g, Carbs 11 g, Protein 6 g

Minty Peas and Tomatoes

Preparation time: 15 min | Cooking time: 3 h | Servings: 2

INGREDIENTS:

- ✓ 1 pound okra, sliced
- ✓ ½ pound tomatoes, cut into wedges
- ✓ 1 tablespoon olive oil
- ✓ ½ cup veggie stock
- ✓ ½ teaspoon chili powder
- ✓ Salt and black pepper to the taste
- ✓ 1 tablespoon mint, chopped
- ✓ 3 green onions, chopped
- ✓ 1 tablespoon chives, chopped

DIRECTIONS:

1- Grease your slow cooker with the oil, and mix the okra with the tomatoes and the other ingredients inside.

2- Put the lid on, cook on Low for 3 hours, divide between plates and serve as a side dish.

NUTRITION(per Serving): Calories 70, Fat 1 g, Fiber 1 g, Carbs 4 g, Protein 6 g

Lemon Artichokes

Preparation time: 15 min | Cooking time: 3 h | Servings: 2

INGREDIENTS:

- ✓ 1 cup veggie stock
- ✓ 2 medium artichokes, trimmed
- ✓ 1 tablespoon lemon juice
- ✓ 1 tablespoon lemon zest, grated
- ✓ Salt to the taste

DIRECTIONS:

1- In your slow cooker, mix the artichokes with the stock and the other Ingredients, and then toss it, put the lid on and cook on Low for 3 hours.

2- Divide artichokes between plates and serve as a side dish.

NUTRITION(per Serving): Calories 100, Fat 2 g, Fiber 5 g, Carbs 10 g, Protein 4 g

Lightning Source UK Ltd.
Milton Keynes UK
UKHW021332080721
386836UK00008B/1463